MUSLIMS AND CHRISTIANS AT THE TABLE

MUSLIMS AND CHRISTIANS AT THE TABLE

Promoting Biblical Understanding Among North American Muslims

BRUCE A. MCDOWELL & ANEES ZAKA

FOREWORD BY HARVIE M. CONN

P.O. BOX 817 • PHILLIPSBURG • NEW JERSEY 08865-0817

Throughout this book we quote from the translation of the Qur'an by Mohammed Marmaduke Pickthall, *The Meaning of the Glorious Koran* (New York: New American Library, n.d.).

Typesetting by Michelle Feaster
Page design by Tobias Design

Printed in the United States of America

Library of Congress Cataloging-in-Publication Data

McDowell, Bruce A., 1956-
Muslims and Christians at the table : promoting biblical understanding among North American Muslims / Bruce A. McDowell and Anees Zaka.
p. cm.
Includes bibliographical references.
ISBN 0-87552-473-7
1. Missions to Muslims—United States. 2. Islam—Relations—Christianity. 3. Christianity and other religions—Islam. I. Zaka, Anees, 1942- II. Title.

BV2625.M38 1999
266'.0088'2971—dc21 99-045496

We dedicate this book to
our sovereign Lord and Savior Jesus Christ,
who said, "I have other sheep
that are not of this sheep pen.
I must bring them also.
They too will listen to my voice,
and there shall be one flock and one shepherd."
—John 10:16

We also dedicate this book to the memory of
two faithful servants of God: my brother
Dr. Clyde B. McDowell
(February 3, 1950 – June 7, 1999),
President of Denver Seminary,
for his encouragement, wisdom, godly modeling
of walking with Christ, vision, and
leadership in equipping the church of Christ
around the world; and our mentor
Dr. Harvie M. Conn
(April 7, 1933 – August 28, 1999),
Professor of Missions at
Westminster Theological Seminary,
for his scholarship, his passion for the unreached
with the gospel, and his compassion for the poor
and oppressed in the world's cities.

Contents

Foreword by Harvie M. Conn xi

Acknowledgments xv

Introduction xvii

PART 1: THE VISION

1. Why Should We Reach Muslims Here? 3
The Growth of Islam in North America — The Black Muslim Movement — Sufism — Motivations for Conversion — The U.S.: An Islamic Intellectual Center — Goals of the Muslim Community — A Lack of Workers

PART 2: UNDERSTANDING MUSLIMS' BACKGROUND

2. An Historical Understanding of Islam 31
The Historical Setting — The Life of Muhammad — Expansion — The Development of Islam

3. Cultural Understanding 49
The Definition of Culture — Cultural Distinctives Common to Most Muslims — Cultural Differences Among North American Muslims — Festivals and Pilgrimages — Assumptions and Stereotypes of Muslims — Islam's Own View of Itself — What Should We Do?

PART 3: THEOLOGICAL UNDERSTANDING

4. Revelation: The Qur'an and the Bible 71
Allah's Mercy in the Final Revelation — The Meaning of Qur'an — Historical Development — Divisional Arrangement — Qur'anic Interpretation — The Relation of the Qur'an to

the Sunnah and the Hadith — Has the Bible Been Corrupted? — Changes Within the Qur'an — Interpreting the Bible and the Qur'an — Using the Bible and the Qur'an for Witness — Handling the Qur'an and the Bible

5. The Nature and Character of Allah 89
The Nature of Allah — The Ninety-nine Names of Allah — The Character of Allah

6. The Person and Mission of 'Isa Ibn Maryam 107
The Person of 'Isa ibn Maryam (Jesus, Son of Mary) — The Mission of 'Isa ibn Maryam (Jesus, Son of Mary)

7. Human Nature and the Effects of Sin 123
Human Nature — The Prophets and Sin — The Muslim Concept of Sin — Righteousness

8. Living One's Faith in the World 135
Our Role in the World — Living One's Faith in the World: the Islamic State — Living One's Faith in the World: The Kingdom of God — Spreading the Vision

Conclusion to Part 3: Theological Understanding

PART 4: REACHING MUSLIMS

9. The Theological Basis for Muslim Evangelism 153
The Sovereignty of God — Salvation Only Through Jesus Christ — The Cross of Christ — Prayer for Muslims — Worship — Missions — Salvation — Eschatology

10. How to Reach Muslims 171
Finding Your Muslim Friends — Methods for Reaching Muslims — Principles of Conduct for Visiting a Mosque — Developing Your Strategy for Muslim Evangelism

11. Guidelines for Friendship Evangelism 195
Know Your Audience — Develop a Friendship and Establish Trust — Pray for Your Friend Regularly — Share the Gospel

Naturally and Biblically — Show Hospitality to Your Muslim Friends — Meet Their Needs — Encourage a Response to Christ — Why There May Not Be a Ready Response to Christ — Continue the Friendship — Cautions — Testimonies of Friendship

12. Meetings for Better Understanding 217
Philosophy of Ministry — Guidelines for Meetings — Topics for Meetings — The Biblical Basis for Meetings — Practical Suggestions for Establishing Meetings — Testimony of God's Blessing — How Meetings for Better Understanding Are Being Used — Muslim Motives for Agreeing to Meetings for Better Understanding — Qur'anic References Used as Points of Contact

13. Studying the Bible with Muslims 239
The Power of the Word — Forms for Presenting the Gospel — Language — Leading Cross-cultural Bible Studies — The Discipleship of New Believers — Contextualized Discipleship

14. Where Do We Go from Here? 255
An Open Door of Opportunity — Vision and Motivation — The Changing Mission Field — Training in Islamics — Literature and Media — House Churches — The Challenge

Appendix 1: The Story of a Muslim Immigrant 263

Appendix 2: A Bible Study Case Study 271

Notes 283

Glossary of Islamic Terms 297

Bibliography 305

Further Ministry Resources 317

Index of Bible References 323

Foreword

by Harvie M. Conn

The image of sharing good news around a table has not always been used to describe the historic encounter of Christians and Muslims. Their first great meeting took place on the battlefields of the Crusades. As romanticized by Christians in the past, those whose chest bore the cross and whose hand wielded the bloody sword were painted with halos of martyrdom. Extermination, cruelty, and greed were sanctified in the name of Jesus.

Among Muslims, a trail of bitterness has left its indelible stain. Since Muslims have not forgotten the Crusades to this day, organizations like Campus Crusade for Christ and Worldwide Evangelization Crusade have searched for new names in their ministry among them. Recently, a group of Christians followed the path of the Crusaders across Europe and the Middle East, meeting with Muslim leaders to confess the sins of the past and to ask for a new beginning to understanding.

The book now in your hands has chosen another path. It is not a dialogue on human rights or the political agendas of development and nation-building, as often promoted by some churches today. Nor is it built around the use of "controversy," a methodology used by Christians in the nineteenth century that, says one author, "sowed the seeds of enmity and hatred in the hearts of Indian Muslims." Undoubtedly, controversy arises around any table where disagreements on crucial issues of the heart are openly shared.

Linked to the church's past, this book promotes evangelism at the table. But this is not evangelism of a proselytizing, triumphalist sort that plots to destroy Islam. Rather, it sets forth Jesus as the fulfillment of the hearts of all of us longing for peace with Allah. It is an expression of hospitality in which one wants to give only one's best to one's companion at the common meal. And the best we can offer is Jesus, the seal of the prophets. It is one beggar saying to another beggar, "We have found bread; come, eat with us."

Although embedded in the mistakes of the past, this message has been heard before. Francis of Assisi (1181–1226) undertook three missions to the Muslims. The last one was an unsuccessful effort to stop the Fifth Crusade, but it gained the marked respect of the sultan of Egypt, Malik al-Kamil. The same desire to share the good news sent Raymond Lull (1235–1315) on four trips to the Muslim world and prompted him to encourage places of learning where Islam could be studied and understood. Some would even argue that in that mutual interchange, Lull himself learned from Islam; out of his study of Sufism may have come some of his mysticism. In the end, he pled that the Crusades had failed; the Holy Land was to be gained only by love, prayer, and tears.

This book focuses on a new day. Francis and Lull traveled to the Muslim world. Now the Muslim world has come to the American table. Henry Martyn (1781–1812) took nine months to reach Calcutta from England. There he devoted the remaining six years of his life almost entirely to Muslims. Now, as we read in chapter 1 of this book, a plane trip of a few hours brings thousands of Muslims daily to our doorstep. And waiting for us in our inner cities are the African-Americans who have turned from our racist pictures of Jesus to find a new unity and self-respect in Islam.

This book encourages us to learn from Martyn's mistakes and from his insights. Hopefully, there will be more room for kitchen conversations about Jesus and God's grace revealed in him than for verbal attacks and public disputes. And, through the disagreements that arise, we will listen again to the repentant words of Henry Martyn: "I wish that a spirit of enquiry may be excited, but I lay not much stress upon clear arguments; the work of God is seldom wrought in this way."

This book is an exciting invitation to that new kind of hospitality.

Acknowledgments

We thank Dr. James M. Boice, senior pastor of Tenth Presbyterian Church in Philadelphia, Pennsylvania, for his preaching and teaching ministry, which has been such a blessing in both of our lives. I (Bruce McDowell) would like to thank the session of Tenth Presbyterian Church for granting me a sabbatical to co-write this book. After being blessed with the opportunity to minister to and through this congregation for over seventeen years, it was a blessing to be able to have a change of pace in my ministry.

We thank our partner in ministry and friend, Rev. J. Lenk, for his comments from his Bible studies with Muslim students while I (Bruce McDowell) was his supervisor for seminary field education. His insights, gentleness, and sensitivity to Muslims make him a great role model.

Great thanks go to Mrs. S. Adam for permission to include her perceptive cultural insights into the experience of a Muslim immigrant.

Thanks go to Mr. I. Coulter of Texas for permission to use one of his ministry reports for a section in the chapter on "Meetings for Better Understanding."

Dr. Harvie Conn's guidance, while studying under his supervision, is greatly appreciated. Some of his comments contributed to the book. We also thank the professors who mentored and influenced us in our studies, Dr. Roger Greenway and Dr. Tim Keller.

Particularly as I (Bruce McDowell) was beginning my study of Islam and ministry to Muslim students around 1983, Mr. Sam Schlorff, a missiologist at Arab World Ministries, had insightful discussions with me. Later we also led Muslim Awareness Seminars together. These discussions and seminars contributed to my thinking in this book. Thanks go to him.

We appreciate the help given by Dr. Philip Ryken, associate pastor of Tenth Presbyterian Church, in reviewing the manuscript. He provided valuable editorial assistance.

We acknowledge and thank the many individuals and churches who pray for and faithfully support our ministries. Without them our work would not be possible.

We also profoundly thank our wives, Susan and Fareda, for their sacrifice, perseverance, and contributions to the writing of this book.

Most of all we thank God for his grace in our own lives and his call to us to bring the good news to those who have never heard it.

Introduction

The title of our book indicates our approach to ministering to Muslims. The main idea of the book is to promote a journey of understanding between Christians and Muslims.

We have known each other since we both began ministering to Muslims in Philadelphia in 1982. We have often shared in the ministry together, prayed together, and encouraged one another with a vision for what God has called us to do in reaching the unreached with the gospel.

We came to believe that this book is needed after noticing a lack of practical guidance on how to witness to Muslims in the North American context. Most of the available literature discusses the theoretical and theological aspects of witnessing to Muslims, but provides little of the practical how-tos.

The purpose of this book is threefold: (1) to set forth the historical, cultural, and theological background of Islam as a foundation for witnessing to Muslims, (2) to encourage witnessing to North American Muslims with the gospel, and (3) to teach how to witness to them more effectively by promoting biblical understanding. This is a practical guide to doing the work of evangelism among North American Muslims. Since much has already been written on responding to Muslim objections, not much of this book addresses those problems specifically.

It is hoped that this book will spur Christians on to witness to Muslims faithfully and effectively in North America. We believe that witnessing must be done with a conviction that the Bible is God's authoritative, inerrant Word and has the words of eternal life through Jesus Christ our Lord. Most of what we have to say does not specifically address reaching African-American Muslims, because that is a specialized topic in itself. However, much of the following material is applicable to reaching them as well. We have included some brief history, which includes the Black Muslim movement. We are writing primarily about reaching foreign-born immigrants, visitors, international students, and visiting scholars.

Much that one sees in the media and literature today about Islam focuses on its militancy, harshness, view of women, and oil wealth. These stereotypes hinder American Christians from reaching out in love to their Muslim neighbors. We would like to present a more realistic view of Muslims, who in many ways are just like each of us. Muslims have hopes and dreams, loving families, work, schooling, and spiritual needs, just as we all do. They make good friends and neighbors and are known for their generous hospitality to guests.

Muslims vary widely in their outlook and perspective. We should not assume that they are all militants seeking to destroy everything that Western civilization holds dear. Most of them are open to friendships and to discussing their faith with Christians. They are often ambitious to convert Christians to Islam, which gives us an opportunity to discuss our faith with them. For most Muslims this would be the first time they have heard the Christian faith made personal to them—or even heard it at all.

Our enemy is Satan, not Muslims. We should regard them as our friends, neighbors, and fellow human beings made in the image of God. We believe that this is God's perspective. Jesus died for, and is seeking to save, a multitude out of Islam. May this book contribute to that cause.

PART ONE

The Vision

The amazing growth of Islam in North America during the last few decades has gone largely unnoticed by the evangelical church. Many people still think that missions is only done overseas, and that unreached people do not live here in North America. After all, we have the gospel on radio and television daily, churches are found every few blocks, and Bibles are easily available. However, what is not realized is that those who are outside of the Christian subculture are rarely exposed to the gospel. Those who have come from an Islamic background have never heard the gospel in terms that they can understand. Even native-born Americans who are converting to Islam out of Christian backgrounds have generally not heard the gospel in a culturally relevant way that addresses issues that concern them.

There is a great need for North Americans to catch the vision that the mission field is not only in the Middle East, Africa, and Asia, but also here as well. Some missionaries from Third World countries have seen the opportunity to reach Muslims here. They are taking advantage of the freedom we have to witness to Muslims, which may not exist in their own country. They have recognized the strategic importance of winning Muslims to Christ here in North America, for many of these Muslims are preparing to become future leaders in their home countries. Additionally, they know that they may be given more of a hearing because they come from the Third World, too.

CHAPTER ONE

Why Should We Reach Muslims Here?

The Growth of Islam in North America

The religious landscape of North America has changed radically during the last couple of decades. As comparative religion scholar Diana Eck says, "Today, the Islamic world is no longer somewhere else, in some other part of the world; instead Chicago, with its 50 mosques and nearly half a million Muslims, is part of the Islamic world."[1] It is difficult not to notice the tremendous changes taking place. Muslims may run the nearby convenience store or service station, sit in class with you at school, or live next door. The United States is now the most religiously diverse country in the world. How has this change in the religious landscape taken place?

Let's begin by looking back to the earliest Muslim presence in America. It is said that Abu Bakari, a Muslim king in Mali, led a series of sea voyages to the New World, beginning in 1310. Mandingan Muslims from Mali and other parts of West Africa arrived in the Gulf of Mexico in 1312 and explored the interior of North America via the Mississippi River.[2] West African slaves began arriving in the Americas in 1510, first introduced by the Spanish. A Dutch ship brought slaves to the English colony in Virginia in 1620.[3] Although accurate statistics are not available, a substantial percentage of the slaves brought to America were Muslim. The immigration of Muslims to North America began as a trickle. In

1717 "Arabic-speaking slaves who ate no pork and believed in Allah and Muhammad" arrived in North America. In 1790 "Moors" were reported to be living in South Carolina and Florida. Some estimate that as many as one-fifth of the slaves brought to the Americas in the eighteenth and nineteenth centuries were Muslim. Those who were brought to the American colonies by and large soon converted to Christianity.

A Muslim named Abd al-Rahman Ibrahima was a leader, the son of a chief of the Fula tribe in Guinea, before being captured during a battle with the Mandingo tribe. He was sold to slave traders and taken to Mississippi. He had been well educated in Islamics in Timbuktu in West Africa. After many years, he was convinced by a printer to write a letter to his tribe for help in securing his freedom. He wrote in Arabic, and his letter was received by Moroccan officials. Seeing that he was Muslim, they appealed to President James Monroe. After forty years of slavery, he was freed from his tobacco plantation in 1829 by order of Secretary of State Henry Clay. Then he was returned to Liberia, where he died the same year.[4]

An 1871 Canadian census recorded only thirteen Muslims in the country, and none appeared in surveys taken ten and twenty years later.[5] Despite these surveys, the first Arab immigrants, mostly from Ottoman Syria, arrived in about 1882. Some of them were Muslim. In the 1931 Canadian census, there were 645 Muslims of Arab origin in the country, mostly in Ontario and Quebec. Canada's first mosque, Al Rashid, opened in 1938 in Edmonton. By 1980 there were almost 16,000 Muslims in Edmonton, making it necessary to build a larger mosque.[6]

A number of Yemenis arrived in America in 1869 after the opening of the Suez Canal. The first Muslim communities in the United States arose from immigration from Syria and Lebanon from 1875 to 1922 as a means of avoiding the Turkish military draft. Many of these immigrants settled in New York, becoming shopkeepers, grocers, or peddlers. Many of them later moved to the Midwest. The earliest recorded Muslim group to organize for communal prayer met in 1900 in Ross, North Dakota.[7] A second wave of immigrants arrived between 1930 and 1938 from Syria and Lebanon, together with some Yemenis and Egyptians. After World War II, Muslims immigrated from the communist countries of Albania and Yugoslavia, dispossessed Palestinians moved from the state of Israel, and educated Syrians and Iraqis fled dictatorships in their countries. By 1970, 300,000 Arabs had immigrated to the United States. Since 1967, Pakistani and Iranian immigrants have particularly enlarged the Muslim community.[8]

The 1960s brought tremendous changes in the country of origin of American immigrants. In 1965 the United States passed an historic immigration act that ended over four decades of legal racism. The Johnson-Reed Act of 1924 had effectively barred Asian and African immigrants, as had the Chinese exclusion act of 1882. With the change in immigration law came immigrants from around the world, including at least sixty Islamic nations. Today 14 percent of legal immigrants to the U.S. each year are Muslims. Since the 1980s, over one million immigrants have arrived each year, mostly from Asia and the Hispanic world. Of course, many Muslim immigrants come for economic reasons. But many of them are coming here for freedom of religion and conscience, which they don't have in their own Islamic countries. Even some of the Islamic fundamentalist groups operate here because of the greater freedom we have. War and revolution have been additional incentives for Muslims to arrive on our shores. In the 1980s many Afghan refugees arrived. In the 1990s Kurds and Algerians arrived because of civil war in their countries. Since the end of the Gulf War in 1991, about 25,000 Iraqis have arrived in the United States to escape the misery of United Nations sanctions on Iraq.

Now "American Muslims are estimated to be 42 percent African-American; 24.4 percent Asian Indian; 12.4 percent Arab; 5.2 percent African; 3.6 percent Persian; 2.4 percent Turk; 2 percent South Asian; 1.6 percent American white; and 5.6 percent other." They live throughout the whole country, but are concentrated in twenty-two major cities.[9] There are estimated to be 1.35 million Iranians in the U.S., 80 percent of them being Muslim. Although this does not correspond to the above figure for the percentage of Persians among American Muslims, a large portion of them go unaccounted for because of such factors as illegal immigration. Over 500,000 Iranians live in southern California, 100,000 in Texas (35,000 in Houston), and 100,000 in the Washington, D.C., area. Los Angeles is the second largest Iranian city outside of Iran, after Istanbul. There are now 250,000 Iraqis in the U.S., with 70,000 of them in the Detroit area, 30,000 in California, and 15,000 in the Chicago area.[10] Although some of them are Chaldean Christian, the majority are Muslim.

Islam is the fastest growing religion in the United States. The growth rate is at least 4 percent annually and could be as high as 6 percent. Growth is due to immigration from Islamic countries, a high birthrate in Muslim families, and conversion, particularly among African-Americans. There are estimated to be over 25,000 conversions to Islam per year. Between three and eight million Muslims live in the U.S., and some say that the most likely figure is about five million.[11] Muslims claim that there are over six million here. This means that there are more Muslims here than in Libya, and more Muslims here than Episcopalians and Presbyterians combined. Their number is expected to exceed the number of American Jews (5.7 million) soon after the year 2000, if it has not already done so. The Chicago metropolitan area alone has 350,000 Muslims and 100 mosques or Islamic centers. The New York City area has twice that many with 700,000 Muslims. Immigrant Muslims and their children comprise 3.5 million people. The largest share of converts from the native-born population are from the African-American community, numbering around two million. Among native-born American converts to Islam, "85% are African American and 12% are White. Sadly, at least 80% of these American converts were raised in the church."[12] Philadelphia has an unusually high number of African-American converts, with two-thirds of the Muslim community being from that background.

Conversion to Islam will not remain an African-American problem, but will continue to increase among non-African-Americans.

White converts in the U.S. number at least 100,000, the vast majority (80 percent) being women, most of whom convert upon marrying Muslim men. One of the earliest white American converts to Islam was Mohammed Alexander Webb, a former Presbyterian, who founded the American Islamic Propaganda Movement in 1893 and was a speaker at the World Parliament of Religions in Chicago that year. Being a jeweler, newspaperman, and diplomat, he converted to Islam while in India. His publishing efforts were funded initially by Indian Muslims and subsequently by the Ottoman sultan Abdul Hamid II. The "brotherhoods" he established in several major cities died out around the time he died in 1916. At that time, North America was not ready for Islam. Now we are likely to see more and more of Islam in the suburbs among whites in the days ahead. Many of the white converts these days are particularly attracted to Sufism. A new trend is that some second-generation Korean immigrants and Hispanics are converting to Islam. A contributing factor among Koreans is the large cultural clash between the first- and second-generation immigrants.

One authority on Muslim evangelism estimates that by 2020 most of our urban centers will be predominantly Muslim. As an example of this, consider what is happening in Philadelphia. It is estimated that

> during the last 20 years . . . the number of Muslim families in the region has quadrupled, and the number of mosques in the city alone has quintupled to 30. Ten years ago, there were perhaps only one or two *halal* meat markets, which obey Islamic dietary rules; now there at least 10. There was perhaps only one *halal* restaurant; now there are at least a half dozen.
>
> A few decades ago . . . both the separatist Nation of Islam and orthodox Sunni Islam established unusually strong footholds among the city's African Americans. . . . The conversion rate has continued to accelerate, fueled by the

> movie *Malcolm X*. Now . . . it is common for five people a week to accept Islam in each of the city's 10 predominantly African American mosques.[13]

Over half of the mosques in North America have been organized since 1980. Now an average of one new mosque per week is opening in the U.S. According to the American Muslim Council, as of 1995 there were 1,200 mosques, 165 Islamic schools, 426 Islamic associations, about 90 Islamic publications, and twelve national Islamic organizations around the country. Nearly 40 percent of these mosques are affiliated with the Islamic Society of North America, based in Plainfield, Indiana. About 20 percent are aligned with Imam Warith Deen Muhammad of Chicago, Illinois, who led a majority of the Black Muslim movement into orthodox Islam. Another 30 percent of the mosques are unaffiliated. In Philadelphia there are sixteen different sects of Islam. Some estimate that there are seventy different Muslim groups in the U.S., some being small African-American groups with various social and religious agendas.

There are two hundred thousand American businesses, from street stalls to major establishments, owned and operated by Muslims. "In creating a support system, Philadelphia Muslims may be leading the way nationally. They have established one of the first and perhaps most ambitious councils of mosques." They have set up an Islamic credit union. It is the first of its kind in North America and will help Muslims obtain money, for instance for homes and cars, without violating the Islamic ban on interest-bearing transactions. Members can also save for the pilgrimage to Mecca, Saudi Arabia. The council is also pushing the city council to make Philadelphia the first major city to adopt the two main Islamic holidays, *Eid al-Fitr* and *Eid al-Adha*. They estimate that there are 15,000 Muslim students in the city schools.[14] Presently, students with parental permission are given an excused absence on *Eid*. Already the Trenton, New Jersey, school district is closed for *Eid al-Fitr*. Muslim students in the Philadelphia public schools are also excused for a couple of hours on Fridays for prayers.

Muslims have also developed social programs with religious aims. A Model Communities Program works in urban centers across the country to improve inner-city housing and provide jobs, schools, and Islamic centers. It is funded by tens of millions of dollars from Saudi Arabia.[15] The Council on American-Islamic Relations tracks incidents of bias against Muslims in the workplace and schools, and provides advocacy on behalf of the victims of such bias.

The Black Muslim Movement

The spread of Islam in the African-American community began in 1913, when Noble Drew Ali founded the Moorish Science Temples in Newark, New Jersey. He is said to have been commissioned to teach Islam to American Negroes by the sultan of Morocco. In 1921 a branch of the Ahmadiyya Movement was founded by Dr. Mufti Muhammad Sadiq in Chicago. Through this movement, many African-Americans were converted to Islam. In 1930 the first Muslim mosque was established by African-Americans in Pittsburgh.[16] By the 1930s, a new sect had developed out of the Moorish Science Temples with the teaching of Fard Muhammad, sometimes called W. D. Fard. He founded the Nation of Islam, which taught black supremacy and that God is black. Elijah Muhammad was discipled by Fard and then succeeded him in 1934 after it was said that Fard had disappeared. Elijah continued the teaching of Fard and spoke of Fard as being divine. Elijah became a prophet of Islam for his followers, taking the place of the seventh-century prophet. He taught that as God, Fard Muhammad "came to destroy the white race and restore the black race to its superior place in the world."[17] The children in their "universities of Islam" (primary and secondary schools) were taught that "America was 'the most vile and wicked nation on Earth' and white people were devils and authors of all manner of wickedness."[18]

During the civil rights movement in the late 1950s and early 1960s, the Nation of Islam grew. In 1959 they had 30,000 followers, and by 1961 they had sixty-nine temples and 100,000 followers. Growth was largely due to the charismatic leadership of Malcolm X. He had been appointed minister of Harlem Temple No. 7 in New York City. He preached, organized, and edited the weekly newspaper *Muhammad Speaks*. As the movement prospered, dissension broke out between Elijah and Malcolm. About this time, Malcolm made the *hajj* to Mecca and discovered that Elijah had distorted Islam in many ways. He withdrew from the Nation of Islam in 1964 to form the black nationalist group, Muslim Mosque, Inc. However, in 1965 he was assassinated while delivering a speech in Harlem.

Elijah Muhammad appointed Louis Farrakhan to be the national minister for the Nation of Islam and the leader of the Harlem Temple, succeeding Malcolm X. Although Farrakhan had been a close friend of Malcolm X, his loyalties were with Elijah. During the 1970s, the Nation grew to having temples in 150 cities, chapters at forty-six universities, and many businesses. By 1975 Islam was seen as a viable religious alternative for African-Americans. It received wide recognition through such athletes as heavyweight boxing champion Muhammad Ali. But the movement was having problems of corruption and deep financial woes.

Elijah Muhammad died in February 1975. Although he was a controversial leader, he played a significant role in raising the dignity and self-esteem of the African-American underclass. C. Eric Lincoln writes, "Elijah Muhammad must be credited with the serious re-introduction of Islam to the United States in modern times, giving it the peculiar mystique, the appeal, and the respect without which it could not have penetrated the American bastion of Judeo-Christian democracy."[19] He must be credited with giving Islam a solid foothold in America.

Elijah Muhammad's son, Wallace D. Muhammad, immediately succeeded him. Wallace was aware of some of the shortcomings of his father and began making some changes in both the beliefs and the practices of the Nation of Islam. He spoke of God being mind rather than black. It was not whites who were devils, but the white devil who was in the mind of whites. Wallace downplayed the divinity of Fard Muhammad and proclaimed a new mission for his people. They now called themselves Bilalian Muslims, and their adherents were called Bilalians, named after Bilal, the first black convert to Islam. Their newspaper was now called *Bilalian News*. In 1975 they claimed a total community of 500,000 African-Americans, 300,000 being militants, in eighty temples, gaining 50,000 converts a year from mostly nominally Christian African-Americans. In 1976 they changed their name to the World Community of al-Islam in the West and opened their membership to nonblacks. By the end of that year, they had established 235 mosques and daily radio broadcasts. By then their teachings were being realigned with orthodox Islam.[20] Wallace grew to appreciate America more, and had the children in his schools pledge allegiance to the flag. The movement's name was changed again in 1980 to the American Muslim Mission. In 1982 their newspaper became the A.M. *Journal*. The Islamization of the movement continued with Wallace changing his name to Warith Deen Muhammad, temples changing to mosques, ministers becoming imams, Arabic and the Qur'an being taught, and the five pillars of Islam being kept. However, the movement had internal dissension and disaffection, and faced financial problems and lawsuits. Soon Warith became simply a symbolic leader for a much smaller group of Muslims. The rest joined other groups or left the movement.[21] The movement's newspaper is now known as the *Muslim Journal*. Warith remains the leading spokesman for Islam in the U.S., even being recognized as such by Islamic governments.

During the reorganization of the World Community of al-Islam in the West because of financial and administrative problems, Louis Farrakhan was transferred from New York to Chicago. He had become a popular leader. In 1978 Farrakhan resigned to begin his own movement based on the teachings of Elijah Muhammad, taking the original name Nation of Islam. Their male adherents dress in white shirts and bow ties, and are often seen selling their weekly newspaper, *The Final Call*, in urban centers. They claim to have the largest circulation of any African-American periodical in the U.S. Farrakhan continues the racist ideology of black supremacy and the denigration of Jews and whites. He believes that Jews control blacks, especially entertainers and sports stars. He has dedicated himself to loosening their "pernicious control" of American life. His theology includes the belief that a black scientist created the white race. He opposes interracial marriages, saying, "Racial harmony does not mean racial mixing." Until blacks are given "freedom, equal justice, and equality" in our diverse environment, he supports a separate state or territory for blacks, either in North America or elsewhere. Farrakhan also says that blacks should not have to pay taxes until they are treated more justly. Imprisoned Nation of Islam converts "should be released on the grounds of their 'righteous' transformation."[22] In a speech at a rally in Philadelphia, Farrakhan said, "It's time for us [African-Americans] to show the world our brilliance in our humanity, in our divinity and in our contributions."[23]

On October 16, 1995, Louis Farrakhan organized a huge rally in Washington, D.C., called the "Million Man March," to promote the dignity of black men, to foster moral renewal, to make national atonement, and to bring reconciliation. Many Christian leaders joined in the march, not because they supported Farrakhan, but because of what the march represented and the issues it was addressing. Despite his racist and fascist statements, Farrakhan has addressed many issues that resonate with the African-American community, and he is therefore admired as a major leader and spokesman for them. He speaks to the anger of many blacks against whites for generations of discrimination, intimidation, and lack of equal opportunity. In 1996 Farrakhan made trips to Libya, the Sudan, Iran, and Iraq, seeking support and goodwill from Islamic leaders. The Nation of Islam is popular with African-American students. There are an estimated 70,000 to 100,000 followers of Farrakhan in the nation, with over eighty mosques.

Another Islamic-oriented American group is the Five Percent. They reject commonly accepted history, authority, and organized religion. They teach that the black man is a god. Their teachings are called Supreme Mathematics, with the "five percent" being those who teach the "truth" concerning black male divinity. Although they teach that Allah is the supreme being, they believe that each black man is the god of his own universe. One's destiny and fate are in one's own hands. Women are known as "earths." So the group is also known as the Nation of Gods and Earths. Members adopt Arabic names. Founded in Harlem in 1964, it has recently been spreading to thousands through American prisons and hip-hop radio.[24]

Sufism

Many Muslims from its early period have sought a more personal, intimate relationship with God. Partly as a reaction against the legalism of some jurists and the rationalism of the philosophers, Sufism developed. In the second and third centuries of the Islamic period, some people wanted to avoid the legal and theological debates of the day and enter a more simple life of seeking God in asceticism and mysticism. They developed the idea of the unity of God into the belief that one can have union with God. Some of the mystics developed a following of disciples. The leader, called a *pir,* was a guide for his disciples in both spiritual and worldly matters. The disciples were subsequently initiated and organized into orders (*tarika*). Many of the Sufis in these orders traveled around, spreading Islam and sometimes performing miracles. The tombs of famous mystics, called "saints," became places of pilgrimage for merit and healing. Sufis are often scorned by orthodox Muslims, although 70 percent of the Muslim world is thought to be influenced by Sufism. However, the Sufis do not reject Islamic law (*Shari'a*), but see their mystical path of devotions as an addition to the observance of the *Shari'a.* Sufis are found among both major branches of Islam, the Sunnis and Shi'ites.

Numerous Sufi orders are present in North America, most having originated from Sufi orders in Iran and the Middle East. One

American order, called Sufis of the West, has centers in Los Angeles and New York. Although it developed in the U.S., its ideas come from abroad.

A Medlevi Sufi order based in Konya, Turkey, has a center in Brattleboro, Vermont. These Sufis publish books on Sufism and have promoted their cause through a national tour of Turkish musicians held at major universities. Their presentation of various wind and string instruments and drums was accompanied by a small group of singers. The music would climax by repeating the names of Allah at a rapid tempo, with rapid breathing leading to hyperventilation. That was followed by a ceremony in which each Sufi would bow to the sheikh, who would spin them off in a whirling dervish dance in an apparently hypnotic state.

The Bawa Muhaiyaddeen Fellowship, another Sufi group, with headquarters in Philadelphia, was founded by Bawa Muhaiyaddeen, a Tamil-speaking illiterate from Sri Lanka. His followers have built a mosque, have published his books, tapes, and videos, and have established centers around the country and abroad. Since Bawa died in 1986, his tomb at the order's farm has become a place of pilgrimage for thousands. His teaching has much in common with New Age teaching, mixing elements of Hinduism and Buddhism with Islam. This quote will give you a taste of his thinking:

> For many years now, people have been spending forty-five minutes, an hour, four hours, five hours a day searching for peace and newfangled techniques. If you want peace, give up these techniques and calm your mind for ten minutes, for twenty minutes, for even five minutes. Please think deeply about this. Do it with firmness, with absolute and complete faith (*iman*), with the certitude and determination to realize God and wisdom. When you have thought about this with your wisdom, say these two words in your heart, "*La ilaha*, other than You there is nothing, *ill-Allah*, only You are God." Say it and look at your heart. . . . Sit in

> one place, look at your heart, and focus intently. . . . As you go on reciting these two words, you will experience more and more bliss. The more of this you gather here in this life, the more bliss you will see over there in the hereafter. You will see a great light there. You will see paradise, a large beautiful palace, and an immense light. . . . You will see the house where you are going to live, where you will be able to experience the bliss you have earned, where heavenly maidens will invite you in and heavenly angels will show you around. . . . It will cure all your diseases and give you long life. . . . When you continue to meditate in this way, your state will display youthful qualities of beauty, light, and color. In this state you will receive whatever you need. You will receive true wealth, and you will have peace."[25]

Americans who are converting to Islamic Sufism are reacting to the extreme materialism of American society. They have seen that material pursuits are not satisfying to the soul. They are part of a growing movement in the country to seek spirituality of all kinds. Americans are losing their faith in science to provide all the answers. Much of the religious establishment has not been able to answer people's spiritual quest with their liberal theology, which leaves out the supernatural. Their psychological theories fail to restore relationships, and their social and political agendas don't touch the heart. In this environment, Sufism presents itself as a good option because it attempts to lead one to union with God through devotional practices and esoteric thought. However, it fails to lead one to true union with God, which is found only through the mediation of Jesus Christ our Lord (1 Tim. 2:5).

Motivations for Conversion

Probably the primary reason why many North Americans turn to Islam is that Muslims here are very aggressive in propagating their faith. They are great at friendship "evangelism" to their family members, friends, and neighbors. As parents, they instruct their children in Islam and have them dress in Islamic style for school. High school students are recruited to attend the *Jumah* prayers on Fridays. When Christians attempt to evangelize a neighborhood, Muslims boldly confront them. They realize that North America is a rich harvest field of many people looking for something to believe in that brings order and discipline to their lives. The millions of young people who have been brought up in public schools and on television generally have no strong religious convictions. Many North American converts to Islam come from either nominal or fervently Christian families. Muslim men are also encouraged to marry Christian women and raise their children as Muslims.

Second, some are attracted to Islam because its teachings are simple and its requirements are achievable. It is easy for the common person to fulfill its obligations, compared to the standards of Christ. In many ways it appeals to human reason, being oriented to law and human work. Islam does not have the difficult "mysteries" of the Christian faith, such as the Incarnation, the Atonement, redemption, the Trinity, and original sin. The simplicity of God as one (*tawhid*) has more rational appeal. Islam does not require theological reflection. Its beliefs are not complicated. Islam has appeal as the culmination of revealed religion, which progressed from Judaism to Christianity to Islam. Some of Islam's practices, such as polygamy and the protection of women, are attractive. But other motivations, particularly social ones, usually play a more important role.

A third reason why North Americans are turning to Islam is that many find a desired sense of community in it. Imprisoned African-Americans, in particular, feel intimidated, culturally displaced, and alienated. Prison officials are often culturally insensitive. Even well-meaning Christians may be using pictures of a light-haired, blue-eyed Jesus, which not only offend Muslim views of idolatry, but confirm that Christianity is a white man's religion. In the Muslim community they find brotherhood, cultural affirmation, and solidarity. This brotherhood is sadly lacking in many

Christian churches, where blacks have not been viewed as equals. This is one of the most important reasons why African-Americans join the mosque. By and large, the American church has not shared power and love with the African-American male, and that has created a spiritual vacuum which is being filled by Islam. What is attractive in a broader sense is that Islam provides the visible manifestation of community and unity across a broad spectrum of people, which is seen especially in prayer and pilgrimage.

Fourth, a strong motivation for African-Americans to convert to Islam is their bitter resentment toward whites as a result of centuries of oppression, which is still felt today. One convert stated that "only in Islam does he feel free to be black, because only Islam admits to the injustices put upon the black people by whites, and so gives him the opportunity to become black again."[26] Christianity is seen as the white man's religion. Now that was largely true for about 1,700 years, but today two-thirds of the world's Christians are non-European. Also, Christianity has been in black Africa since the first century. Today Christianity is the fastest growing religion in black Africa. But Islam is still seen as being particularly for blacks, even though Muhammad had black slaves. Many of the slaves brought Islam with them from Africa. White Christians are seen as those who enslaved the black man. Although this is true, Muslims and black Africans were equally involved in the slave trade, which extended to North Africa, the Middle East, and India. It was evangelical Christians[27] in Great Britain, led by William Wilberforce, who initially brought a stop to the slave trade. Slavery has continued up to the present day in Islamic countries such as Mauritania and the Sudan, without objection from Islamic religious leaders. The Nation of Islam, with its racist teachings, is the door through which many of the converts to Islam enter, although most of them move on to more orthodox, nonracist groups.

Fifth, since the end of Reconstruction (which followed the Civil War), the dominant society has tried to terrorize and intimidate the African-American community. This was originally expressed in "Jim Crow" laws of segregation and discrimination, the imposition of voting requirements designed to exclude African-Americans, church burnings, and lynchings. This forced African-American churches to abandon their concern for identity and missions and to move into a survivalist mode. This was the model of the church during slavery. As a result, the church had little to offer to define the African-American experience. The rise of Islam was one of several non-Christian attempts to fill this theological vacuum. As the African-American community became more urbanized, there were new social and cultural challenges that needed to be addressed. But, in large measure, the church was not addressing the issues of African-American identity and significance in the plan of God. As a result, the "Christian consensus" began to erode and a state of crisis arose in the community. Islam appeals to African-Americans because it offers a sense of African identity and significance in God's rule over the affairs of men.[28]

Sixth, there has been not only a theological vacuum in the African-American community, but also a leadership vacuum. Ronald Potter points out three ways in which this has been manifested. First, a number of ministers have failed to stand up for the gospel of Jesus Christ in events such as the Million Man March, while Muslim speakers have unashamedly expressed loyalty to Allah, Muhammad, and Farrakhan. Potter asks, "Are we as black Christians affected by a new radicalism, where it is more important to be identified with blackness than Christianity, where racial loyalty is more important than seeking and telling the truth? Is it cool to say 'Allah' or 'Mohammad' because they are supposedly identified with blackness, while God and Jesus—because of their allegedly white identification—are becoming politically incorrect in black society?" Second, more emphasis has been placed on "the experiential and expressive dimensions of Christian life than upon the doctrinal aspects of faith." Black Christian leaders, often biblically and theologically ignorant, have been disarmed and confused by Islam. Third, many Christian leaders' beliefs have not made much of a difference in their personal and corporate lives in a way that would encourage others to take the Christian faith seriously.

The gospel has not been communicated to the urban underclass in a way that addresses important aspects of their lives: violent crime and police brutality; disintegration of the community as manifested in drugs, AIDS, and unwed juvenile mothers; and a spirit of hopelessness and despair. As a result, Islam has become a real challenge to the black community.[29]

Seventh, related to the two previous reasons, African-American churches have largely failed to meet their community's deepest needs. The black male has been largely absent and irresponsible in the church, where women predominate. Issues of poverty and injustice are not addressed from a biblical perspective, but are ignored by looking to "the sweet by-and-by." Jesus is seen as a wimp hanging on a cross, rather than as a man's man and the conqueror of sin and death.[30]

Eighth, some are tired of the immorality, drugs, and family breakdown that have become so prevalent in Western society. They have a desire for godliness. As Carl Ellis notes from his experience in prison ministry, "Often, an inmate realizes he has been taken in by illusions of instant wealth through crime. He may also realize he has been alienated from God and so consequently desires to achieve God's favor. Perhaps he wants to purge himself from those false values that led to his incarceration. Therefore, when he witnesses the Islamic community with its disciplined, rigorous approach to life, he might see this as the means to satisfy his desire for righteousness."[31] Additionally, many North American churches have become centers for emotional outlet, political agendas, and social activism. But they have little spiritual vitality, Bible teaching, or ministries to meet the real needs of the family. So when an alternative comes along with strong but simple teaching, a sense of community, and a desire to meet family needs, it provides a strong pull for those looking for answers.

Ninth, as mentioned above in connection with Sufism, Americans are turning to Islam because they are looking for a spiritual alternative to extreme materialism and the secular trust in science to answer life's questions. Sufi mysticism and passion offer an attractive means to find spiritual reality. Also, the all-encompassing view of Allah as the source of good and evil, faith and unbelief, who has preordained all things, is attractive. Many are looking for a God who is bigger than their problems and on whom they can rely. Islam's code for all areas of life, including politics, economics, war, peace, art, family, morality, and worship, provides a blueprint for how to live. People are looking for direction in their lives.

What may be seen in all of this is the great need for American Christians to live godly lives, incorporating biblical principles in all of society, acting justly, bringing reconciliation between races, and witnessing boldly. A clear response to Islam is needed and should be taught in our churches.

The U.S.: An Islamic Intellectual Center

In the last four decades, the United States has become a center of Islamic intellectual ferment, as an increasing number of Muslim students have enrolled in American colleges and universities. American universities have become in the 1990s "the new microcosms and laboratories of a new multicultural and multireligious America."[32] Numerous students are even coming to the United States from the Islamic world to get a Ph.D. in Islamics. The estimated number of Muslim students varies from 77,000 to over 100,000 per year, possibly up to 30 percent of all international students. Prior to the Iranian revolution in 1979, there were about 70,000 students in the United States just from Iran alone. We are now also seeing the children of first-generation Asian Muslim immigrants (who came here after the 1965 Immigration Act) graduating from college.

Thousands of Muslim students have become active in student groups like the Muslim Student Association of the United States and Canada (MSA), which has offices in Plainfield, Indiana. Shi'ite students have their own organization. Since its beginning in 1963, the MSA has grown to over 150 chapters in North American colleges and universities. They publish newspapers and magazines and hold conferences and youth leadership camps promoting Islam. They are also in the forefront of promoting social justice and making political statements about Muslim concerns around the world.[33] The MSA is now known as the Islamic Society of North America (ISNA) and is the parent organization for many Muslim organizations in North America.

Rabitat al-Alam as-Islami, or the Muslim World League, is a Saudi-funded organization which heavily supports many of the Islamic student organizations in the West, including several in the United States and Canada. They are responsible for much of the Islamic propaganda used to proselytize around the world.

Of concern to some are the scientists from radical Islamic countries who receive their training at American universities. Upon returning home, they are capable of producing chemical, biological, and nuclear weapons. "In the seven years since the end of the Gulf War in 1991, nearly 11,000 visas have been issued to students from nations that sponsor terrorism—including 503 Iraqis, 5,154 Iranians, 113 Libyans, 3,227 Syrians, 1,604 Sudanese."[34] Although these countries are prohibited from receiving American aid or technology with military applications, they can send students. Members of Hezbollah, the Lebanese terrorist organization, have used student visas to enter the United States. Of course, what these students study in science can be used for either good or evil. They all need the gospel. God presents us with an open door of opportunity to make the good news of Jesus known to them.

A major recruiting ground for Islamic fundamentalism is on American university campuses. Recruiting is done by well-funded, professionally organized student organizations targeting Muslim students. "The Muslim Brotherhood; the Indian subcontinent's equivalent, Jamaat-i-Islami; Sheikh Omar's organization, Takfir wal Hijra [responsible for the bombing of the World Trade Center]; and Lebanon's virulent Iranian-backed Hizbullah—which was responsible for the Beirut kidnappings of Americans and suicide bombings, including the one that killed 250 U.S. Marines at their barracks in 1983—all have active student programs at colleges throughout America. From Berkeley in the west to Florida University in the east and many points in between such as Michigan State and Southern Illinois University, well-funded, professionally organized student organizations target Muslim students."[35] Shielded from the watchful eyes of police in their own countries, these Muslim students are recruited into a variety of Islamic organizations that are often outlawed back home. Here they are able to forge links with Muslim students from other nations to develop a network of international leaders. One of the largest and most active Muslim student organizations is at the University of Southern Illinois in Carbondale. Involving students from the Middle East and Southeast Asia, it produces large amounts of literature and proselytizes widely beyond the campus.

Muslim students are often easily recruited into fundamentalist Islamic organizations because they have become isolated from other students. They are often mocked and patronized for their religious beliefs, with bigotry being shown by both students and faculty. One American-educated Arab engineer in the Gulf said, "Muslims are the only ethnic group about whom it is still acceptable to be racist in America. We have replaced blacks in this regard."[36] Whenever headlines speak of violent acts being done by Muslims, Muslim students at American campuses are insulted and sometimes assaulted. To avoid such problems, some Muslim students deny they are Muslims while living in America.

Muslim students' understanding of Islam and its role in the world is being shaped in the American setting. Muslim intellectuals and leaders who have become a significant part of the American academic scene have been able to provide an interpretation of Islam that is relevant to life in the U.S. and the modern world. Their writings and ideas have been exported by students returning to their home countries to assume leadership positions in the Muslim world. In this manner the opinions and interpretations of American Muslims have influenced people in the Middle East, Africa, and Southeast Asia. Their Islamic worldviews have also been attractive to many indigenous Americans, both black and white, who have converted to Islam in recent decades.

In light of the strategic nature of this segment of the Muslim population, North America is one of the greatest mission fields for reaching Muslims. What happens here will affect many countries overseas as well. These people will have an impact on their societies, governments, and nations. God and Satan are contending for the minds and commitments of these future leaders, who have the capacity to be a dynamic force for change.

Goals of the Muslim Community

The Muslim community has five primary goals in the United States. Their first priority is to organize local mosques. In the past ten years, mosques and Islamic centers have quadrupled to approximately 1,250 or more. On average, a new one opens each week in America. By 1986, about two-thirds of the mosques were operated by African-Americans.

Second, the Muslim community desires to train their children in Islamics. According to one Islamic source, "There are over 500,000 Muslims studying in the United States. Of these, 10,000 attend Islamic schools."[37] All fifty states have Islamic training schools. A school in Denver has the goal of providing a place for learning their language, culture, and history. In New Mexico, a Muslim boarding school seeks to provide a place that protects children from the immorality, violence, and drugs that are found in public schools.

Many public schools are now accommodating the needs of Muslim students, especially during Ramadan. Students who are fasting gather with a Muslim instructor in the library during lunch. Upon request, students are being given a room in which to pray. Rules prohibiting the wearing of hats in school are relaxed so that boys may wear a *kufi* (skullcap) and girls may wear a *hijab* (scarf). On January 28, 1998, Syracuse University in New York closed its doors to become the first university in the U.S. to recognize *Eid al-Fitr* as a holiday.

Several new Islamic publishing houses have started up to meet the growing demand for Islamic literature. Because Muslim children are growing up in a predominantly non-Muslim culture, a need for literature affirming their identity and faith has been strongly felt. Muslim immigrants who entered the country as students now direct publishing houses of Islamic children's books, such as Iqra' International Educational Foundation, al-Meezan International, Kazi Publications, Amica International, and American Trust Publications. They produce texts for the 150 full-time Islamic schools in the United States and Canada and 1,800 Islamic "Sunday schools." A Pakistani-born editor produces a magazine for Muslim teens called *Young Muslim,* which has a circulation of 25,000.[38]

Third, Muslims seek greater access to the media in order to present Islam in a positive light. Muslims rightly object to the negative stereotypes of Muslims presented in children's textbooks, political cartoons, and news reports. In 1985 the Islamic Information Service was launched by a professor at the UCLA School of Medicine. They produce a weekly program called *Islam,* which is distributed to television stations in various cities. The most widely heard Muslim radio personality is Warith Deen Muhammad, the leader of what used to be called the American Muslim Mission. His weekly broadcasts are carried by over thirty stations. Other local programs are heard in New York City and Houston. United Press International is now Saudi-owned. Public displays of religious symbolism have now come to include Islam. For the first time in 1997 at Christmas, an Islamic star and crescent were displayed at the White House along with the national Christmas tree and a Hanukkah menorah.

Fourth, Muslims are seeking to become politically involved in America, ultimately to Islamize the country. Some are petitioning their state legislatures and city councils to declare Muslim holidays such as the *Eids* as legal holidays to be observed by Muslims in schools and offices. "On a tour of USA in 1977, Dr. Abdel-Halim

Mahmoud, of Islam's renowned Al Azhar University, Egypt, was asked if American Muslims might one day try to replace the Constitution with the Sharia. 'We cannot deny such a possibility,' he replied. 'If America one day adopted Islamic law in an enlightened way, America would be adopting the law of God. And He is not subject to making a mistake.' "[39] The Washington-based American Muslim Council facilitates Islamic participation in the American political process. In 1980 the U.S. Congress adopted a resolution in recognition of fourteen centuries of Islam and promised to improve the understanding of Islam in America. Leaders of every Muslim country received copies of this resolution.[40] In 1991 Charles Bilal of Kountze, Texas, became the first Muslim to become mayor of an American city. A Muslim became deputy mayor in Detroit. The American Muslim Council established a legal department in 1992, which has as one of its goals to set up a Muslim American Bar Association. Muslim prayers have been led before state legislatures and the U.S. Congress. Imam Siraj Wahaj of Brooklyn opened a session of the U.S. House of Representatives with prayer on June 25, 1991. Then in February 1992, Imam Warith Deen Muhammad delivered the opening prayer for the United States Senate. At the end of the month of Ramadan, on February 20, 1996, Hillary Clinton welcomed Muslims to the White House to celebrate the *Eid* there for the first time. She said, "This celebration is an American event."[41] The Qur'an was read at the ecumenical service before President Clinton's second inauguration in January 1997.

The fifth and final step for Muslims in America is to develop *da'wah* (calling people to the way of Islam). Propagating Islam among Americans is looked upon not only as a duty for Muslims here, but also as an inherent part of their culture. To promote Islam, Saudi Arabia and other Arab countries have provided large grants to establish Islamic studies departments at major American universities. Examples include recent grants of $5 million to Harvard University and $23.5 million to the University of Arkansas.[42] Another means being used to propagate Islam has been to gain access to major American institutions. Imam Abdul-Rasheed Muhammad was sworn in as the first Islamic chaplain in the American military in January 1994. The Muslim Student Association, with chapters at most of the major universities in North America, has *da'wah* as one of its major functions. They distribute literature, hold public meetings on Islamic topics, give lectures to classes and church groups, and sponsor conferences and youth camps. Hundreds of Muslims are arriving in the United States especially to propagate Islam. They provide instruction in Islam in state prisons. Some come as international students, with the goal of winning Americans to Islam. Foreign Islamic governments (even the "secular" government of Turkey) provide financial support to Muslim missionaries in the U.S. They also finance the distribution of free books on Islam and the building of mosques and Islamic centers. Saudi Arabia has given public libraries beautiful editions of an English translation of the Qur'an parallel with the Arabic. Included in it are appendixes on how Muhammad is prophesied in the Bible and how the Bible has been corrupted.

A Lack of Workers

Some people are under the false impression that many Christian missionaries are reaching Muslims. The church is growing so slowly among Muslims not so much because Muslims are "hard" to convert, but because they have been largely ignored by the church. There are comparatively few people ministering to Muslims. Only about 2 percent of the Protestant missionary force is ministering to the over one billion Muslims, who make up almost 20 percent of the world's population. Even many of those ministering in Muslim countries are not reaching Muslims, but the nominal Christians in those lands. One prayer letter put it this way:

> Did you know that 90% of the church mission resources are spent among English speaking people and they are the

> most evangelized people in the world! But, less that 1% of these resources are given to work among Muslims, the least evangelized people of the world who make up 19% of the world population.[43]

There is not only a lack of workers reaching Muslims with the gospel overseas, but also a lack of workers reaching Muslims in North America—where there is complete freedom to reach them and where most of them speak English. Few Christians seem to have the patience or the willingness to get the training it takes to reach Muslims when so many other groups are more responsive to the gospel. This is often the case among some who may catch a vision for reaching Muslim students, but then shift their focus to a more responsive group.

God seems to have a plan for bringing the gospel to many Muslims by bringing them to Christian communities. Many international students and immigrants are coming from completely unreached Muslim ethnic groups around the world. For example, there are in the U.S. about 100–300 Muslim Uyghurs from Xinjiang Province in western China. They will be influential leaders among the seven million Uyghurs in China and Central Asia. Perhaps God is allowing the massive migration to the West from Muslim countries so that many among them will hear the gospel and believe it, since otherwise they would not have the opportunity to do so. We have a responsibility to fulfill God's commission to lovingly disciple Muslims in all that he has commanded us.

For Reflection/Action

1. What are you going to do in light of the above information? Here are some suggestions:
   (a) Pray, asking God to show you where he is working, so that you may join him.
   (b) Discuss with your pastor or your church's missions committee how to reach out to the Muslim community.

   (c) Seek help from groups that are already involved in Muslim ministry in your area.
2. How can you find out how many Muslims live in your city? How can you find out where they live? What is the closest mosque?
3. How well are you prepared to reach them with the gospel?
   (a) Ready
   (b) Not ready
   (c) Hesitant
   (d) Need help

Part Two

Understanding Muslims' Background

In order to minister effectively to Muslims, it is necessary to understand the history of Muhammad's life and the development of Islam, because they are foundational to Muslims' worldview and our ability to relate the gospel to them. Additionally, understanding some elements of Islamic culture will help in building relationships. This understanding will assist us to know how to respond to their viewpoints, pray for them, or meet their needs.

CHAPTER TWO

An Historical Understanding of Islam

The Historical Setting

To get an historical perspective on Islam, we must understand the environment in which it developed. Polytheism, consisting of a hierarchy of stone gods, dominated the religious life of pre-Islamic Arabia. Archaeological evidence shows that worship of the moon god as the greatest of all gods was prevalent. The moon god was married to the sun goddess and had daughters who were stars. In Mecca many pilgrims were attracted to a shrine of a black meteorite and a sacred well. Associated with this polytheism were fertility ceremonies and rituals to control the demonic spirits who were believed to rob graves, eat human flesh, and terrorize ordinary people's lives.

Into sixth- and seventh-century Arabia were coming ideas from Greek mythology, Persian Zoroastrianism and Manichaeism, Judaism, and Christianity. However, the Bible had not yet been translated into Arabic, and so there was not an accurate understanding of the faith among Arabic-speaking people. No attempts at translating the Scriptures had been made, partly because few Arabs could read. In Abyssinia (Ethiopia) and Syria there were large Christian communities, but in Arabia, especially in the Mecca area, there were evidently very few Christians.

The Byzantine empire was the major power in the area, competing with the Persian empire for control of the Middle East.

There was no dominant power in Arabia at this time; rather, there were various warrior monarchs, who were recruited to side with the competing powers. No central authority ruled the Arabs; no binding law or authority existed above that of the tribe.

The Life of Muhammad

Beginnings

Hazrat (an honorary title) Muhammad was born in A.D. 570, the year of the elephant, in Mecca. In that year a general from Yemen attacked Mecca, leading his army on an elephant. Muhammad was born into the dominant Quraish tribe, to the Hashimite clan. Muhammad's father, Abdullah, died two months before Muhammad's birth, and his mother, Amina, died at the age of twenty-one, when he was only six. His mother called him Ahmad, "the praised one." From age six to eight, Muhammad was raised by his grandfather, Abdul Muttalib. After his grandfather died (in his eighties), Muhammad was raised by his uncle, Abu Talib, a shopkeeper. Muhammad grew up as a shepherd, and then became a caravan trader until he was twenty-five. He led successful trade caravans to Syria and Yemen.

Muhammad married Khadija, a wealthy businesswoman with an Ebionite Christian background. Ebionites developed from the Jewish-Christian church after the fall of Jerusalem and were influenced by the Qumran community. They "exalted the Law, though they considered it contained false pericopes, rejected the Pauline epistles, and regarded Jesus as the son of Joseph and Mary, but elected Son of God at his baptism when he was united with the eternal Christ, who is higher than the archangels, but not divine. . . . His work was that of a teacher rather than savior. From Qumran they learned dualism, vegetarianism, and hatred of sacrifices. They had their own gospel, now called the 'Gospel of the Ebionites.' "[1] Many of these beliefs have parallels in Islam. Khadija apparently had an important influence on Muhammad.

When they got married, Muhammad was 25 years old and

Khadija was 39 or 40. Khadija had been twice widowed before her marriage to Muhammad. She bore him two sons and four daughters, and died at the age of 65. Their youngest daughter, Fatima, was the only one to live to adulthood. She married 'Ali, the son of Abu Talib, Muhammad's uncle.

Can one not assume that Muhammed, having been raised in an idolatrous and animistic culture, was an idol worshiper in his youth? Did he not sin, just as all others do, before his call to be an apostle almost two-thirds of the way through his life? "The main effort of Muslim scholars was and still is to argue that Muhammad was granted immunity from sin before he was honored with his apostleship. The ambiguity surrounding Muhammad's pagan life and his inner beliefs, influenced by various monotheistic factions, eventually resolved itself into the concept of monotheism, a concept that Jews and Christians already shared."[2]

Prophethood

In 610, at the age of forty, Muhammad became a prophet. He claimed to have received a revelation from the angel Gabriel in a cave on Mount Hira. He often went there alone to meditate, usually for a month each year. His initial experience was visual. Mostafa Vaziri suggests that Muhammad may have seen Halley's comet, which was visible in Arabia in 607–608. Muhammad doesn't explicitly say that he saw an angel, but he saw a masculine being of some sort. This extraordinary experience may have been a divine sign, he thought, preparing him to receive divine revelation, for he understood each people to have their own prophet.[3] Interpreted as the angel Gabriel, this masculine personage came to Muhammad while he was asleep and told him to "read" (or "recite") three times some writing on a coverlet of brocade. Muhammad replied that he didn't know how to read. Then the angel said,

> Read: In the name of thy Lord who createth,
> Createth man from a [blood] clot.

Read: And thy Lord is the Most Bounteous,
Who teacheth by the pen,
Teacheth man that which he knew not. (Surah 96:1–5)

When Muhammad awoke, it was as though the words were on his heart. At first he wasn't sure what to think of these revelations. Initially, he thought he might be possessed by a spirit. Khadija was the first to believe in Muhammad's prophethood, and she encouraged him in it. Soon others, such as his cousin 'Ali and some of his friends, like Abu Bakr, believed that he was a prophet of Allah. After three years, Muhammad began publicly preaching a message of one God and of coming judgment. He enjoined the giving of alms (*zakat*) to the poor out of one's surplus. He condemned the rich for their neglect of the poor and orphans, and he opposed the Meccan usurers. His own status as an orphan must have influenced his teaching. During his time in Mecca, most of his converts were from among the poor and insignificant, who were more receptive to a message of judgment and paradise. However, Muhammad did not attack big business, such as the caravan trade or the promoting of pilgrimages to the Ka'aba in Mecca. Slavery was accepted as a natural institution, and he made no attempt to dismantle it. In fact, he owned slaves himself. He continued to receive purported revelations for twenty-three years, until he died in 632.

The Ka'aba and Idols

The Ka'aba was believed to have been built originally by Adam and then rebuilt by Abraham and Ishmael as the house of God. It was the center of Arabian pilgrimage and festival in Mecca. Muhammad's grandfather was the head of the Quraish tribe and the guardian of the Ka'aba and the holy well of Zamzam. Inside, the Ka'aba was filled with 360 idols of as many gods. The Black Stone in the corner of the Ka'aba had been the object of worship for centuries before Muhammad. (The fall of the meteorite was mentioned by a Roman historian as early as 60 B.C.) Although

Muhammad preached against the idolatry of the Meccans, he preserved the pilgrimage rituals that had been practiced in the preceding period.[4] These *hajj* rituals included circling the Ka'aba seven times and, if possible, kissing the Black Stone. By claiming Abraham as his religious ancestor, Muhammad was able to depaganize the Ka'aba and devote it to the cult of Allah.

At one point early in the Meccan period, in order to win the friendship of the Quraishites, Muhammad praised three of their goddesses, Al-Lat, Al-'Uzza, and Manat (Surah 53:19–20, which became known as the Satanic verses). He proposed that they were really angels or exalted goddesses to whom one could appeal before Allah. For a time, these remarks caused Muhammad to be suspect by his followers. Jews and Christians thought he had reverted to his original polytheism. Gabriel is then said to have come to Muhammad, rebuking him for giving as a revelation something that Allah had not revealed. Satan is blamed for putting something into his desires and on his tongue.[5] And so the surah continues, "Are yours the males and His the females? That indeed were an unfair division! They are but names which ye have named, ye and your fathers, for which Allah hath revealed no warrant. They follow but a guess and that which (they) themselves desire. And now the guidance from their Lord hath come unto them" (Surah 53:21–23). Although many Muslim scholars try to dismiss this incident, several of the earliest biographers of Muhammad include it, and there is no reason why it would have been made up.

Literacy

Most Muslims staunchly defend the view that Muhammad was illiterate. This helps to uphold their view that the Qur'an was miraculously revealed from heaven. They deny that Muhammad's own ideas and knowledge may have influenced his revelations. Later Muslims advanced this theory to remove any possibility of a human element in the development of the Qur'an. One verse, Surah 29:48, seems to speak to this: "And thou (O Muhammad) wast not a reader of any scripture before it, nor didst thou write it with thy right hand, for then might those have doubted, who follow falsehood." However, this may be a reference to the accusation that Muhammad was merely plagiarizing the Jewish and Christian scriptures, not a reference to his literacy in Arabic.

Muhammad came from a prestigious tribe, where being illiterate would have disqualified him from operating a caravan. Also, when Muslims from Medina captured Meccans, they were required to pay money or teach their captors how to read and write in return for their freedom. This suggests that the Meccans were more cultured and literate than the Medinans. Thus, it is difficult to think that Muhammad, with his background, would have been illiterate. Several *Hadith* sources indicate that Muhammad could write, including one in which he asks for paper and ink to write his will.[6] On his deathbed, he motioned for A'isha to bring him something on which he could write the name of his successor, but he was too weak to do it. When Muhammad made a treaty with the Meccans, they refused to acknowledge him as the apostle of Allah. So, in relenting to their demands, he struck out that phrase and wrote "Muhammad, son of Abdullah," and then signed the peace treaty. Another illustration of Muhammad's writing ability is found at St. Catherine's Monastery, where a letter dated 632 and said to be signed by Muhammad guarantees the monks' freedom because they honored Islam by building a small mosque in their walled fortress. Finally, in the first surah revealed to Muhammad, the angel Gabriel tells him, "Read: And thy Lord is the Most Bounteous, Who teacheth by the pen, Teacheth man that which he knew not" (Surah 96:3–5). If Muhammad could read, could he not also write? Here Allah refers to Muhammad as teaching by the pen.[7]

Knowledge of Christianity

Islam developed within the context of Judaism, Christianity, and paganism. On the Arabian peninsula, the major Christian influences were Byzantine, Nestorian, and Monophysite. Fundamental ideas in Islam were clearly borrowed from Judaism and Christianity, but they were often distorted. Analysis of several historical factors shows that Muhammad was influenced by both religions as he formulated his own religious views, although his understanding of them was sketchy. Muhammad's direct knowledge of Christianity was very limited. He had little understanding of Christian teaching or of what the Christian church was. There are phrases here and there throughout the Qur'an which remind one of phrases in the *Injil* (the Gospels) or in Christian liturgies.[8] The full witness of the Christian Scriptures seems never to have been available to the prophet of Islam. The Bible did not then exist in the Arabic language, and the Greek, Syriac, and other versions could have been available to him only indirectly, through personal contacts. From the contents of the Qur'an, it seems clear that Muhammad's Christian knowledge was completely oral in origin. It also seems evident that the quality and range of his contact with Christianity was insufficient to give him an authentic encounter with Christ.[9] We know that he had esoteric conversations with the monks Bahira and Nestur. His view of Christ seems to have been influenced by Nestorian Christianity.

There is also linguistic evidence that indicates Judaic and Christian influences on Muhammad. Numerous terms and names find their origin in the Bible, apocryphal literature, and Syrian Christianity. In addition, Islamic liturgy appears to be shaped by various Judaic and Christian sources, such as in their use of Scripture and *salat* (prostration). As a young man, Muhammad made caravan journeys to Syria, where he had contact with Nestorian Christianity.[10] But much of Muhammad's contact with Christianity occurred in the later period of his career, as a result of his political relations with Christian communities on the borders of Arabia and through a few of his wives, who had some Christian background. But there is no evidence that he had firsthand knowledge of Christian practices. Harold Coward writes,

> In the Arabian peninsula there were a number of scattered Jewish communities, and some at least nominally Chris-

tian communities. Indeed Muhammad understood his revelation to be a continuation and fulfillment of the Jewish and Christian biblical tradition. Muhammad's respect for the biblical tradition is exemplified in his teaching that in prayer one should face Jerusalem. It was only when the Jewish community of Medina refused to accept Muhammad as the sole leader of the one community of Allah that the Prophet ordered that prayer be offered when facing the direction of Mecca.[11]

Hijra

As Muhammad preached his message of judgment, belief in one God, resurrection, heaven, and his apostleship, conflict arose between him and the Quraish tribe of Mecca. They hated the Prophet for attacking their gods and teaching that their fathers who had died in unbelief were lost. According to Tor Andrae, this conflict had closely related religious and social aspects. Muhammad was preaching against the polytheistic religion of their ancestors, in which sacred customs were closely tied to tribal tradition. These religious traditions also reinforced the social order, keeping people in their proper place. The leading citizens of Mecca opposed Muhammad out of their arrogance and pride. They ridiculed him, saying, "Is it a mortal man, alone among us, that we are to follow? Then indeed we should fall into error and madness." They accused him of being a liar (Surah 54:24–25). Muhammad's opponents insinuated that he was simply seeking power and privilege, trying to exalt himself and desiring to have the leading role. They were indignant that a common man, with no natural claim to authority, should put himself forward as a prophet with authority over others. So the religious conflict led to a social conflict in which only one side could ultimately be victorious. Physically, Muhammad did not suffer much, but many of his poor and unprivileged followers were tortured and abused, and some were even killed.[12]

During the pilgrimage season, Muhammad met with six men from Yathrib (later called Medina), five of whom agreed with his monotheism, since they were familiar with Judaism. During the next two pilgrimages, he met them again and worked out an agreement to come to Medina and be their leader. Two feuding tribes would join together under the agreement, which included the provision that they had to obey him. Muhammad's charismatic personality, more than his doctrine, appears to have won them over.

Meanwhile, the Meccan polytheists were plotting to kill Muhammad. To escape from them, he and all of his 150 converts fled from Mecca to Medina on September 25, 622. So important was this event, called the *hijra* (the Hegira), that the year 622 became the first year of the Muslim calendar. (Their lunar calendar year is approximately eleven days shorter than the solar calendar year.)

Muhammad set up a religious government in Medina headed by himself as the one who knew the will of Allah. He gathered many followers and sought the allegiance of various Jewish groups. At first he was quite conciliatory toward the Jews. But because some of them refused to give their allegiance to Muhammad and even criticized him, he opposed them. Eventually, he became bitterly opposed to them and left the message to his community, "Let not two religions be left in the Arabian peninsula."[13]

Conquests

One lesson Muhammad learned while in Mecca was that the faith he was preaching would not gain many adherents through preaching alone. War and the use of force were incorporated as a doctrine of faith.[14] A part of the *Hadith* called *Sirat* describes the conduct of Muhammad during his wars. (Muhammad's sword and bow can be seen in the Topkapi Palace in Istanbul, Turkey.) Moral authority and religious doctrine were not enough to convert Arabia.

While in Medina, Muhammad established the first Islamic

state. As the leader of the new Islamic community, Muhammad led his followers into battle against those who refused to submit to his leadership or acknowledge his prophethood. In order to support the growing Islamic community, Muhammad led his followers on raids to plunder caravans, particularly those going to Mecca. This not only brought them wealth, but deeply affected the economy of Mecca.

The three most important battles occurred during Muhammad's consolidation of power. First there was the battle of Badr in 624 against the Quraishites of Mecca, in which the Muslim forces were victorious. They interpreted their victory as a divine judgment on the polytheists. During this battle, Muhammad received a revelation that one-fifth of the war booty was to go to him and the cause of Allah. The second major battle was again fought against the Quraishites, this time at Uhud in 625. This battle was lost by the Muslims, due to the defection of hypocrites seeking to gather valuable goods. Another battle, known as Khandaq, ensued when ten thousand Quraishite troops came to attack Medina. But the inferior force of Muslims was prepared, for at the advice of a Persian named Salman Farsi, they had dug a trench across the vulnerable part of the city. As a result, the Meccans gave up their siege and returned after a few skirmishes. But, during the siege, a Jewish group in Medina turned against the Muslims. The Muslims defeated them and had all their captured men killed and their women and children taken captive.

By 629 the central government in Yemen collapsed after being under Persian rule since 572. When the Yemenis turned to Muhammad for governance, his power greatly increased. This helped make the vital victory over Mecca possible. In 630, within eight years of arriving in Medina, Muhammad attacked Mecca with an army of ten thousand warriors. The inhabitants were forced to accept Islam. Because of the powerful leadership and influence of the Quraish tribe and Umayya clan, Muhammad assigned many of their leaders to high positions in the government and the military. Thus he was able to affirm their loyalty through partnership in power. As a result of their military conquest of the Arabian peninsula in eighty military operations, they acquired much wealth and power.

The Arabs converted to Islam not because of spiritual revival or religious persuasion, but because of their fear of Muhammad's army. The new religion, which began by merely seeking to introduce monotheism to the Arabs, developed into a means for military conquests. Muhammad was able to take control of Arabia because of intertribal strife, the lack of foreign domination, and the cultural backwardness of the people.

Marriage

Muhammad remained monogamous until Khadija died.[15] But in the ten years following her death, he married eleven other women.[16] First he married Sauda, but simultaneously showed affection for A'isha, who was six or nine years old.[17] She was the daughter of Abu Bakr, his closest companion. At her father's request, their marriage took place about three years later. A'isha was Muhammad's favorite wife during this period. Montgomery Watt thinks the marriage between Muhammad and A'isha must have been more like a father-daughter relationship, but Mostafa Vaziri comments, "The purpose of this marriage in light of the age difference has still not been satisfactorily explained."[18] There were many other women who gave themselves to Muhammad out of devotion to him. In addition, he had sexual relations with slave girls whom he owned. The motivation for Muhammad's later marriages is a matter of conjecture, but most Muslim scholars see them as having religious, political, social, economic, and strategic importance. Many of his wives were widows from the military campaigns, and two were daughters of his enemies.

One marriage that created some controversy was between Muhammad and Zaynab. One day Muhammad went looking for Zayd ibn Haritha (as was his custom), his adopted son, whom Khadija had given to him as a Christian slave—and whom he had freed. Upon entering Zayd's tent, he saw Zayd's attractive wife Zaynab naked behind a thin veil and was attracted to her. While she went to get dressed, she heard Muhammad murmuring, "Gracious Allah, good Lord who turns the heart." Proud Zaynab boasted of this to her husband, who then went to Muhammad and offered to divorce his wife for him. Muhammad refused, since it would have been considered incest for him to marry his adopted son's wife. But then Muhammad, in a trance, received a revelation while with A'isha that Allah had married them (Surah 33:36–40). A'isha responded, "Truly thy Lord makes haste to do thy pleasure."[19] Said to have been in an unhappy marriage arranged by Muhammad, Zayd divorced Zaynab so that Muhammad could marry her. Zayd continued to have a good relationship with Muhammad. Vaziri comments, "This incident involving Muhammad's personal life shows him relying on revelation to suppress any doubt about his worldly desires or any suspicion of possible error in his private conduct."[20]

The pre-Islamic custom of taking as many wives as one wished continued after Muhammad. It served the purpose of establishing political and religious ties between clans, besides the pleasure of having a harem. Muslim scholars generally agree that Surah 4:3 means that men are allowed to marry up to four women. But at the time of its revelation, many Muslims already had six to eight wives. Even 'Ali, after the death of Fatima, took more than four wives. It may be that originally the verse was meant to encourage those Muslims with only one or two wives to take more, not to set an upper limit, particularly since many men were killed in battle. If Muhammad had intended the limit to be four, he probably would have limited himself to four and instructed those with more than four wives to divorce those that exceeded the limit.

What Do You Think of Muhammad?

One of the most common questions that Muslims ask Christians is, "What do you think of Muhammad?" In answering this question, bear in mind the following things. Because Islam is both a religion and a political system, do not offend your Muslim friend culturally by saying anything derogatory. But be careful not to refer to Muhammad as a prophet. To say to a Christian with a Muslim background that Muhammad was "a prophet who went astray" would be incomprehensible, because a prophet is one who is rightly guided by God. To say he was a "false prophet" would offend and alienate an inquirer.

On the other hand, we as Christians must be honest theologically in answering the question. We could say something to this effect: "Since Muhammad was not mentioned or prophesied to come by the prophets of the Old Testament (see Deut. 18:15, 18, compared with John 1:21, 25, 45; 6:14; 7:40; Acts 3:22–26; 7:37) nor by the apostles as the Counselor or 'praised one' in the New Testament (see John 14:16, 26), we cannot recognize him as a prophet or apostle. Moreover, the test for a prophet of God is, 'If what a prophet proclaims in the name of the LORD does not take place or come true, that is a message the LORD has not spoken' " (Deut. 18:22). In presenting this truth, we must do so in a kind and humble way. This will help to build a relationship that will lead to further discussion. It is wise not to spend too much time on this question, for Muslims are very sensitive about their prophet. In fact, in many Muslim countries, to say something derogatory about Muhammad is punishable with prison or worse.

An honorable title of courtesy, such as Hazrat Muhammad, could be used when referring to him. You could mention the positive things about him, such as his strong leadership, his hatred of idolatry, his belief in one God, and his improvement of the life of the Arab people. Then Muslims will ask, "But do you believe that he was a prophet?" One good answer is, "If I did, then I would be a Muslim," but they may have trouble accepting that response. Dudley Woodberry, dean and associate professor of Islamic studies at Fuller Theological Seminary, writes in response to this question,

> Knowing that part of my answer might offend, I might answer with a question like "What would you think if I said

> a major prophet came after Muhammad?" Knowing they will affirm that Muhammad is the seal of the prophets, I can say that I feel the same way about Jesus. My point is made without saying anything negative that could be counterproductive.[21]

It would be helpful to point your Muslim friend to Hebrews 1:1–12 as an indication of why we need no new revelations through prophets. In these verses we see that after sending many prophets, God spoke to us through Jesus as the final revelation of God himself. After Jesus' redeeming work on the cross, which purifies us from our sins, he sat down in the place of honor beside God the Father. This indicates that Jesus had completed his work of redemption and is now ruling with God as Lord over all. The passage tells us that Jesus' name is superior to that of the angels, that he is worshiped by them, that he is called God and Lord, that he created the universe, and that he is eternal.

Succession

After the death of Muhammad on June 8, 632, leadership of the Muslim community was hotly contested. Muhammad was succeeded as ruler and religious leader of the Islamic state by the "four righteous caliphs," Abu Bakr (632–34), Umar (634–44), Uthman (644–56), and 'Ali (656–61).

Abu Bakr was a close friend of Muhammad from the days before his call to prophethood. Muhammad supposedly said that if the faith of all men were weighed against the faith of Abu Bakr, his faith would outweigh all of theirs.

Umar was known as "a man of sincerity and power, with hard hands but with an upright heart."[22] He lived a simple life, though he ruled over the largest empire in the world at that time. His rule was characterized by strict enforcement of the Qur'an and Muhammad's regulations.

Uthman succeeded him at age 70. He was weak in character,

indecisive, and favored his friends and relatives. He compiled one authoritative Qur'an and burned all other copies. After twelve years of rule, he was assassinated.

'Ali, Muhammad's cousin and son-in-law, was elected as the next caliph and ruled for five years. Uthman had appointed his nephew Mu'awiya governor of Syria. 'Ali recalled him, but he refused to give up his position. Instead, he formed an army which fought 'Ali's forces at Siffin. Out of this conflict, a splinter group formed, a member of which murdered 'Ali in 661.[23]

The Shi'ites believe that only 'Ali and his descendants were the rightful successors to the Prophet. Allah appointed prophets and spiritual leaders from Adam to Abraham to Muhammad to the twelve Imams, who were all physical descendants of their predecessors. The Shi'ites believe that a divine spark was transferred from one Imam to the next. 'Ali's two sons, Hasan and Husain, were the successive Imams after him. Husain's defeat in battle and death at the hands of his Muslim enemies in 680 at Karbala is mourned annually by the Shi'ites. The last Imam disappeared in 874, and they are waiting for his reappearance as the Mahdi, "the guided one," to establish righteousness and justice on earth. This idea appears to have come from the Christian belief in Jesus' return. There is disagreement among Shi'ites as to the number of Imams. The largest of the several Shi'ite sects, the Twelvers, are dominant in Iran. Muhammad's succession has continued to divide the Sunnis from the Shi'ites. It is not a theological division, but a question of who should have the power to control the world.

Expansion

After 'Ali's death, Mu'awiya became caliph. He had been Muhammad's secretary when they conquered Mecca. He directed the conquest of Egypt and Syria, and became the governor of Syria. He was of the Umayyad clan of the Quraish. Muhammad and 'Ali were of the Hashimite clan of the Quraish. The Umayyads consolidated their power and formed a dynasty (661–750) with its center in Damascus, Syria. They took the name Sunni after the *Sunnah* of the Prophet (his customs and precedents).

As early as the 640s, the Arabs had conquered most of Syria, Iraq, Persia, and Egypt. Within another thirty years, they were taking over part of Europe, North Africa, and Central Asia. By 750, the Muslim armies had conquered land from Spain in the west to India in the east. The Umayyad dynasty was succeeded by the Abbasid dynasty (750–1258), centered in Baghdad, Iraq. In 1258 the Mongols invaded Baghdad and other parts of the Islamic empire. Although they destroyed much of Islamic civilization and killed many people, they soon adopted Islam.

In the first one hundred years of Islam, Muslims conquered extensive lands that were about 90 percent Christian. In some places, such as Syria, the Christians preferred Muslim rule to that of the oppressive Byzantine empire. About 3,200 churches were either destroyed by the Muslims or converted to mosques. Many nominal Christians converted to Islam because of the poll tax imposed on non-Muslims and the social advantages of becoming a Muslim.

The Crusades, from the eleventh to the thirteenth century, in which Christians sought to retake the Holy Land from the Muslims, has had a profound impact on the Muslim world up to today. In 1095 Pope Urban II called for the first Crusade, saying, "God wills it." The secular motivations for the Crusades were wanderlust, economic gain (encouraged by repeated famine in Europe), expanded trade (particularly by Italian cities), and the desire to win glory, fame, and power in battle. The spiritual motivation at the outset was to assist the Byzantine emperors against the Muslim Seljuk Turks. Related to this was the desire to heal the breach between the western and eastern wings of the church. Most people desired to rescue the sacred places in Palestine, especially Jerusalem, from the Muslims. John Taylor's assessment is, "The Crusades were not launched in the spirit of Christian love of one's neighbor or enemy; they were launched for reasons of greed for wealth and territory, of intolerance towards the Eastern Churches, and of ignorance and arrogance towards Islam."[24] Many atrocities and massacres were committed in the name of Christ against Muslims, and they are remembered as if they just happened yesterday. K. S. Latourette says, "Here was an effort to achieve the kingdom of God on earth by the methods of that world which the New Testament declares to be at enmity with the Gospel."[25] Middle Easterners today view Christian missionaries as modern Crusaders.

When Columbus discovered the New World, Islam had more adherents than any other religion in the world, extending from Senegal, West Africa, to the Philippines. But it had lost the unity that it had in its early period. It had broken up into various empires. The colonization of most of the Islamic world by European nations from the eighteenth to the early twentieth century marked a period of decline in Islam. It was difficult for Muslims to understand how Allah could allow them to be subjugated by Christian nations. But in the latter part of the twentieth century, there has been freedom from colonial powers, a resurgence of Islam, and the blessing of tremendous oil wealth. But with the revival of Islam and a booming population have come deep divisions and strong nationalistic movements.

The Development of Islam

The Islamic religion arose after Judaism and Christianity had developed as powerful religious forces. Muslim theologians deny this fact by saying that Islam was the religion of earlier biblical prophets. In their denial, Muslim theologians appeal to the Qur'an, which states that Islam is the religion of Allah. They believe that Adam, Noah, Abraham, Isaac, Jacob, Moses, Jonah, Job, Zechariah, Jesus, and all the other prophets were Muslims. All these prophets had a message for their own nation, but Muhammad has been sent to all mankind. The *Hadith* says, "Every Prophet used to be sent to his nation only, but I have been sent to all mankind" (*Sahih al-Bukhari*, I, 331). Thus, Jesus is believed to have been sent only to the children of Israel. Nevertheless, it remains true that Islam, with its Qur'an, began during Muhammad's life, 570–632. Its message is not the same as that found in the Bible, although there are some similarities.

Recent research points to the possibility that much of Islam's development may actually have taken place during the Abbasid Caliphate, 150–300 years after Muhammad's death. Some Orientalist scholars contend that the Qur'an that we have today is not the one compiled by Uthman sixteen years after Muhammad's death. "The Qur'an was the product of an evolving revelation, more than likely canonized during the early Abbasid period towards the end of the 8th century, and in or around, what is today Iraq and Iran (see Crone 1980:3–17)."[26]

The traditions of Muhammad (*Hadith*) were passed down orally and compiled in written form during the eighth to the tenth centuries. Of the tens of thousands of traditions, only several thousand are considered authentic. But during the 150–300 years after the life of Muhammad, many embellishments were probably added to the story of his life.

For Reflection/Action

1. Compare the life of Muhammad with that of Jesus in the Gospels. What are the significant differences? How would you make this evident to your Muslim friend?
2. How do the pilgrimage to Mecca, the rituals related to it, and Muslim prayer facing the Ka'aba fit in with the worship of an unseen God who abhors idolatry?
3. How could you present a Christian view of marriage to your Muslim friend that would be more attractive than Muhammad's model?
4. Was Jesus a preacher of Islam? In what ways was he and was he not?

CHAPTER THREE

Cultural Understanding

The Definition of Culture

Culture, in its broadest sense, is the patterned way in which people do things together. Culture is a dynamic, creative, and continuous process that includes behavior, values, and substance, which are learned and shared by people and which guide them in their decisions and give meaning to their existence. If there is to be any common life and corporate action, there must be agreement, spoken or unspoken, about a great many things. Culture implies a measure of homogeneity. But if the cultural unit is larger than a clan or small tribe, it will contain a number of subcultures, and subcultures of subcultures, within which a wide variety and diversity is possible. Culture holds people together over a span of time. It is learned anew by each generation by absorption from the environment, especially in the home. Action in accordance with the culture is generally at the subconscious level. An accepted culture covers everything in human life. At its center is a worldview, that is, a general understanding of the nature of the universe and of one's place in it. From this basic worldview flow both standards of judgment or values and standards of conduct. Culture is closely bound up with language, and is expressed in proverbs, myths, folk-tales, and various art forms, which form part of the mental context of all members of the group. Cultures are never static; they are in a continual process of change.

Culture is people constantly interacting. It involves things that are repetitive, giving people a unified existence. Participation in a culture is one factor that provides a sense of belonging.[1]

There are three characteristics of culture: it is not innate, but learned; the various facets of culture are interrelated—you touch a culture in one place and everything else is affected; it is shared and in effect defines the boundaries of different groups.

Foreign-Born and American-Born

Among Muslims, there are thousands of cultures and subcultures. These various cultures from around the world have come to North America. As Muslims come here, their culture is impacted by the surrounding culture, creating some changes. The greatest impact is made on the second generation of immigrants. But influencing all of the Muslim cultures are the traditions and many cultural forms passed on by the Islamic faith.

The worldview and culture of the immigrant Muslim and the American convert to Islam are very different. The immigrant will likely retain most of the traditional Islamic customs and understanding of events, as found in his culture of origin. The American convert will likely have some basic Christian background (without having been a believer), which influences his or her outlook. The American convert, like secular non-Christians, will usually be familiar with many Christian words, but will not necessarily have an accurate understanding of their meaning.

Cultural Distinctives Common to Most Muslims

Muslims generally have certain cultural distinctives that come from their religion, setting them apart from the rest of North American society. However, the extent to which individual Muslims follow these distinctives varies widely. These distinctives fall under the following categories:

Clothing

According to Islamic tradition, men must be covered with clothing from their waist to below the knee. Women must be completely covered with clothing except for their hands, feet, and face (and some do not except the face). They may display their beauty only to their husband or close relative. They are not to wear tight fitting or see-through clothing. Many modern Muslim women believe that the head covering was useful in the early period of Islamic history, but that it is not applicable to them today. However, the rise of Islamic fundamentalism has generated a renewed interest in women wearing a head covering. Tor Andrae says that the tradition of head covering actually arose later than Muhammad's time, being adapted from Persian and Syrian Christians.[2] Men are forbidden to wear pure silk and gold, whereas women can wear both.

Food

No pork or pork products may be eaten, since pigs are unclean animals. However, some Muslims raise pigs to sell to non-Muslims. All meat must be *halal*, meaning that it must be butchered by having the name of Allah invoked as the animal's neck is slit and the blood is drained out. Many *halal* meat markets are now appearing around North America. Muslims will eat fish, but not shellfish.

Hygiene

The bathroom is considered unclean and the place of the devil. A Muslim would be surprised to find a Bible for reading in the bathroom of a Christian's home. Wiping or cleaning oneself after using the toilet is done with the left hand. Therefore, it is considered improper to hand someone something with the left hand.

Ablution (*wudu*), the ritual cleansing required before prayers, is done in the bathtub and sink when at home. Complete ablution by bathing (*ghusl*) is required after sexual intercourse, a wet dream, or giving birth. The body of a dead person is also ritually washed and buried within twenty-four hours.

If ceremonial washing with water is not possible, a Muslim can cleanse himself by putting or lightly striking his hands on clean earth, passing the palm of each hand over the back of the other, blowing off the dust, and then passing his palms over his face (Surah 4:43).

Shoes are removed when one enters a house, but slippers are worn to go into the bathroom or kitchen. Muhammad brushed his teeth with the fibrous root of a certain plant. Some Muslims use the same method, and these roots can be found in Muslim stores. Dogs are considered unclean animals and are not kept in the house. The thought of shaking hands with someone who has just petted a dog is repulsive. Cats, however, are considered clean, as Muhammad had pet cats.

Social relations

More conservative Muslims have women stay in the home rather than work in the marketplace. *Purdah* is the term used for the seclusion of women from the onset of puberty. Those who keep this custom mix only with near relatives and women friends. They also wear a veil (*hijab* [Arabic], *chador* [Iranian], or *burqa* [South Asian]) in public. Other Muslims think it is perfectly appropriate for women to take any position in the professions, politics, and business. Usually it is considered inappropriate for men and women to look each other in the eye or shake hands. Women are to cast their glance downward in the presence of men. Muslim men who come here as immigrants or students often misunderstand the motivations or intentions of North American women who are friendly, talkative, and outgoing in their relationships with men. A Christian woman should never attempt to witness to a Muslim man. Immigrant men will automatically assume there is marital or sexual interest. Women should seek to build relationships with other women, rather than Muslim men. A Muslim man must never be invited into a woman's apartment while she is alone.

When my wife and I (Bruce McDowell) were invited to a Muslim home for a dinner party with several other Muslim international student couples, the men and women ate and talked in two separate rooms the whole evening. When I went to a Nigerian Muslim's apartment regularly to teach the Bible, my friend never introduced his wife to me, nor did I even see her, even though she was there and would prepare lunch for me. A Sudanese student invited me and a mutual Muslim friend to his apartment for lunch. His wife served lunch to us, but stayed in the kitchen the whole time. Other Muslim friends were happy to have me meet their wives, talk with them, and enjoy a meal together.

Among immigrant Muslims, it is the practice to shake hands when you meet and when you leave your friends, even when you see each other regularly.

One should never sit cross-legged, because showing the sole of your foot is considered offensive. It is a sign of disrespect, especially to elders.

Marriage

Traditionally, marriages in Muslim families are arranged by the parents of the couple. It is quite common for these arranged marriages to be made between cousins so that family ties remain strong. Sometimes international students studying in North America will return to their home country toward the end of their studies to get married to someone arranged for them by their parents. However, it is becoming more common for Muslims here to marry for love. Many of the family connections for marriage are missing for immigrants who have been uprooted. It is common to see advertisements in Muslim publications of persons looking for marriage partners. Some Muslim groups, particularly among the Shi'a, believe in temporary marriage. This is seen as a way of getting around infidelity while a man is on a long business trip. A Muslim woman may not marry a non-Muslim, but a Muslim man may marry a non-Muslim wife. Thus it is ensured that the head of the home will be a Muslim, and so the children will be brought up as Muslims.

Cultural Clashes

Many of the counseling problems for which a Muslim will seek help from his or her imam are related to learning "to survive in an environment which is often unsupportive of Muslim ideals and values."[3] Several examples of the differences in values have been in the news recently. Two Kurdish refugees in Oklahoma were charged with seeking to arrange to marry underage girls. A twenty-nine-year-old Muslim man was charged in Maine for allegedly buying into marriage a fifteen-year-old girl for $250 and some used furniture. This payment was made to obtain the written permission from the girl's parent, as required for someone under eighteen. A Muslim flight attendant for U.S. Airways sued her company because she was not allowed to wear a head scarf on the job. She now teaches in the training department, where there are no uniforms.

Some of the cultural clashes Muslims encounter pertain to society at large and its view of Islam. Recently, sixteen American Muslim organizations called for the removal of a marble frieze of Muhammad on the north wall of the Supreme Court building. He is depicted as a lawgiver along with numerous others. The image shows Muhammad with a sword in one hand and the Qur'an in the other. The Muslims wrote the high court, "This imagery reflects long-held stereotypes of Muslims as intolerant conquerors and perpetuates misconceptions that continue to have a negative impact on the lives of ordinary American Muslims." They also said that Muslims discourage the use of "created images" of the Prophet. They offered to replace the image with quotations of the Qur'an. Chief Justice Rehnquist replied that the image would stay because it is "not intended as a form of idol worship," but simply recognizes him as "an important figure in the history of law." With regard to the sword in Muhammad's right hand, he said, "Swords are used throughout the Court's architecture as a symbol of justice." The Court did, however, revise its literature, which described Muhammad as the "founder of Islam" rather than as "the last in a line of prophets that includes Abraham, Moses, and Jesus."[4]

Some of the cultural clashes Muslims encounter in North America are not only with American society, but between various Muslim cultures. Often in Muslim student associations on college campuses, even among students from the same country, there will be a keen sense of competition and a power struggle. For example, Turkish students from small towns, with a more conservative background, will clash with students from major cities who have a more secular outlook. There may be major philosophical differences between Turkish students and Saudi students over music. Saudi students, with the Wahhabite interpretation of Islam, will say that music is not part of the Islamic tradition. However, for Turkish students, music is an integral part of their Islamic cultural heritage.

Cultural Differences Among North American Muslims

Yvonne Haddad and Adair Lummis summarize some of the distinctive characteristics of Islam in America:

> Throughout this century different waves of immigrants have brought to America different ideas and expectations of what it means to be Muslim. They come representing the consensus of what their fellow Muslims overseas think Islam is and should be at any given time. In the 1950s nationalist Muslims emigrating to America brought a rational interpretation of Islam in which the particulars of Islamic observance such as regular prayer and attendance at the mosque are considered less important than living an ethically responsible life. At the same time, a few imams came holding up the ideals of specific Islamic practice

> with a stress on law and ritual. More recently there has been an influx of Muslims from abroad with financial support from Saudi Arabia representing what they understand to be "official" Islam. These people are generally unwilling to compromise what they see as the incontrovertible principles of Islam in its pure form. All of these perspectives continue to characterize the whole picture of Islam in the United States and make it very difficult to generalize about "American Islam." One must take into account differences in nationality and ethnic affiliation, in educational level and economic status, in the interpretations of Islam current at the respective time that immigrants arrived in this country, and in the adaptations that occur over the years as a result of interaction with the American culture.[5]

Haddad and Lummis have categorized American Muslims into five groups:

1. Liberals are the most Americanized, with no recognized religious leadership.
2. Conservative, Westernized Muslims adhere to the minimum requirements of Islam concerning personal piety, diet, and prescribed practices.
3. "Evangelical" (their term, borrowed from Christians) Muslims emphasize what the Qur'an says and the example of Muhammad in defining the faith. They are concerned to adhere to all the details of keeping the faith. In order to do so, they remain isolated from all but a small group of like-minded Muslims.
4. Another group is similar in all respects to those in the third group, except that they seek to apply Islam to all of society. They want the U.S. to be an Islamic state.
5. The final group are the Sufis, who focus on the mystical aspects of Islam. Most of this group are converts to Islam.[6]

Festivals and Pilgrimages[7]

The following festivals play an important part in the life of a Muslim each year.

Ashura: Sunni Muslims celebrate this day as a day of thanksgiving for the mercies of God shown to various prophets: Adam was forgiven for eating the forbidden fruit, Noah was delivered from the Flood, Abraham was delivered from Nimrod's wrath, and Moses led the Israelites through the Red Sea. Shi'ite Muslims observe the day as one of penance and mourning in commemoration of the massacre of Imam Husain, the Prophet's grandson, and his followers in 58 A.H. (A.D. 680). Often it is observed by self-flagellation with chains in the streets until there is bleeding.

Eid al-Fitr (the Festival of Fast Breaking): This is a three-day feast at the end of the month of Ramadan, beginning on the first day of the month of Shawwal. After the 29 or 30 days of fasting during Ramadan (the end of which is determined by the sighting of the new moon), great feasting ensues. On the following morning, the whole community comes together, usually in a park or field. A speaker gives a short speech encouraging everyone to follow the ways of Islam, they pray together, and gifts are distributed to the needy. Friends and relatives give thanks, rejoice, and exchange greetings during the following days. Candy or gifts are often distributed to the children.

Eid al-Adha (the Festival of Sacrifice): This feast commemorates Abraham's offering of his son (Ishmael, not Isaac) as a sacrifice, and Allah's provision of a ram. The first day of the four-day celebration marks the end of the *hajj* (pilgrimage) observances in Mecca and commemorates the end of Muhammad's pilgrimage to Mecca. It starts on the tenth day of the month of Dhul-Hijja. Muslims all over the world join with the pilgrims in giving thanks, rejoicing, and sharing. Rams or camels are sacrificed in each community and the extra meat is given to the poor. It is roughly equivalent to the American Thanksgiving. This festival can be used as a bridge to show the necessity for a sacrifice for our sins.

Eid Ras el-Sannah/Yennair Festival: This commemorates the *hijra*, Muhammad's flight from Mecca to Medina in September 622. This event marks the beginning of the Islamic lunar year.

Hajj (Pilgrimage): This is the pilgrimage to Mecca that Muslims are to make once in their lifetime, if they can afford to do so. In Mecca they go through a number of rituals, including circling the Ka'aba seven times and sometimes kissing or touching the Black Stone (a meteorite) in the corner of the Ka'aba. The rituals also include the sacrifice of sheep and cows. In recent years the meat has been shipped to poor Islamic countries like Bangladesh. One can also pay to have the sacrifice made on one's behalf in one's hometown. All pilgrims wear the same white clothes during the *hajj*, putting the rich and the poor on an equal footing. Making the *hajj* is one of the five pillars of Islam. One who has made the *hajj* acquires the title of *hajji*.

Throughout the Islamic world, many Muslims make pilgrimages to the tombs of Muslim saints and relics of Muhammad. They believe that this will increase their merit on the Day of Judgment.

Isra-wa-al-Mi'raj (Night of Ascension): This commemorates Muhammad's nighttime journey from Mecca to Jerusalem and then his ascension to paradise (to the seventh heaven) from the Dome of the Rock (Masjid al-Aqsa) on a white-winged, horselike animal named Buraq. At each level of heaven, he was welcomed by various prophets. Upon coming to Allah's House, he was told of the obligatory five daily prayers for Muslims, after speaking to Moses and Allah. However, not all Muslims accept this tradition of the conversation with Moses and Allah (*Sahih al-Bukhari*, IV, 429). There is also debate as to whether it was just the soul or the soul and body of Muhammad that ascended.[8] But the *mi'raj* is mentioned in the Qur'an (Surah 53:13). This night is celebrated by reading the Qur'an, praying, and relating the story of *Israwal Mi'raj*.

Mawlid al-Nabi (Birthday of the Prophet): This celebration honors Muhammad's birthday, which is seen as a mercy not only to Muslims, but to all humanity. This form of veneration of the Prophet is held on 12 Rabi' ul-Awwal, the third month of the Muslim calendar. The practice began in the late eleventh century. Special assemblies are held, in which poems are recited, songs are sung, and stories of the Prophet's birth, childhood, preaching, suffering, and character are narrated. Special candies are made to share with the children, and folk music is played for the occasion. It is a time for inner joy and happiness.

Nisf Shaban (Half of Shaban): This commemorates the change in the direction (*qibla*) of prayer from Jerusalem to Mecca. Muhammad encouraged Muslims to fast during this day and to keep vigil on this night.

Saum of Ramadan (Fast of Ramadan): This is a month of fasting, when no food, drink, or sex is allowed from sunrise to sunset. One is not even supposed to swallow one's own saliva or smoke. Young children, the ill or weak, the elderly, and pregnant or nursing women are exempt. People are expected to help the needy instead of satisfying themselves. This month is sacred because of the many significant events in Islamic history that occurred during it, including the "coming down" of the Qur'an as the revelation of God's will for mankind to Muhammad. Fasting begins when there is enough daylight to distinguish a white thread from a black thread, or a half hour before dawn. There is no limitation on eating and drinking at night, so most people feast then and take it easy during the day. A meal (*sahur*) is eaten just before dawn and right after sunset (*iftar*). Often the community gathers together for the *iftar* meal at the neighborhood mosque.

Keeping the fast of Ramadan is one of the five pillars of Islam. It is a community effort, with everyone watching to see that others do not cheat. In Islamic countries it is enforced by law. This time of year can be especially difficult for those ministering to Muslims or for converts from Islam because it tends to tighten the grip of Islam on the community. It is a time of intense spiritual warfare.

During Ramadan, one is to learn to control one's actions, mind, and feelings. For a whole month, one's faith is tested by taking stock of one's personal weaknesses. It is a time for purifying both body and soul by doing good deeds. Emphasis is put on kindness, tolerance, patience, and mending fences. During this month, special prayers in the evening, called *tarawih*, are encouraged, along with the reciting of the entire Qur'an.

The beginning of Ramadan varies annually, in accordance with the Islamic lunar calendar of 354 days in a year. Each year Ramadan begins about eleven days earlier (on the solar calendar) than the year before. Ramadan is the ninth month of the lunar year, and it begins by the sighting of the moon and the making of astronomical calculations.

The last ten days of Ramadan are considered particularly blessed. This is especially true of the twenty-seventh day of Ramadan, which celebrates *Nazul al-Qur'an*, the revelation of the Qur'an. This is one of the holiest days in the Muslim calendar. On that night, the revelations began to be sent down (Surah 17:85) to the lowest of the seven heavens. From there, the angel Gabriel (Jibril) revealed it to Muhammad piecemeal, as the need arose. That night of initial revelation is called *Lailat al-Qadr'*, the Night of Power (or Majesty, or Destiny), which is described as better than one thousand months. The one who worships Allah at this time by performing optional prayers and reciting the Qur'an will get a better reward than worshiping him for one thousand months. At this time, the mosque is brightly lit, and the story of the revelation of the Qur'an to Muhammad is related. Orthodox Muslims gather in mosques to pray and recite the Qur'an until dawn. It is a time of heightened spiritual intensity. This night is described in the five verses of Surah 97 called "Power" (see *Sahih al-Bukhari*, III, 231, and chapter 2).

Youm al-Jumah (the Day of Assembly): Every Friday, Muslim men are obliged to assemble for prayers at noon. Women and children are not required to attend, but are welcome. They sit at the back of the mosque or in a section by themselves, possibly separated by a screen or curtain. A sermon is preached at the congregational meeting. This day is not similar to the Sabbath rest of the Bible, for Muslims do not believe that God becomes weary from his work and needs to rest. Of course, this is a mistaken understanding of the Sabbath. Muslims engage in business before and after the assembly, just as on other days.

Assumptions and Stereotypes of Muslims[9]

Some writers are saying that the twentieth century marked the confrontation between Christianity and Communism. The twenty-first century may well see the confrontation between Christianity and Islam. But Islam will also confront secularism and modernity.

There are many stereotypes that both Muslims and Westerners have of each other and of themselves that contribute to building barriers between them. The following list of typical stereotypes can be helpful to understand the outlook of ourselves and others. But stereotypes have a dangerous side, in that they depersonalize individuals. Stereotypes categorize people and reduce complex issues to their simplest forms without understanding the whole picture. We must be careful, particularly when relating to the individual we are befriending. But we also need to be careful in regard to the attitudes we develop, since stereotypes throw up barriers, rather than building bridges of understanding.

Stereotypes Muslims Have of the West

- The U.S. is a Christian country and a decadent colonialist empire.
- America is a materialistic society with no moral standards. Its people are sexually free, drink alcohol, and are racist.
- Independence and individuality are highly valued by Americans.
- Westerners are scientific wizards.
- Westerners don't value life, as evidenced by their practice of abortion and euthanasia.
- There is widespread disrespect for, and lack of authority in, the North American family.
- People in the West are irreligious, as demonstrated by the absence of public prayer.

These are some pros and cons of the West:

+ freedom
+ opportunity
– permissiveness
– decadence
– adversariness

Stereotypes Muslims Have of Themselves

- We are a very religious people.
- The West has questions; we have the answers.
- We are following the truth.
- There is one united Muslim world.
- We are more enlightened, since Muhammad was the last of the prophets.
- We have a fixed Qur'an, which cannot be translated and has not changed.
- We have a long history, which has proven itself.

- We have a fear of being backwards. The West both attracts and repels.
- We are peace loving. We prefer a war of words to a war of guns.
- Islam is very tolerant.
- Islam is realistic and reasonable.

These are some pros and cons of the Muslim world:

+ religious, not secular
+ a young religion, spreading across the world
+ triumphing over decadence, championing morality
+ growing world power
– ambiguous regarding modernity

Stereotypes We Have of Muslims

- Many are rich oil sheikhs.
- Many are camel jocks.
- They are Arabs.
- They are terrorists and fanatics.
- They are sinister and dangerous.
- They are backwards.

Stereotypes We Have of Ourselves in Regard to Muslims

- We are incapable of reaching them.
- God is on our side.
- The success of the West shows we are right.

The West's Assumptions

- Muslims must assimilate into our culture. We run into problems because Muslim immigrants don't fit the pattern of earlier immigrants.

- Religion is a private matter, making it is harder to witness in the U.S.
- As Muslims are Westernized, they will be more open to the gospel.

Muslim Assumptions

- The West is decadent, and Muslims must convert it. Muslims have a message that will change the world to right living.
- Muslims must maintain a separate Islamic subculture. Muslim children should be educated in Islamic schools.
- The West is misinformed, ignorant, and prejudiced against Islam by the media, politicians, orientalists, and missionaries.

Islam's Own View of Itself

There are eight presuppositions about Islam, which Muslims believe to be the most fundamental features of their religion:

1. *Islam is universal.* Although proclaimed in Arabic to the Arabs of Muhammad's time, Islam is a religion for all mankind. Muslims base their claim on the qur'anic verse, "We have not sent you but as mercy for all the nations" (Surah 21:102). Muslims believe that Islam is the only hope of humanity, and its victory over other religions and cultures is assured because all men have come from one community (*ummah*) without distinction of race, color, language, or culture.
2. *Islam is all-inclusive.* It is not a mere creed, but the basis of a whole way of life for nations and individuals. It has economic, social, civil, criminal, and international legal systems.

3. *Islam is eternal.* Muslims believe that Islam is the one true religion of Allah. It is the religion that God made known on the day when man first appeared on earth. In every age, in every country, and among every people, all God-knowing and truth-loving men have been Muslims, irrespective of whether they called their way "Islam" or something else.
4. *Islam is not the religion of the sword.* Muslims are concerned to refute the allegation that Islam achieved its conversions at the point of the sword. Their theory of *jihad* (holy war) often stresses (a) that certain conditions surround warfare "in the way of Allah," notably the requirement that it should be defensive, and (b) that warfare is the "lesser *jihad*," the greater *jihad* being the struggle against self, which takes place within each devout Muslim. They use the following qur'anic verses to show that Islam is not a religion of the sword:

> And fight in the way of Allah against those who fight against you, and not aggressively; surely Allah does not love the aggressor. (Surah 2:190)
>
> Let there be no compulsion in religion. The right Path has surely been made distinct from the wrong. (Surah 2:256)
>
> God will not change the conditions of a people until they change what is in their hearts. (Surah 31:11)

5. *Islam is rational.* Commentators and Muslim scholars stress that Islam is not antiscientific. "O my Lord! Advance me in knowledge" (Surah 20:114). Muslims argue that nothing in the Qur'an opposes reason, and that there is nothing in it that can be proved to be wrong. Not one of its injunctions is unjust; nothing is misleading.
6. *Islam is realistic.* Muslim writers argue that Islam accepts human nature as it is, without damaging it by describing it

as sinful, as the people of the book (Jews and Christians) believe. Islam proclaims that polygamy is the most balanced approach to social relationships between men and women. Through the institution of polygamy, divine guidance has steered a middle course between the two extremes that are devoid of rationality, decency, and justice. It is a balanced way between celibacy and promiscuity.

7. *Islam is harmonious*. Again, Muslim scholars and teachers (*'ulama*) emphasize that through Islam alone can harmony be achieved both for the individual and for society. They claim that Islam reconciles the conflicts of people and nations, faith and science, the material and the spiritual, the terrestrial and the transcendent. They claim that Islam has a twofold objective in this regard: (a) for the individual, it teaches how to live a clean, decent life; (b) for the community (*ummah*), it provides the basic principles for social, economic, and spiritual life, promoting progress and civilization. Islam is a religion for individuals and communities, without making any distinction between them.
8. *Islam is misunderstood.* Most Muslims believe that their religion is misunderstood, especially in the West. If we understood it, we would naturally embrace it. Many Muslims have rejected the Christian gospel because of Westerners who have sought to downgrade Islam.

What Should We Do?

1. Stereotypes hinder us in our outreach. We must get beyond stereotypes and deal with reality and truth. Begin where Muslims are, and find out where they are by getting to know them. Take time to do this.
2. We must separate Christianity from modernity. We must establish a new kind of relationship with Muslims to bring them to Christ.

3. Since Islam addresses the needs of both the individual and the community, in reaching Muslims for the gospel we must reach out to both the individual and the community. We need a holistic, biblical, world-and-life view that address the Muslim's concerns. A simply pietistic, individualistic, or ascetic faith does not appeal to Muslims.
4. To reach Muslims for Christ, we must open ourselves up to them and hear their point of view concerning their religion. It is clear from our experience with them that the right approach to Muslim evangelism is an educational one. A teaching ministry is needed for both Christians and Muslims, in order to remove the misunderstandings on both sides.

For Reflection/Action

1. What steps do you need to take to relate culturally to Muslims? How may it affect how you relate to your Muslim friend at a meal, in your home, in a mosque, or in a church?
2. What are some of your assumptions about Muslims?
3. Invite a Muslim to your home for a meal or tea and try to discover if any of each other's stereotypes are confirmed or found to be wrong.
4. How can you present the Christian faith in such a way that it is not identified with modernity and the West?

Part Three

Theological Understanding

It is crucial for understanding the relationship between Islam and Christianity to know what Muslims think about major Christian doctrines. Part 3 is an investigation of Muslim views of the Christian doctrines of the nature and character of God, the person and mission of Jesus Christ, human nature, and the effects of sin. Both traditions are compared with respect to their goals for society—the Islamic state and the kingdom of God.

In its cultural background and religious ideas, Christianity is closer to Islam than to any other religion, except Judaism—which is, in its pure form, a part of the total Christian revelation. The frequent mention in the Qur'an of Old Testament characters like Adam, Noah, Abraham, Ishmael, Joseph, Moses, David, Solomon, and others, together with such New Testament characters as Zechariah, John the Baptist, Mary, and Jesus, demonstrates a close relationship between the Bible and the Qur'an and therefore between Christianity and Islam. However, the stories about these people in the Qur'an are quite different from the accounts in the Bible, often including miraculous incidents and purported sayings that are quite foreign to the biblical characterization of the individuals involved. The qur'anic stories are actually closer to the midrashic tales of the Jews and the stories of Christian tradition and apocrypha, than they are to the canonical accounts. There is also a lack of chronological or historical background to the qur'anic accounts. For example, Miriam, the sister of Moses, appears to be confused with Mary, the mother of Jesus. But the chief point of difference between the Qur'an and the Old Testament is the absence from the Qur'an of any profound conception of sacrifice and a sacrificing priesthood.

Muslims and Christians have widely divergent understandings of the nature of man, man's role in the world, and how one should live out one's faith in the world. Muslims believe that an Islamic state must exist to live out fully one's submission to God. Christians believe that the kingdom of God is manifested in the lives of believers by a spiritual transformation that can exist in any type of external situation, but which brings external transformation as God works through believers. These divergent views also lead to differences in how these visions will spread. As we look at these matters, we will see that the kingdom of God is the Christian answer to the Islamic state.

The principle beliefs that Muslims and Christians hold in common are these:

1. God is the creator and sustainer of the universe, and he relates to people in a way that appears to them to be personal.
2. The whole universe is a coherent and ordered structure that is open to scientific investigation and research.
3. God controls history, and he himself will bring it to an end in judgment.
4. God has revealed his will to people through prophets and apostles, and through sacred scriptures.
5. Men and women, angels, and all created beings have the privilege and duty to worship God.
6. Part of our duty to God is to exercise social and moral responsibility.
7. Security in life is dependent upon the mercy and compassion of God.
8. Men and women may bring their requests to God in prayer, knowing that he will hear them and that he is able to effect his will in the world.[1]

CHAPTER FOUR

Revelation: The Qur'an and the Bible

Allah's Mercy in the Final Revelation

Although Christianity and Islam have different conceptions of man, they both believe that humanity needs revelation. For the Muslim, revelation consists of divine guidance for man in the form of law, while for the Christian, revelation is primarily concerned with redemption from sin to restore a right relationship with God.[1]

Muslims believe that human reason is imperfect and is unable alone to apprehend the real nature of the Good or indeed any reality at all. Absolute good and evil can therefore be known only by divine revelation through the mediation of prophets. In God's providence, there has been a succession of prophets from Adam to Muhammad, as long as men have been on earth. In principle, the revelations given to all the prophets were the same, although there was gradual development in accordance with the development of man. Each revelation expanded, modified, and abrogated the preceding revelations. Since the Qur'an is the final revelation, it contains the final and most perfect answers to all questions regarding belief and conduct.

The Qur'an makes it clear that Islam is the last and most complete of the revealed religions; that the sacred book, the Holy or Noble or Glorious Qur'an, cannot be abrogated; that the prophet Muhammad is the "Seal of the Prophets"; and that the Islamic religion embraces all religious duties. Islam sees itself as the culmination of a gradual development in which the *shari'a* (divine law) brought by each prophet was more complete than the *shari'a* preceding it.[2] Muslims agree that 104 books have been given by God. Muhammad is the last in the line of 124,000 prophets sent to peoples of all ages and nations. Twenty-five of these prophets are named in the Qur'an. Muhammad claimed not to have brought anything new, but to have restated the truth claimed by all the previous prophets and to have reestablished the primordial tradition (*al-din al-hanif*), which is the truth lying within the nature of things.[3]

As already mentioned, Muhammad is said to have been illiterate. This point is emphasized to show the miraculous nature of the Qur'an. It could only have been a revelation from Allah. How could such a perfect book have been written by an illiterate in such beautiful poetry and classical Arabic? Some Muslims say the Qur'an is the only miracle in Islam. They will refer you to Surah 10:38–39 to emphasize its unreproducible, sophisticated literary style and pure Arabic. "And this Qur'an is not such as could ever be invented in despite of Allah. . . . Or say they: He hath invented it? Say: Then bring a surah like unto it, and call (for help) on all ye can besides Allah, if ye are truthful."

Great reverence and awe of a somewhat mystical quality is given to the Qur'an by Muslims. It is treated as something almost worthy of worship. It is commonly read from an ornate stand made for holding it. Those who have memorized the whole Qur'an are shown great respect, even if they do not understand Arabic and cannot explain what it means. They are given the title *hafiz*. Muslims often comment on the beauty of the Arabic text, particularly as it is chanted. Merit is acquired from the rote reciting or reading of it, without any need for understanding.

Although the Qur'an asserts otherwise, it is a very difficult book for contemporary readers to understand, even for highly educated Arabic speakers. Frequently there are dramatic shifts in style, voice, and subject matter from one verse to another. It assumes a familiarity with words, events, and stories that were lost even to its earliest readers. At times Allah is referred to in both the first and the third person in the same sentence. Divergent accounts of the same story appear in different places. Some portions abrogate other portions of the text, and defend the right to do so.

The Meaning of *Qur'an*

Qur'an means "that which is read, recited, or rehearsed." Many believe that the first revelation to Muhammad was,

> Read: In the name of thy Lord, who createth,
> Createth man from a clot.
> Read: And thy Lord is the Most Bounteous,
> Who teacheth by the pen.
> Teacheth man that which he knew not. (Surah 96:1–5)

According to the Qur'an, Allah revealed the name Qur'an to Muhammad (12:2–3; 43:3).

> "Lo! We have revealed it, a Lecture [Qur'an] in Arabic, that ye may understand. We narrate unto thee (Muhammad) the best of narratives in that We have inspired in thee this Qur'an, though aforetime thou was of the heedless." (Surah 12:2–3)

The Qur'an is said to have been "sent down to the Prophet Muhammad (Surah 47:2), having been revealed to his heart through the Holy Spirit [understood as the angel Gabriel or divine inspiration] (Surah 26:193, 194) in the month of Ramadan (Surah 2:185)."[4] It is said to be a verbal revelation given to Muhammad during a period of about twenty-three years at Mecca (610–22) and Medina (622–32). The revelation came piecemeal to provide for the needs of the moment and is said to be adequate for all unforeseen contingencies. The first need was to create faith in the Creator, the One, the Supreme, the Mighty, the Wise, the Gracious, the Merciful.

Muslims hold to a dictation view of revelation, that the angel Gabriel dictated the very words of God from an eternal book in heaven. About three centuries after Muhammad's death, Muslim theologians asserted that the Qur'an was uncreated and coeternal with Allah. Essentially, one could say that the Qur'an means to Muslims what Jesus means to Christians. Muhammad is said not to have taken any initiative in being a prophet. He resisted the revelation, but was forced to be Allah's prophet by the angel. So Muhammad could not claim any special qualities or knowledge in himself for this revelation.[5]

Historical Development

Muhammad received revelations in Mecca for thirteen years, during which time he received ninety surahs. During the ten years after the *hijra* to Medina, he received another twenty-four surahs, which comprise one third of the Qur'an. The Meccan surahs can be divided into the early (612–17), middle (617–19), and late (619–22) periods.[6] The Medinan surahs were revealed over a long period of time, but the dates are quite certain. That is, portions of a surah were revealed at one time and other portions of the same surah were received later. Some early Medinan surahs contain verses that were added during the last days of Muhammad's life.

At the time of Muhammad's death, there was no complete manuscript of the Qur'an. The complete revelation was committed to memory by many of his companions, and surahs were written on scattered pieces of bone, leather, flat stones, and leaves. According to Islamic tradition, Abu Bakr, the first caliph, made the first complete written copy of the Qur'an. The Qur'an in its present form was compiled around 646 by Zaid ibn Thabit under the direction of Uthman, the third caliph. The followers of Muhammad who had memorized the surahs were assembled, together with the pieces of bone, leather, and leaves on which surahs had been written, in order to compile an authorized, authentic Qur'an. A manuscript in the possession of the daughter of Umar was used to produce the chief text of the official version. Uthman then made seven copies of this official version and distributed them to the Islamic learning centers in such places as Mecca, Medina, Basra, and Damascus. He had all other copies burned after 646–50, so there could be no challenge to the authentic text.

However, orientalists have been studying the earliest known manuscripts of the Qur'an. In 1972 in Sana'a, Yemen, the oldest known manuscripts of the Qur'an were discovered, dating from before 750. In 1981 the German scholars Puin and Von Bothmer began studying these ancient texts. However, they have been reluctant to publish more than brief articles on their research, partly for fear that the Yemeni government might deny them further access to the manuscripts, due to the repercussions of their findings. Puin discovered that these documents "revealed unconventional verse orderings" and "minor textual variations." They were written in the rare and early Hijazi Arabic script and were palimpsests—texts written over earlier, washed-off texts—which could be read with ultraviolet light. This seemed to indicate an evolving text, rather than one that has been unchanged since the time of Muhammad. Such a text would have less authority than has been claimed by Muslims. As R. Stephen Humphreys, a professor of Islamic Studies at the University of California at Santa Barbara says, "To historicize the Koran would in effect delegitimize the whole historical experience of the Muslim community. . . . If the Koran is a historical document [that is, one that developed over time], then the whole Islamic struggle of fourteen centuries is effectively meaningless."[7]

Aside from these Yemeni manuscripts, there are no other primary sources for Islam prior to 750. As Crone and Cook state, "There is no hard evidence for the existence of the Koran in any form before the last decade of the seventh century."[8] All of our sources come from a formative period of Islam 150–300 years after the events they describe, and so are quite distant from those events. There is no evidence for the original qur'anic text, nor of the recension distributed by Uthman. Although Muslims claim to have copies of Uthman's recension, not one has proved to be so. Two of the oldest copies of the Qur'an are the Samarkand manuscript in the Soviet State Library in Tashkent, Uzbekistan, and the Topkapi manuscript in Istanbul, Turkey. Both of these manuscripts were written in the Kufic script, which did not appear until the 790s or later. They are also written in a landscape format due to the elongated style of the Kufic script, which was not used in earlier Arabic manuscripts. Thus, these manuscripts must be dated 100–150 years after the supposed compilation by Uthman.[9]

Since Arabic culture had a strong oral tradition, the early qur'anic writings were written mainly as an aid to memorization. They were written without vowel markings or consonantal dots. In Arabic, five different variations are possible with one little jog (letter consonant), with either one, two, or three dots above or below the jog. Of course, this could change the meaning of words. In 705 Hajjaj, the governor of Iraq, introduced the system of pointing the letters, which made it much easier to read. But that could have introduced new meanings to words that could have been pointed differently.

Divisional Arrangement

The Qur'an is not arranged according to the order in which it was revealed. The very first verses revealed were Surah 96:1–5, and the last verse revealed was Surah 110. As a revelation came, Muhammad would tell the recorders and reciters the text and its placement in the whole. He dictated his revelations to half a dozen scribes. They had primitive methods of transcription, writing on pieces of leather or bone. However, the principal and most reliable method of preserving the text is considered to have been memorization. As Ajijola says, "The accuracy of the written or printed text needs to be attested by at least two persons of good repute who can recite it from memory, and not the other way about."[10]

There are 114 surahs, the longest comprising one-twelfth of the book (286 verses), and the shortest being only three verses. The longer surahs are divided into sections called *rukus*, which generally deal with a particular subject. Surahs are further divided into verses called *ayat*. The last 35 surahs are so short that they have no *rukus*. There are a total of 6,247 verses—or 6,360 if you include the *bismillah* that begins each surah. As an aid to recitation, the Qur'an is subdivided into thirty parts of equal length, called *juzw*. Each of these is further divided into four parts. The Qur'an has also been divided into seven *manzils* for its complete recitation in seven days.

Why does the Qur'an have its present arrangement? As Ajijola says, "It is not a book of history or biography, nor a book of recitations. It is a book designed as guidance for man in matters of belief, and for man's intellectual, moral, and spiritual welfare. The arrangement of the book is to be judged in terms of this purpose." It "is to guide man, to reform him, and to raise him in the moral and spiritual scale. Because of this, the Surah Al-Fatihah takes first place, this being the portal or porch of the Holy Qur'an; the Surahs Al-Ikhlas, Al-Falaq and An-Nas take the last places, being the finale of the Holy Book."[11]

The order of the Qur'an is considered to have been arranged by Allah. As Surah 75:17 states, "Lo! upon Us (resteth) the putting together thereof and the reading thereof."

Ajijola says:

> This order—the Divine order prescribed for the reading of the Qur'an—has a grand purpose. It is that a reader of the Book should become so drawn by the subject matter of the first Surah, that he should wish to go on with the reading rather than turn away from it. . . . The Surahs Al-Falaq and Al-Nas make him attached to it. The two last Surahs, therefore, are called Mu'awwadhatain, two refuges, two shelters, or if you like, two amulets for the reader of the Qur'an.[12]

Qur'anic Interpretation

Muslims believe that the Qur'an gives its own rules of interpretation in Surah 3:7:

> He it is Who has revealed the Book to thee: some of its verses are decisive, they are [the] basis of the Book, and others are allegorical; then as for those in whose hearts there is perversity, they follow the part of it which is allegorical, seeking to mislead and seeking to give it their own interpretation; but none knows its interpretation except God; and those well-grounded in knowledge, say, "We believe in it, it is all from our Lord" and none do mind except those having understanding.[13]

The "decisive" verses are those that are clear, to be taken at face value. They form the basis of the Qur'an and the fundamental principles of the religion. The "allegorical" verses are those that are susceptible to various interpretations.

In the eighth century a group known as the Mu'tazilites sought to develop a rationalistic means to define and defend the Islamic faith as it encountered other religions. They used the rational procedures of Greek philosophy, which raised many questions about predestination, moral responsibility, and the nature of God. The Mu'tazilites adopted a metaphorical, rather than simply a literal, understanding of the Qur'an. They believed that the Qur'an was created in time, as is anything that is not God himself, in opposition to those who believed it was uncreated and the eternal word of God. The Mu'tazilites' views were considered orthodox for a brief time under Caliph al-Ma'mun (813–33).

However, this movement was stamped out in the tenth century. The official doctrine became *i'jaz*, the inimitability of the Qur'an (making it untranslatable into other languages). This was a crucial turning point in Islamic history, determining the course of qur'anic interpretation down to this day. Instead of rationalism, legalism was developed as an application of the eternal revelation to social and political situations. Reason was employed by the orthodox only to apply the Qur'an to specific situations and to defend what the text stated. So Muslim theologians became legal experts. They did not explore the rational principles upon which the laws were based. They gave authoritative interpretations of proper behavior. The *'ulama* were concerned not with what people should know, but with what they should do. This theological method leads to inner conflict. Muslim theologians do not seek to resolve conflicting statements, but to assert both at once. We see an example of this in their statements about God being both one (a unity) and having attributes. The Mu'tazilites said this meant that God's attributes are the same thing as God. Otherwise, we could say that God is made up of parts. The orthodox settle this question by saying that God's attributes "are not He nor are they other than He."[14]

Various Muslim intellectuals from Egypt, Iran, Algeria, and Pakistan who have upheld Mu'tazilite views in recent years have been declared apostate, resulting in their death or exile. They have sought to reinterpret Islam for the modern world, hoping to bring about its renaissance. But there is a huge gap between these intellectuals and the majority of Muslims, who will never question the orthodox understanding of the Qur'an and Islamic history.[15]

The Relation of the Qur'an to the *Sunnah* and the *Hadith*

The *Sunnah* is the mode of life of the prophet Muhammad, which has become the body of social and legal custom. It includes both his practices and his sayings. *Hadith*, originally meaning "news," has essentially the same meaning, but more specifically refers to Muhammad's sayings. The *Sunnah* and the *Hadith* are the second source of the law in Islam. One must be careful to assign neither too much nor too little importance to the *Sunnah*, relative to the

Qur'an. Muhammad was required in one revelation to give an explanation of the Qur'an (Surah 16:44). This he did by both example and words. This explanation is considered to be by divine inspiration. Muhammad did not receive a revelation recited in words for this explanation, but was guided by inner revelation. Since the Qur'an revealed not just a religion of certain beliefs, but a whole way of life, a code was needed for all aspects of man's life. The broad principles of life found in the Qur'an were given specific application in the example of Muhammad. The Qur'an says, "Surely you have in the Apostle of God an excellent exemplar" (Surah 33:21). The Qur'an repeatedly says to obey God and the Apostle.

From the beginning, the *Sunnah* of Muhammad was seen as a second source for Islam, and so the companions of Muhammad preserved his sayings by memory and occasionally in writing. However, Muhammad discouraged the writing of the *Sunnah*, so that it would not get inadvertently mixed up with the Qur'an. After Muhammad's death, schools developed in which the *Hadith* was passed on, by memory and in writing, in short narratives and reports on the sayings and deeds of the Prophet. But *Hadith* seemed to grow as new situations were encountered and new teachers sought to give qur'anic application to those situations. In the ninth and tenth centuries, collections were made of the *Hadith* by famous people like al-Bukhari and Muslim, 120–290 years after the death of Muhammad. Bukhari had received much of his traditions from Imam Malik ibn Anas (712–95). It is said that especially in regard to the practice of Muhammad, the *Hadith* forms a reliable source of Islamic teaching. If any errors have crept into the *Hadith*, they are seen as being corrected by the Qur'an itself. So only *Hadith* that comes from the most reliable collections and does not contradict the Qur'an is accepted.

The transmitters of *Hadith* accepted by the Sunnis are al-Bukhari (d. 870), Muslim (d. 875), Ibn Majah (d. 886), Abu Dawud (d. 888), At Tirmidh (d. 892), and An Nasa'i (d. 915). There are 7,413 *Hadith* sayings that are considered to be authentic. Various editions have been published, one in six volumes. To have a good understanding of Muslim thinking, you have to read the *Hadith*.

Islamic tradition comes in four genres: (1) the *Sira*, biographies which speak of the Prophet's traditional life (including battles); (2) the *Hadith*, thousands of short narratives on the life and sayings of the Prophet; (3) the *Ta'rikh*, histories and chronologies of the Prophet's life; and (4) the *Tafsir*, commentaries on the Qur'an. However, the latter two sources are not considered primary, except in the absence of any earlier source on the subject matter. The best known of these were written by at-Tabari (d. 923).

Has the Bible Been Corrupted?

When Muhammad was in Medina, he encountered Jews who opposed his claim to prophethood. When it became evident that there were basic differences between the Qur'an, on the one hand, and the Scriptures of the Jews and Christians, on the other hand, the Muslims accused the Jews and Christians of dividing up their Book (into Torah and Evangel) and corrupting it. Jews were accused of concealing verses in the Bible foretelling the coming of Muhammad as a prophet.[16] According to Muhammad, previously written Scriptures, being prophecies of the future, must have contained references to his own coming. Therefore, if Jews and Christians would not admit it, they must have been concealing something that was in the Book revealed to them. Other qur'anic passages accuse the Jews and Christians of deliberately "corrupting" or "altering" the Scriptures with their mouths, which seems to mean playing with words to make fun of the Muslims. The Qur'an does not say that the *text* has been corrupted. Muhammad maintained that the message of the *Taurat* (Torah) and the *Injil* (Evangel) must have been the same as his own. When he discovered that Christian teaching differed from his own in essential respects, he inferred that they must have corrupted the Evangel.[17] But the developed form of the doctrine that Jews and Christians had corrupted the Scriptures did not appear until some time after Muhammad's death. As this doctrine of *tahrif* developed, Muslims generally came to regard the existing Jewish and Christian texts as valueless.[18] This view is seen in the *Hadith:*

> Why do you ask the people of the scripture about anything while your Book (Quran) which has been revealed to Allah's Apostle is newer? You read it pure, undistorted and unchanged, and Allah has told you that the people of the scripture (Jews and Christians) changed their scripture and distorted it, and wrote the scripture with their own hands and said, "It is from Allah," to sell it for a little gain. (Bukhari, [Vol. 9], 339).[19]

Here Jews and Christians are accused of having changed their Scriptures for unethical gain.

However, it should be known that

> the earliest extant manuscripts of the whole of the Old Testament and New Testament (the Codex Sinaiticus) date from the fourth century A.D. (i.e., 200 years before the time of Muhammad). The Old Testament [containing the *Taurat* and *Zabur*] texts among the Dead Sea Scrolls date from the last few centuries B.C. and the earlier part of the first century A.D.; and they confirm the accuracy of our accepted texts. Similarly with the New Testament [*Injil*], there are several manuscripts or parts of the New Testament which date from the third century. And the earliest fragment of the New Testament that has been found dates from around 125 A.D. (the Chester Beatty Papyrus). If, therefore, Muhammad believed that the revelation which came to him confirmed the previous Scriptures, which he knew were in the hands of Jews and Christians at that time, at what stage could they have been corrupted, and by whom? Muhammad could hardly accuse the Jews and

> Christians of corrupting the text of their Scriptures and, at the same time, claim that the Qur'an was confirming all that the Scriptures revealed before.[20]

Christians today are confident that the Bible we have is fully trustworthy, being essentially the same as the originally inspired documents.[21] There is no historical evidence of a *Taurat, Zabur,* or *Injil,* as the Qur'an speaks of it. Also, there is no shred of evidence for any written text of the Old Testament apart from what we already have. We have the same Bible today that the Jews and the Christians had long before Muhammad lived.

Qur'anic teaching itself indicates that God would not allow his word to be changed. The following passages support this view:

> Shall I seek other than Allah for judge, when He it is who hath revealed unto you (this) Scripture, fully explained? Those unto whom We gave the Scripture (aforetime) know that it is revealed from thy Lord in truth. So be not thou (O Muhammad) of the waiverers. Perfected is the Word of thy Lord in truth and justice. There is naught that can change His words. He is the Hearer, the Knower. (Surah 6:115–16)

> Theirs are good tidings in the life of the world and in the Hereafter—There is no changing the Words of Allah—that is the Supreme Triumph. (Surah 10:65)

However, modern Islamic interpreters may not interpret these verses in a way that supports the integrity of the Bible.

A mere accusation that the Bible has been corrupted does not constitute proof that it has been corrupted. Ask your Muslim friend to show you where the Bible has been changed. Ask him when it was changed. Can he tell you what historical documents the charges are based upon? Help him to see that accusations need to be backed up with evidence. Thus he may be led to see the infallibility of the Bible. Also ask him, "Cannot God, being all-powerful, protect his Word from corruption?"

Changes Within the Qur'an

The Qur'an itself affirms that it has been changed:

> And when We put a revelation in place of (another) revelation,—and Allah knoweth best what He revealeth—they say: Lo! thou art but inventing. Most of them know not. (Surah 16:101)

Islamic scholars differ on what portions of the Qur'an have been abrogated by later revelations. There are twenty cases where one revelation has been said to supersede, contradict, or abrogate a previous revelation. One change acknowledged by all Muslims is the change in the direction for prayer (Surah 2:142). Originally Muhammad had directed that people were to face Jerusalem when praying. However, after he had a conflict with the Jews in Medina, he received a revelation that prayer was to be directed toward the Ka'aba in Mecca. Why would Allah not have given this important revelation at the beginning, since the Ka'aba is supposedly the center of the universe, established at the beginning of human history? The qur'anic reason is that Allah was distinguishing "who followeth the messenger, from him who turneth on his heels" (Surah 2:143).

Interpreting the Bible and the Qur'an

When comparing Islam and Christianity, Christians cannot interpret the Qur'an by the Bible, nor can Muslims interpret the Bible by the Qur'an. Each can be rightly interpreted only within its own context: the Qur'an by the Qur'an, and the Bible by the Bible. (Of course, the Bible, as the authoritative Word of God, does judge the Qur'an.) Many, both Muslim and Christian, have attempted to interpret the other's scripture when comparing the two religions, but this has generally led to more misunderstanding.[22] Biblical language does not help us understand qur'anic language. For example, Muslims speak of 'Isa (Jesus) as the "word of God" and "a spirit from God," but Christians understand these terms in a different sense than Muslims do. The Word of God in Christianity is a "person," while Islam has ordinary speech in mind. The Muslim idea is that Allah created 'Isa (Jesus) through his speech. "A spirit from God" for Muslims refers to the angel Gabriel breathing into Mary a subtle body which conceived Jesus. But for the Christian, the Spirit of Jesus is the Holy Spirit, the third person of the Godhead.

Using the Bible and the Qur'an for Witness

Many Christians who witness to Muslims use the Qur'an to prove their arguments and point to the gospel. Some converts from Islam have even testified to becoming interested in the Christian faith because of the exalted things the Qur'an has to say about Jesus. While using the Qur'an as a source for Christian witness has had some success, it has a number of problems.

Generally, avoid using the Qur'an to prove your arguments. This only emphasizes the authority of the Qur'an to the Muslim. Pointing to the similarities between the Qur'an and the Bible only confirms to the Muslim that the Qur'an is right and that it is the final part of the progressive revelation. To account for the differences between the Qur'an and the Bible, he will argue that the Bible has been corrupted.

As you point to a qur'anic verse to make a point, the Muslim will often offer a different interpretation of it. That is why it is best that Muslims and Christians each interpret their own scriptures by their own rules of interpretation. Muslims will certainly misinterpret the Bible whenever they attempt to use it for their arguments.

Also, use discernment in quoting from the Qur'an. If someone from a Christian background points to errors in the Qur'an, that may cause the Muslim to take a more entrenched position. That could put the Muslim in a defensive mode that would close him off from seeking the God of the Bible. When challenged, a Muslim may become more fervent in his faith and adopt a more fundamentalist view of Islam. However, Christians can lead their Muslim friends to discover the theological and historical errors in Islam if the time is right for such things (see Prov. 25:11; Surah 16:125). A Muslim will discover many of these errors on his own as he is confronted with the truth of the Bible.

Another danger in using the Qur'an is that you could be accused of blasphemy against Allah by denigrating his prophet or the Qur'an. Even if you do not intentionally do that, sometimes it can be misconstrued that way. In some Islamic countries, that could mean imprisonment or death.

When witnessing to Muslims, let the Bible speak for itself. This does not mean that we do not explain its meaning, or answer objections, or give a defense of our faith through reason. But man's reason has been corrupted through the noetic effects of sin. Even our ability to understand has been affected by Adam and Eve's fall from a relationship with God in the Garden of Eden. The ability to understand spiritual truth comes from the Spirit of God. "The man without the Spirit does not accept the things that come from the Spirit of God, for they are foolishness to him, and he cannot understand them, because they are spiritually discerned" (1 Cor. 2:14). Consequently, our carefully reasoned arguments may fall on deaf ears. But "the word of God is living and active. Sharper than any double-edged sword, it penetrates even to dividing soul and spirit, joints and marrow; it judges the thoughts and attitudes of the heart" (Heb. 4:12). It will penetrate the heart of a Muslim. The Holy Spirit works in a person's heart through hearing the word of God. Therefore, do not put an emphasis on reasonable arguments outside of Scripture. They will usually not be convincing to a Muslim, and will be countered by Islamic apologetic arguments. God's word "judges the thoughts and attitudes of the heart." This is what is missing in Islam.

Handling the Qur'an and the Bible

Avoid offending your Muslim friends by putting the Bible on the floor, near your feet, or below your waist. Muslims treat the Qur'an with special care by keeping it on a stand and storing it on a high shelf. Do not share with your Muslim friend from a Bible that has been written in, underlined, or highlighted. This, too, would be seen as not treating it with proper honor. What is more important for most Muslims is conformity to outward forms of respect, rather than understanding the meaning of the text. Most Muslims around the world memorize the Qur'an without understanding the Arabic they are memorizing. For Muslims, the Qur'an in the form of paper and ink is sacred, not just its content.

In folk Islam, the Qur'an is thought to have magical powers. Portions of the Qur'an may be written on a piece of paper with ink that is then washed off to be used for magical purposes. For example, the washed ink may be drunk for its healing powers. The Qur'an is used in divination by closing one's eyes, saying God's name, reciting the *Fatiha,* and drawing one's fingers from the back of the Qur'an through its pages. The Qur'an is opened where one's finger enters and one reads the first verse on the page. From these words one concludes what one should do or advise. The Qur'an is used throughout the Islamic world as a talisman; miniature copies are often hung on children's clothes for protection. Daily recitation of the Qur'an is said to keep Satan away from that person's home.

As we have seen, there are some major differences between Christianity and Islam on the nature of revelation, the authority and accuracy of the Bible and the Qur'an, and Muhammad's value as a model. Some confusion arises when Christians attempt to use the Qur'an in their witnessing, because that vests the Qur'an with authority and because Christians and Muslims use certain terms with different meanings. We ought to expose Muslims to the words of the Bible and let it speak for itself. Then the Holy Spirit will do his work in their hearts.

For Reflection/Action

1. To what degree is it useful to use the Qur'an in one's witness to Muslims? How might it be used?
2. Ask a Muslim you are befriending to respond to the qur'anic verses that affirm the authority of the Bible.
3. Encourage your Muslim friend to read the Bible and become familiar with it. You could begin by giving him a copy of the Gospel of Luke. Giving him a whole Bible at first may be too overwhelming. If you do, give him some advice on where to start.

CHAPTER FIVE

The Nature and Character of Allah

The Nature of Allah

The term *Allah* in Arabic means "the One and Only True, Universal God of all." The same term is used in the Arabic Bible for "God." So the terms *Allah* and *God* are synonymous. However, this does not mean that the Allah of the Qur'an and the God of the Bible are revealed to have the same nature and character.

Allah's Transcendence

The qur'anic view of God is deistic in the sense that God and the world stay apart. In orthodox Islam there is no entrance of God into the world or any human fellowship with God.[1] However, Sufis would probably say that God is everywhere in nature, as they seek to experience him through spiritual exercises (*dhikr*). Orthodox Muslims understand God as being beyond every quality and state that belongs to creatures, which would make the incarnation of Jesus impossible. In fact, belief in the oneness of Allah means that "none can be named or qualified with the Names or Qualifications of Allah."[2] In common with Christians, Muslims understand that God is without any limit or boundary. He is not material or corporeal or limited to space and time. Every divine quality is free from the notion of limitedness, as the Qur'an says:

"Nought is as His likeness" (Surah 42:11).[3] However, Christians believe that God, in Christ, willingly humbled himself in the form of a man, thus putting limits on himself for a time in the person of Jesus.

Christian assertions concerning the nature of God are positive statements, such as: God is a spirit; God is light; God is love. However, Allah is defined by a series of negations. Allah is understood to have absolute sovereignty and omnipotence. His character is impersonal—infinite and eternal. He has neither a body nor a spirit. Al-Ghazali says, "Neither does He exist in anything nor does anything exist in Him."[4] A Muslim never thinks of God as having any particular image, whether physical, human, material, or otherwise.

Islam teaches that God does not reveal himself to anyone in any way. God reveals only his will, which is found in the Qur'an. God is transcendent, so any thought of God's self-revelation or immanence would compromise his transcendence.[5] But Allah is not just a philosophical concept or a remote deity. A Muslim would say that Allah is a personal God, who is close, easily approached, loving, forgiving, and merciful. "Allah is closer to the human than his jugular vein."[6] However, his closeness and personality are of a different kind than is understood among Christians. As al-Hilali and Khan put it, "He is with us by His Knowledge only, not by His Personal Self, 'There is nothing like unto Him, and He is the All-Hearer, the All-Seer' (Surah 42:11). . . . It is not like as some people think that Allah is present everywhere, here, there and even inside the breasts of men."[7] For the Muslim, the reduction of God's transcendence is not permissible. God's relationship to man is didactic, hortatory, and educational; it is revelatory only in terms of propositions. Harold Spencer explains: "Between the nature of Allah and that of man there is an absolute 'opposition'. Allah remains inaccessible and man can know nothing of His nature. By contrast with the language of the Bible this means that man may not 'participate in the divine nature' (see 2Pe 1:4); as the Qur'an says, 'There is no participation in Him'."[8]

Misconceptions of the Trinity

One of the most familiar objects of Christian teaching attacked by Muslims is the doctrine of the Holy Trinity, because it is understood as not only blasphemous but irrational. How can one plus one plus one equal one? But most Muslims have neither seriously tried to understand this doctrine nor examined its implications.[9]

The Qur'an takes a sympathetic attitude toward Christians (Surah 5:82) and distinguishes them from the *mushrikun* who worship other gods than Allah. However, many verses from the Medina period exhort Christians not to fall into the crime of "associating," but rather to bear witness to the one and only God. Thus, in regard to the Trinity, the Qur'an says, "Say not 'Three'—Cease! (it is) better for you!—Allah is only One God" (Surah 4:171). And in another surah we find: "They surely disbelieve who say: Lo! Allah is the third of three; when there is no God save the One God. If they desist not from so saying a painful doom will fall on those of them who disbelieve" (Surah 5:73).[10]

For the Muslim, monotheism does not mean simply the unity of God, because there can be different persons in unity. Monotheism in Islam is the absolute oneness and uniqueness of Allah, which precludes any doctrine of persons sharing a Godhead. It also excludes all forms of God-incarnate philosophies.[11] God is absolute and transcendent. The oneness of God is emphasized in Surah 112: "Say: He is Allah, the One! Allah, the eternally Besought of all! He begetteth not nor was begotten. And there is none comparable unto Him." The Arabic word used here for "one," *ahad*, is different from the word *wahed*, which indicates numerical oneness. *Ahad* has the specific meaning of "one" in the sense of "solitary, excluding a trinity." Arabic-speaking Christians use the word *wahed* when referring to the Triune God. So when King Hussein of Jordan was buried and Surah 112 was recited eleven times, they were declaring to the world that their Unitarian God is the only true God, while the Trinitarian God of Christians is false.[12]

Muslims accuse Christians of tritheism, which is *shirk*—ascribing companions or plurality to the Deity. It is natural for Muslims to use this term for Christians because Christians believe that the Son of God is omniscient, independent of the creation, a powerful intercessor, and worthy of worship. Therefore, almost all the passages in the Qur'an which speak against idolatry and assert God's unity are used by Muslims to deny the doctrine of the Trinity.[13]

Christians, no less than Muslims, believe in the unity of God (Mark 12:29; 1 Cor. 8:4–6; James 2:19). The mystery of the Trinity does not mean that there are three gods or that two other beings are associated with God.

Both Christian and Muslim scholars tend to read later controversies into the Qur'an. Thus, the rejection of the doctrine that "God is one of three" is usually taken to be a denial of the Christian doctrine of the Trinity. Strictly speaking, however, what is rejected is a doctrine of tritheism, which orthodox Christianity also rejects. Similarly, when Muslims reject the fatherhood of God the Father and the sonship of Jesus, they misunderstand that a physical relationship is being claimed, which Christians also reject.[14] Muslims who try to refute Christian teaching have misunderstood the doctrine of the triune God to mean that there is plurality of substances in God. Others, who have been more sympathetic toward Christianity and have recognized that Christians really are monotheists, such as al-Ghazali, Ibn Rushd, and Ibn Qayyim, have understood only a heretical modalist view of the Trinity and the Incarnation as the language of theophany. Generally speaking, Muslim refutation of Christian teaching has come from an obsessive urge to defend the transcendence of divine unity. Christian doctrines are dismissed because they are seen as an affront to the divine nature. Although both Muslims and Christians believe in the unity of the divine substance, Muslims usually think that Christians either deny it or at least distort it.[15] The word "begotten" in the King James Version of the Bible (John 1:14, 18; 3:16) only adds to the confusion.

Qur'anic formulas reject heterodox formulations of the mystery of the Trinity (such as God, Jesus, and Mary) that are not related to the Trinity of authentic Christianity. The Qur'an rejects the Nestorian[16] formulation of the Incarnation ("to take a son to oneself") as well as the Monophysite[17] formulation ("God is the Messiah"). Some scholars believe that Muhammad never knew the doctrine of orthodox Christianity; therefore, he was unable to reject it. What he rejected were distortions of Christianity. Nonetheless, Muslim theologians have exploited qur'anic texts that deny Christian teachings, not understanding the precise meaning of those denials. This has caused centuries of regrettable misunderstanding.[18]

It is difficult to understand why the Qur'an would reject a trinity consisting of God, Jesus, and Mary. Did Muhammad not comprehend the basic doctrine of the Trinity as believed by Christians? Christian scholars have often thought so. But Muhammad came into contact with Christianity in several ways: from Yemeni Christians visiting Mecca; probably during his merchant caravan trips to Syria; from his favorite concubine, Miriam, a Christian Copt from Egypt; from returning Muslim refugees from Abyssinia; and from the learned deputation to Muhammad from Najran, headed by a bishop of the Orthodox Church. There were probably other contacts, too, such as Khadija's cousin Waraqah. Although the Christian groups in that region adored and prayed to the virgin Mary, none of them understood the Trinity to include her rather than the Holy Spirit. Therefore, some writers conclude that Muhammad's idea of God includes a deliberate rejection of the Christian idea of the Godhead—the Father, the Son, and the Holy Spirit.

One possible source for the confusion between Mary and the Holy Spirit in the Trinity could be the fact that the Syriac word *ruha*, "spirit," is feminine, and some Syriac-speaking Christians used to think of the Holy Spirit as "she." Also, an early apocryphal gospel, *The Gospel According to the Hebrews*, contained this sentence, referring to the temptation of Jesus: "Even now did my Mother, the Holy Spirit, take me by one of mine hairs, and carried me away unto the great mountain Thabor." This idea of the Spirit became widespread. Additionally, this confusion could be explained by the extraordinary veneration of the virgin Mary by the Abyssinian Christians.[19] Finally, research has revealed that a heretical Christian sect known as the Choloridians, who held a view similar to that described in the Qur'an, had contact with Mohammad during his tenure in Mecca.

The Holy Spirit or Gabriel?

When we say that God is a spirit, the Muslim believes that we are speaking a horrible blasphemy. The Qur'an does use the word *spirit* twenty times, but each time the word is understood to refer to a created being that has a subtle body capable of penetrating a coarse body. Angels and *jinn* have such subtle bodies. So to say that God is a spirit is understood to mean that he is a created being. The "holy Spirit" is mentioned several times in the Qur'an. Surah 16:102 speaks of him as the inspiring agent of the Qur'an: "Say, the holy Spirit hath revealed it from thy Lord with truth." Also, Surah 2:87 and 2:253 say, "We supported him (Jesus) with the holy Spirit." All Muslim commentators agree that these passages refer to the angel Gabriel. Only one passage (Surah 2:97) asserts that Gabriel was the channel of Muhammad's revelation. The angel is mentioned only one other time in the Qur'an, in Surah 66:4. It is not clear why this confusion between "the holy Spirit" and the angel Gabriel developed. The New Testament says that Jesus was conceived by the Holy Spirit in the virgin Mary, whereas the qur'anic commentator Zamakhshari says that the virgin conceived "when the angel Gabriel blew up her garment."[20]

An African-American Muslim explained to one of the authors that, in his view, Jesus' conception took place through the angel Gabriel. However, he understood Gabriel and other angels to be supermen with extraordinary powers, such as the Nephilim (sons of God) who had children by the daughters of men (Gen. 6:4). Gabriel, he thought, was not a spiritual being who announced the power of the Holy Spirit coming upon Mary to conceive (Luke 1:34–35), but a specially empowered man who impregnated Mary.

The Qur'an also mentions "the Spirit," or "the faithful Spirit," in association with angels. In these passages the Spirit is regarded as one of the angels.[21] So we conclude that there is no place for, or even mention of, the Holy Spirit as God, coeternal with God the Father and God the Son.

God as Redemptive Love

The Christian teaching about God is that he is triune. This is necessary in order for God to show his redemptive love. The doctrines of the Trinity and the Incarnation are significant for the Christian only in relation to the redemptive purpose of God offering grace to sinful men. One way to understand the Trinity would be the following: God, in his transcendent Being, as inscrutably above the universe; God made manifest to men in the life, death, and resurrection of Jesus Christ; God present, unseen but very near, in the hearts of men.[22] The Christian witness emphasizes the self-disclosure of God himself, while in Islam it is the will and guidance of God that are revealed. Thus, we cannot say that the God of Islam is the same as the God of Christianity. For the triune God has in love planned our salvation before the foundation of the world (Eph. 1:4–5).

The Ninety-nine Names of Allah

The Qur'an assigns the best names to Allah:

> Allah! There is no God save Him. His are the most beautiful names. (Surah 20:8)
>
> Allah's are the fairest names. Invoke Him by them. (Surah 7:180)
>
> He is Allah, than whom there is no other God, the Knower of the invisible and the visible. He is the Beneficent, the Merciful. He is Allah, than whom there is no other God,

> the Sovereign Lord, the Holy One, Peace, the Keeper of Faith, the Guardian, the Majestic, the Compeller, the Superb. Glorified be Allah from all that they ascribe as partner (unto Him). He is Allah, the Creator, the Shaper out of naught, the Fashioner. His are the most beautiful names. All that is in the heavens and the earth glorifieth Him, and He is the Mighty, the Wise. (Surah 59:22–24)

There are several lists of Allah's names. The lists differ somewhat in the names included and in the translations from Arabic. Muslim theologian al-Ghazali (d. 1111) popularized a list that was originally attributed to Abu Hurairah. Interestingly, three of the ninety-nine names of Allah are not found in the Qur'an, but in the *Hadith*. Sixteen names for Allah found in the Qur'an are not included among the ninety-nine names. These names (with four alternates) are often repeated to obtain merit, using a rosary of beads to count them.

1. Al-Rahman: the Compassionate, the Gracious
2. Al-Rahim: the Merciful
3. Al-Malik: the King, the Sovereign
4. Al-Quddus: the Holy One
5. Al-Salam: the Peace, the Author of Safety
6. Al-Momin: the Faithful, the Giver of Peace
7. Al-Mohymin: the Protector
8. Al-Aziz: the Incomparable, the Strong, the Mighty One
9. Al-Jabbar: the Benefactor, the Compeller
10. Al-Mutakabbir: the Mighty Doer, the Majestic, the Proud
11. Al-Khaliq: the Creator
12. Al-Bari: the Maker
13. Al-Musawwir: the Former, the Fashioner
14. Al-Ghafar: the Forgiver
15. Al-Qahhar: the Powerful, the Dominant
16. Al-Wahhab: the Giver, the Bestower
17. Al-Razzaq: the Sustainer, the Bestower of Daily Bread, the Provider

18. Al-Fattah: the Opener, the Reliever
19. Al-'Alim: the Omniscient, the Knowing One
20. Al-Qabiz: the Restrainer, the Withholder
21. Al-Basit: the Expander, the Enlarger, the Spreader of the Hand
22. Al-Khafiz: the Depressor, the Abaser
23. Al-Rafi': the Exalter, the Elevator
24. Al-Mu'iz: the Strengthener, the Honorer
25. Al-Muzil (Muthill): the Lowerer, the Humiliator, the One Who Leads Astray
26. Al-Sami: the Hearer, the All-Hearing
27. Al-Basir: the Seer, the All-Seeing
28. Al-Hakam (Hakim): the Judge, the Wise
29. Al-'Adl: the Just
30. Al-Latif: the Benignant, the Subtle, the Gracious
31. Al-Khabir: the Knower, the Aware, the Cognizant
32. Al-Halim: the Clement, the Forbearing
33. Al-'Azim ('Adhim): the Great, the Mighty, the Grand
34. Al-Ghafur: the Great Pardoner, the Forgiving
35. Al-Shakur: the Rewarder, the Grateful, the Appreciative, the Acknowledger of Thanksgiving
36. Al-'Aliyy: the Most High, the Sublime, the Exalted
37. Al-Kabir: the Great Lord (meaning "the possessor of pride")
38. Al-Hafiz: the Guardian, the Protector, the Preserver
39. Al-Muqit: the Giver of Strength, the Feeder, the Sustainer
40. Al-Hasib: the Reckoner, the One Who Takes Account
41. Al-Jalil: the Glorious, the Beneficent, the Majestic
42. Al-Karim: the Munificent, the Bountiful, the Gracious, the Generous
43. Al-Raqib: the Watcher, the Watchful
44. Al-Mujib: the Approver of Supplications, the Responsive, the Harkener, the Answerer
45. Al-Wasi': the Expander, the Vast, the All-Embracing
46. Al-Hakim: the Physician, the Judge of Judges

47. Al-Wadud: the All-Loving, the Affectionate
48. Al-Majid: the Glorious
49. Al-Bais (Ba'ith): the Awakener, the Raiser (from death)
50. Al-Shahid: the Witness
51. Al-Haqq (Hak): the Truth, the True
52. Al-Wakil: the Provider, the Trustee, the Agent
53. Al-Qawwi: the Powerful, the Strong
54. Al-Matin: the Firm
55. Al-Waliyy: the Protecting Friend, the Helper
56. Al-Hamid: the One to Be Praised, the Praiseworthy, the Laudable
57. Al-Muhsi: the Counter
58. Al-Mubdi: the Cause, the Originator, the Beginner
59. Al-Mu'id: the Restorer, the Reproducer
60. Al-Mohyi: the Life-Giver, the Restorer
61. Al-Mumit: the Death-Giver, the Destroyer, the Slayer
62. Al-Hai: the Living, the Alive
63. Al-Qaiyyum: the Self-Subsisting
64. Al-Wajid: the Finder, the Perceiver, the Inventor or Maker
65. Al-Majid: the Grand, the Most Illustrious, the Most Glorious

[65. Al-Mugheeth: the Refuge, the Helper]

66. Al-Wahid: the Unique, the One

[66. Al-Ahad: the Only One]

67. Al-Samad: the Perpetual, the Independent, the Eternal
68. Al-Qadir: the Powerful (as in "the One who predestinates all")
69. Al-Muqtadir: the Prevailing, the Overcomer
70. Al-Muqaddim: the Bringer Before
71. Al-Muwakhir: the Bringer After, the Retarder, the Deferrer
72. Al-Awwal: the First
73. Al-Akhir: the Last
74. Al-Zahir (Dhahir): the Evident, the Manifest, the Substance
75. Al-Batin: the Hidden, the Essence

76. Al-Wali: the Governor
77. Al-Muta'a: the Sublime, the High Exalted, the Lofty One
78. Al-Barr: the Beneficent, the Benign
[78. Al-Bar: the Doer of Good, the Righteous]
79. Al-Tawwab: the Propitious, the Relenting
80. Al-Muntaqim: the Avenger
81. Al-Afu: the Eraser, the Forgiver, the Pardoner
82. Al-Rauf: the Benefiter, the Compassionate, the Kind, the Indulgent
83. Malik-ul-Mulk: the Ruler of the Kingdoms, the King of Kingdoms, the Owner of Sovereignty
84. Zuljalal-wal-Ikram: the Lord of Glory and Honor, the Lord of Majesty and Bounty
85. Al-Muksit: the Equitable, the Quotable
86. Al-Jami': the Assembler, the Gatherer, the Collector
87. Al-Ghani: the Rich, the Self-Sufficient
88. Al-Maghani (Mughni): the Enricher, the Profiter
89. Al-Mu'ti: the Giver
90. Al-Mani': the Withholder
91. Al-Zarr: the Afflicter, the Distresser, the Harmful
92. Al-Nafi': the Benefactor, the Propitious, the Profiter
93. Al-Nur: the Light
94. Al-Hadi: the Guide
95. Al-Badia: the Incomparable
[95. Al-Asili: the Eternal in the Past]
96. Al-Baqi: the Eternal, the Everlasting, the Enduring
97. Al-Waris (Warith): the Inheritor, the Heir
98. Al-Rashid: the Director, the Guide to the Right Path
99. Al-Sabur: the Patient[23]

Some Christians have found, in studying these ninety-nine names of Allah from a biblical perspective, that they can be used for Christian witness. Scripture references using the title may be used to give a Muslim a biblical perspective on the attribute. However, one must be careful not to synthesize the two religions, merging perspectives. Instead, careful analysis must be done to understand the terms from each one's holy book. Ask a Muslim what the term means to him. Afterwards share what a biblical perspective is on the subject. In that way, one avoids reading biblical meaning into qur'anic terms.

The Character of Allah

"God is one" is a statement made by both Muslims and Christians, but it could also be said by the heathen worshiping their idols. What is important is the character of this one God. The Muslim says that because Allah is one, Allah and the God of the Bible are the same. This belief that Allah and the God of the Bible are identical is foundational to Islam.

The Qur'an describes how the Arabs of Muhammad's day associated Allah with the worship of the Ka'aba and worshiped him along with goddesses such as *Allat*, female angels, Satan, and the *jinn*. The Prophet of Islam denounced these associations of other deities with Allah and gave greater impact to his teachings by identifying Allah with the God of the Bible. He made the Ka'aba the House of God, and declared that Abraham and others in the Old and New Testament had worshiped Allah as the one supreme God. Muhammad declared that Allah sent down not only the Qur'an, but also the Torah (*Taurat*), the Psalms (*Zabur*), and the Gospels (*Injil*). Therefore, the Qur'an and the Bible are said to come from the same source, the same God.[24] But do these books all give the same image of who God is, and do they therefore come from the same source?

A God of Good and Evil

What does the Qur'an reveal about Allah's nature? It emphasizes his creative power, and it teaches that not only the moral and material good of the world, but also its moral and material evil, are his creation. So when Muslims speak of the unity (*tawhid*) of Allah, they combine in that unity some creative activities that Christians say are contradictory and cannot be reconciled. This Muslim teaching can be compared to that of the Manichaeans, who believed that there were two powers in the universe, one being the creator of good and the other of evil. These two creative activities are combined in Allah, so that the doctrine of the unity of Allah is a unified dualism. Allah creates all man's acts, both good and evil, and allows man only the power to appropriate (*iktisab*) the acts that he has created for him. This appropriation is not even a free acceptance on man's part, to which he can say, "I don't want to act thus." Man's every thought and act, his every intention and purpose, are created by Allah. Man creates nothing, neither thought nor action (Surah 37:96). Allah is unconditioned in his creative activity.[25] According to the *Hadith* of the Prophet, Allah created all unpleasant things on Tuesday. The Qur'an says, "Say: I seek refuge in the Lord of Daybreak from the evil of that which He created" (Surah 112:1, 2).[26]

God as Righteous

In Islam there is no law of righteousness in the being of Allah. The Qur'an states that Allah does as he pleases; he guides men aright and he leads men astray. In twenty passages of the Qur'an, Allah is said "to lead men astray." He created a multitude of spirits and men specifically for the purpose of torturing them in hell, "that I will fill hell with jinn and mankind together" (Surah 32:13). Even true believers have no sure hope of not spending time in hell, for Surah 19:71 says, "There is not one of you but shall approach it."[27] However, in Shi'ite Islam, the fifth and sixth Imams said that "God loves His creation so much that He will not force it to commit sin and then punish it. And God is so powerful that whatever He commands comes to be."[28] If a man appears to keep Allah's laws, Allah is not obliged by any standard of justice to put such a man in paradise. Allah's character is also seen in Surah 15:29–43, where Satan says to him, "As Thou has beguiled me I will beguile them." This lack of justice or consistency is reflected in other ways. For the Muslim, it is a heinous sin to worship a creature of Allah, but Satan is punished by Allah for not being willing to worship Adam (Surah 2:28–31). Allah is merciful in overlooking the sins of his prophets and those who fight in the way of Allah, but he is the quick avenger of all infidels and idolaters, whom he has led astray.[29]

In contrast to this view of Allah, the God of the Bible is righteous. He hates evil, and does not create moral evil, lead men astray, or initiate Satanic activity. Central to the biblical teaching is its emphasis on the unity of God's moral character. The God of the Bible is conditioned by his holy nature. He sets life and death before people and says to them, "Choose."[30]

God's Immutability and Truth

The Qur'an does not attribute unchangeableness to Allah. His decision can never be changed by any outside power, and his will has neither limits nor obstacles. This means that Allah is never bound to a decision that he once made. He cares nothing about being consistent. Therefore, he did not hesitate, when circumstances required, to change and rescind his earlier revelations, even when they contained specific commandments and instructions to believers. This created conflict for Muhammad, since he claimed to be transmitting a divine message that was inscribed upon tablets preserved in heaven, and which therefore should be eternal and unchangeable. But, as circumstances changed, Muhammad did not hesitate to assert that Allah had abrogated his earlier revelation and substituted another. "Whatever verses we cancel or cause thee to forget, we bring a better or its like. Knowest thou not that God hath power over all things?" (Surah 2:100). This early Medinan verse had already been preceded by changes in earlier revelations or by giving revelations new content by adding explanations or restrictions (Surah 16:103). In Surah 53 it can be seen how Muhammad kept on revising his revelations concerning the Meccan goddesses as his views changed to a stricter monotheism.[31] Allah's moral law changed, like the ceremonial law, according to times and circumstances.[32] According to the qur'anic conception of God, Allah cannot be held to a word that he has once spoken. Not only could Allah change what he previously decreed, but he could even have withdrawn the whole revelation which he gave Muhammad (Surah 17:86). Another aspect of the irrational nature of Allah's will is that he often makes offensive or misleading statements in order to "prove" men or stir up unbelievers to contradict the revealed word (Surah 74:31; 17:46).[33] This is all utterly opposed to the Christian view of God as one who is immutable and true.

Allah's Ninety-nine Names and Moral Character

God's attributes are called *Isma-ul-Sifat* by Muslims and are called in the Qur'an *Isma-ul-Husna,* the excellent or beautiful names (Surah 20:8), of which there are ninety-nine. They are divided by some into three classes: wisdom, power, and goodness. But more commonly they are divided into two classes: his terrible attributes and his glorious attributes. Of these attributes, only four may in a special sense refer to his moral character, although his merciful attributes are in a sense moral, too. Two of these four attributes, El-'Adl (the Just) and El-Muksit (the Equitable) are found only in tradition. The other two, found in the Qur'an, El-Kuddus (the Holy) and El-Hak (the Truth), are of doubtful significance in Muslim theology. For all of these attributes are really just expressions of his will, rather than characteristics of his nature. Contradictions exist in Allah's attributes because they are not essential to his nature, but descriptions of his inscrutable will. Therefore, Allah may not be holy, righteous, and loving in every situation.[34]

For the Muslim, there is no absolute truth in Allah or in ethics. Abu Hanifah says that if a man should swear "by the truth of God," this does not constitute an oath. El-Kuddus (the Holy) is used of Allah only once, but without the same meaning as for the Christian.[35]

For the Muslim, "holy" does not imply moral purity or perfection, but the complete absence of anything that would make Allah less than he is, or ceremonially clean.[36] Although many impressive titles and descriptions are given to Allah in the Qur'an, there is no suggestion that he is holy and unapproachable by sinful man. Among the ninety-nine names for Allah are many that refer to different aspects of his wisdom and power, but none that speak of holiness or righteousness. The emphasis is on power rather than purity.

This lack of emphasis on the moral nature of Allah is in marked contrast to that of the Bible, where God's holiness, truthfulness, faithfulness, love, and justice are emphasized. From a Christian perspective, Muhammad had a generally correct view of the incommunicable attributes of God (omnipotence, omniscience, etc.), but had a false concept or no concept at all of his communicable attributes (holiness, truthfulness, etc.). The reason why Muhammad never had an understanding of God's holiness and justice is that he never had a true knowledge of the nature of sin and its consequences.[37]

God's Love

One also fails to find in the Qur'an an emphasis on God's love for us and on our obligation to love God and our neighbor, as is found in the Bible. In 1 John 4:7–21 one finds the word *love* twenty-seven times in fourteen verses. The Bible tells us that God loves us even though we are sinners in rebellion against him. By contrast, one can only find a few verses in the Qur'an that speak of God's love. There is one that says that Allah loves those who love him, but "loveth not the disbelievers" (Surah 3:31–32).[38] Also, "Allah loveth not the corrupters" (Surah 5:64). Another verse speaking of love says, "O ye who believe! Whoso of you becometh a renegade from his religion, (know that in his stead) Allah will bring a people whom He loveth and who love Him, humble toward believers, stern toward disbelievers, striving in the way of Allah, and fearing not the blame of any blamer. Such is the grace of Allah which He giveth unto whom He will. Allah is All-Embracing, All-Knowing" (Surah 5:54). In a verse that speaks of not going in unto a woman during her menstruation, the Qur'an says, "And when they have purified themselves, then go in unto them as Allah hath enjoined upon you. Truly Allah loveth those who turn unto Him, and loveth those who have a care for cleanness" (Surah 2:222). Al-Wadud, "the Loving" (Surah 11:90), is one of the ninety-nine beautiful names for Allah, but it does not mean that love is part of his character. Love implies a relationship. But Allah is unknowable. Al-Wadud comes from the verb *wadda*, which means "kind" and some aspects of "love," but without its full depth of meaning. Allah's love is what Christians would call common grace, in that he shows his mercy and care for his creation. But it is not a personal or sustaining love. There is no redemptive love in Islam, unlike Christianity: "But God demonstrates his own love for us in this: While we were still sinners, Christ died for us" (Rom. 5:8; cf. Rom. 8:35–39; Eph. 3:17–19).

The Sufis emphasize the love of God through experiencing God, who is everywhere in nature. Some Sufis have pantheistic tendencies. Experiencing God comes through developed devotional techniques, such as controlled breathing, chanting the names of God in an accelerating tempo, and whirling into a trance. In performing *zhikr* exercises, where one is remembering or being mindful of God to perceive the oneness of all being, a Sufi concentrates on one of the names of God. Sufi scholar Annemarie Schimmel writes:

> . . . in performing a *zhikr* based on one of the names of God, the wisdom of the mystic leader must be shown to a particular degree, because it is his responsibility to instruct and carefully watch over the pupil, lest the pupil be exposed to serious mental and psychic dangers. The rules for use of these names of God have been worked out by the Sufis in painstaking detail. The name Al-Fa'iq, "the Overwhelming One," [for example,] should never be used by a beginner, but only by a high-ranking gnostic. The wrong

> use of a name of God can have serious consequences for the person affected or those close to him or her, which can even be displayed in the form of physical symptoms, as I know from the personal experience of friends.[39]

In reading this, one wonders how a God who loves and is personal with his people would pose "serious mental and psychic dangers" and cause "serious consequences . . . in the form of physical symptoms" to those who are remembering him. From a Christian perspective, this activity appears rather to invite demonic powers to enter the Sufi. This is sometimes manifested by supernatural abilities, such as piercing oneself with a knife without harm.

Imitate Muhammad or God in Christ?

Muhammad did not demand that his followers follow God—they only had to submit and obey. Rather, he required them to follow him—Muhammad. In contrast, the apostle Paul writes, "Be imitators of God, therefore, as dearly loved children and live a life of love, just as Christ loved us and gave himself up for us as a fragrant offering and sacrifice to God" (Eph. 5:1–2). John emphasizes this point as well: "This is how we know we are in him [God in Christ]: Whoever claims to live in him must walk as Jesus did" (1 John 2:5–6).

Christians believe that God is righteous, holy, self-giving, and loving. This is essential to the Christian belief in one God. God's character gives meaning to all that is written in the Bible. Man's nature and destiny find their meaning in the light of God's character.

For Reflection/Action

1. How do the different views of God in Islam and Christianity affect how a follower of each faith relates to God?
2. How can the different views of the moral character of God in Islam and Christianity affect a follower's pattern for living?

CHAPTER SIX

The Person and Mission of 'Isa Ibn Maryam

The Person of 'Isa Ibn Maryam (Jesus, Son of Mary)

Qur'anic References to Jesus

A Muslim believes that what the Qur'an says about Jesus ('Isa) is final and authoritative, superseding the corrupted Gospels. Accordingly, he accepts Jesus as one of the most distinguished apostles of God. A Muslim can never think of Jesus in any derogatory terms. He believes that the Islamic conception of Jesus does not belittle his role, underestimate his character, or degrade his great personality in any way. He thinks Jesus is depicted most respectfully in the Qur'an, reflecting his high, God-given status.[1]

What does the Qur'an say about Jesus? He is called a sign from God, a mercy from God, a servant of God, and a prophet. The Qur'an affirms the virgin birth of Christ and that he is the Word of God (Kalimat Allah) conveyed by God to Mary. He is said to be a "spirit proceeding from God" (Surah 4:171); he is "strengthened by the spirit of sanctity"; "his name is the Messiah" (Surah 3:45). Christ is presented in unparalleled grandeur as the only prophet "after the image of Adam" (Surah 3:59), that is, like Adam in having no human father. According to the Qur'an, God's creative word *kun* (let there be) was said for three things: the creation of the world, the creation of Adam, and the conception of Christ. We also find Jesus prophesying his death and resurrection in the Qur'an. It speaks of the return of the Lord with thousands of angels. This word for "Lord" is *rab*, referring to Jesus. He is acknowledged as having given sight to the blind, cure to the lepers, and life to the dead.

Muslims believe remarkable things about Christ and his mother. The Qur'an contains numerous narratives that remind us of the apocryphal gospels: the story of Mary in the temple, her marriage to Joseph, the birth of Christ under a desert palm tree, his witness to his mother from the moment of birth, and the miracles Jesus performed as a child and a youth, such as making clay pigeons come alive.[2] The Sufis (Ibn Arabi) take Christ as a rule of life, and the Tirmidhi consider him as the "seal of sanctity."[3] As the "seal of sanctity," Jesus is the preeminent example, and the direct and miraculous manifestation, of esotericism, in its aspects of love and wisdom.[4]

Nonetheless, "Jesus is the center of Christianity, but only peripheral in Islam."[5] Of the 6,236 verses in the Qur'an, only 74 are expressly concerned with Jesus Christ, and 42 of them refer to him only indirectly and incidentally.[6] Furthermore, Muslim Christology is woefully inadequate by Christian standards.

Jesus' Deity and Incarnation Denied

Muslims believe that Christianity is of divine origin, and they revere its founder, but from a different perspective. They do not accept his incarnation or his filial relationship with God. Jesus was not a God-man or the Son of God. But he is recognized as a major prophet and spiritual leader in the Abrahamic tradition.[7] Although the Qur'an and the *Hadith* give Jesus Christ a high place among the prophets and affirm his sinlessness and power to work miracles, this does not distinguish his person from that of other prophets. The preexistence of the Word of God is denied.[8] The biblical title of "Messiah" (*masih*) is accepted and applied to Jesus, but there appears to be little awareness of its original significance.

The virgin birth is taught in the Qur'an, but is interpreted simply as a miracle.[9] The divinity and the eternal sonship of Christ are denied. He is a creature like Adam. "Lo! the likeness of Jesus with Allah is as the likeness of Adam. He created him of dust, then He said unto him; Be! and he is" (Surah 3:59). The Qur'an stresses that Jesus never claimed to be a god or the son of God, and that he was only the servant and apostle of the Lord, as were the prophets before him. Even when the Qur'an says that Jesus was a spirit from Allah, that is interpreted to mean a soul created by Allah.[10] Muslims are confounded by the relationship between the Father and the Son in the Christian Godhead. How can Jesus, a man, be God? The assumption behind this question is that Jesus, in Christian theology, somehow *became* God. It is thought that Jesus' followers gave him this divine status. But, according to the Scriptures, Jesus has always been God from the beginning (John 1:1).

Explaining the Term Son of God

In explaining the term *Son of God* to a Muslim, it is helpful to keep several things in mind. When the term *son of . . .* is used in everyday speech, it is often used metaphorically. It does not mean that one is physically a son of someone. Examples would be "son of the road" and "sons of thunder." In an evangelistic discussion, emphasize that *Son of God* refers to the spiritual relationship between God the Father and Jesus the Son. Then show that in the Bible the Son is a "picture" to us of God the Father. As it says in John 14:9, "Jesus answered: 'Don't you know me, Philip, even after I have been among you such a long time? Anyone who has seen me has seen the Father. How can you say, "Show us the Father"?' " And Hebrews 1:3 says, "The Son is the radiance of God's glory and the exact representation of his being." The Son has the most intimate knowledge of the Father (Matt. 11:27), and speaks and does exactly what his Father has taught him (John 8:28–29). The Son represents the Father to the highest degree, as described in the parable of the tenants (Mark 12:1–9). At Jesus' baptism, a voice *from heaven* says, "You are my Son" (Mark 1:11), meaning that he was not physically begotten. When Peter confessed that Jesus was "the Christ, the Son of the living God," Jesus responded by saying that this had been revealed to him not by man, but by his Father in heaven (Matt. 16:16–17). Even after being shown these passages, a Muslim may find it hard to accept the title *Son of God* because of the Muslim tradition. Have patience; in time, God may make things clear to him.

Most Muslims will not deny that God could become a man, since God can do anything. Usually Muslims ask the wrong question: "How can Jesus be God or the Son of God?" or "How could God have become a man?" Rather, they ought to ask, "Why did God become a man?" The answer to this question makes the previous questions irrelevant.

You may refer to Jesus as the Messiah or the Word of God, which are qur'anic terms.[11] But again, these terms need to be given biblical content. A Muslim usually will not understand that Jesus, as the Messiah, was God's "Anointed One"—the one who was anointed by the Spirit of God at his baptism to be our prophet, priest, and king. Muslims understand Jesus to have been the "Word of God" in the sense of a message conveyed to Mary (Surah 4:171), not as the eternal One who was with God from the beginning, was God, became flesh, came from the Father, brought grace and truth, and made God known (John 1:1–2, 14, 18).

The Influence of Christian Heresies

Muslims often consider the Christian teaching concerning the Incarnation and the Trinity to be rejected by passages from the Qur'an. But these passages do not accurately represent Christian teachings. What they reject are heretical views that the church itself repudiates.[12] Islamic Christology was influenced by heretical doctrines that confused Muhammad as he sought the unity of Allah. One of these heretical influences was Nestorianism, which failed to understand the two natures of Christ. The Qur'an's condemnation of the Incarnation condemns not the orthodox doctrine of Chalcedon (that Christ has two natures, being fully divine and fully human), but the distorted views of Monophysitism (according to which Christ had a single divine nature, clad in human flesh) and Nestorianism (which taught a unity of wills rather than of personhood).[13] The Qur'an represents the Incarnation in various ways. Sometimes Christ is spoken of as a human being clad in divinity. This view is suggestive of the Nestorian heresy. More frequently, Christ is spoken of as a human-divine person brought into being in the flesh by the divinity itself. Regarding this view, we find this: "Far is it removed from His transcendent majesty that he should have a son" (Surah 4:171). The Mariamist heresy, which believed in three gods—God, Mary, and Christ—appears to come out in Surah 5:116: "O Jesus, son of Mary! Didst thou say unto mankind: Take me and my mother for two gods beside Allah?"

It is understandable how statements that are believed to be aimed at Christian teaching could have been made, when one considers that the Qur'an was condemning the multiple idols at the Ka'aba in Mecca, where the "sons and daughters of God," such as Al-Lat, Al-'Uzza, and Manat (Surah 53:19–20), were idolatrously worshiped. Because of this, the very expression "son of God" was taboo. Later Muslim apologists read into the qur'anic texts a refutation of Christian teaching. However, not one of the qur'anic texts gives an accurate account of Christian teaching. Therefore, rather than saying that the Qur'an repudiates Christian teaching, it would be more accurate to say that it misunderstands Christian teaching.[14]

Muhammad's response to his understanding of the Christian doctrine of the divinity of Christ was sheer unbelief: "They surely disbelieve who say: Lo! Allah is the Messiah, son of Mary. The Messiah (himself) said: O Children of Israel, worship Allah, my Lord and your Lord. Lo! whoso ascribeth partners unto Allah, for him Allah hath forbidden Paradise. His abode is the Fire" (Surah 5:72). This same denial of the Messiah's divinity is given earlier in the same surah in verse 17: "They indeed have disbelieved who say: Lo!

Allah is the Messiah, son of Mary." And in verse 75 we read, "The Messiah, son of Mary, was no other than a messenger, messengers (the like of whom) had passed away before him. And his mother was a saintly woman. And they both used to eat (earthly) food." This clearly indicates that Jesus was only human. Even the omniscience of Jesus is denied when he responds to Allah, "Thou knowest what is in my mind, and I know not what is in Thy mind. Lo! Thou, only Thou art the Knower of Things Hidden" (Surah 5:116).

Biblical Response

The witness we find in the biblical revelation is quite a contrast to what we have seen in Islam:

> In the past God spoke to our forefathers through the prophets at many times and in various ways, but in these last days he has spoken to us by his Son, whom he appointed heir of all things, and through whom he made the universe. The Son is the radiance of God's glory and the exact representation of his being, sustaining all things by his powerful word. After he had provided purification for sins, he sat down at the right hand of the Majesty in heaven. (Heb. 1:1–3)

Here we see Jesus as Son, Word, Creator, revealer of God in his incarnation, Lord of the universe, Savior of sinners, and King ruling in heaven from a position of power and glory.

Jesus had a discussion with two of his disciples in which he revealed who he was:

> Thomas said to him, "Lord, we don't know where you are going, so how can we know the way?"
>
> Jesus answered, "I am the way and the truth and the life. No one comes to the Father except through me. If you

> really knew me, you would know my Father as well. From now on, you do know him and have seen him."
>
> Philip said, "Lord, show us the Father and that will be enough for us."
>
> Jesus answered: "Don't you know me, Philip, even after I have been among you such a long time? Anyone who has seen me has seen the Father. How can you say, 'Show us the Father'? Don't you believe that I am in the Father, and that the Father is in me? The words I say to you are not just my own. Rather, it is the Father, living in me, who is doing his work. Believe me when I say that I am in the Father and the Father is in me; or at least believe on the evidence of the miracles themselves." (John 14:5–11).

Jesus is clearly telling us that he is the way to God, that he embodies the truth, and that we have eternal life in him. In seeing Jesus as he has been revealed to us, we see God, for God the Father is in Jesus and Jesus is in the Father. Jesus' words are the same as God's words. Jesus' work is the work of God.

The Mission of 'Isa Ibn Maryam (Jesus, Son of Mary)

Jesus as the Warner and Bringer of a Spiritual Way

Christians were held in special esteem by the prophet Muhammad because of the role of Christ. His function was that of every prophet: to transmit the warning of God. Stress is laid on Christ's preaching. Sayyidna 'Isa (Jesus) was a messenger to the children of Israel, according to the Qur'an. Jesus had a mission to the Jews of both purification and esotericism. He is the "Seal of Sanctity" both for Muslims and *a priori* for the Jews.[15] Jesus was different from other men in that he was born of the Word of God given to Mary, but he was just a prophet among other prophets, although one of the greatest of them. He is viewed by Muslims as lesser than Muhammad and equal to Abraham.

In the Qur'an, Jesus has a very close association with Mary. For example, we read: "And We (Allah) made the Son of Mary and his Mother to be a miraculous sign, and We gave them refuge on a height offering tranquility (and safety) and watered with springs" (Surah 23:50). This association appears even in the trinity of God-Jesus-Mary that the Qur'an attributes to Christianity. The message of Jesus is also the message of Mary, because she is the "Spouse of the Holy Spirit" and an aspect of the Way and Life.[16]

From the Qur'an it is seen that only five prophets of God brought *shari'a* (divine law) to his people: Noah, Abraham, Moses, Jesus, and Muhammad. Jesus is honored as one of these "possessors of determination": "He hath ordained for you that religion which He commended unto Noah, and that which We inspire in thee (Muhammad) and that which We commended unto Abraham and Moses and Jesus" (Surah 42:13).[17] Jesus is referred to in the Qur'an as "the Spirit of God" (*ruhallah*). His special function was understood by some (Sufis) to be that of bringing a spiritual way, rather than a religious law.[18]

Jesus' Prediction of Muhammad's Coming

According to the Qur'an, the message of Jesus had three aspects, concerned with the past, the present, and the future. First, Christ confirmed and preserved what had been previously revealed in the Torah. For the present, the gift of a meal came down from heaven at Christ's request. This is identified as the Eucharist (Surah 5:112–14), which he celebrated and perpetuated. Christ predicted that in the future a messenger would come after him whose name would be Ahmad, the Prophet of Islam.[19] "And when Jesus son of Mary said: O Children of Israel! Lo! I am the messenger of Allah unto you, confirming that which was (revealed) before me in the Torah, and bringing good tidings of a messenger who cometh after me, whose name is the Praised One (Ahmad)" (Surah 61:6).

Muslims understand this announcement of the coming of Muhammad to be in Jesus' prediction that the *parakletos* would come (John 14:16, 26; 15:26; 16:7). Muslims claim that the Greek word *parakletos*, which is translated "counselor" or "ever-present helper," should be read *periklutos*, or "praised one," which would have the same meaning as *Ahmad*. *Ahmad* is derived from the same root—*hamada*, "to praise" or "to exalt"—as the name Muhammad. Ahmad is the heavenly name of the Prophet, which reflects the inward dimension, the intellect. Many Muslims believe that when Muhammad came, Christians changed the word *periklutos* to *parakletos*, so that Christ's reference to Muhammad would be hidden. Muslims consider it inconceivable that Christ would have had nothing to say about a major religion like Islam. So this announcement of the coming of the Paraclete is understood to be a reference to Islam.

However, there are several defects in this argument. Proof that Christians did not change the word *periklutos* to *parakletos* is found in the many extant New Testament manuscripts that were written many years before Muhammad's time. Not one Greek manuscript has been found that reads *periklutos* instead of *parakletos*.[20] Also, the Muslim contention is refuted by the time and purpose of the prediction. It was given by Jesus to his disciples on the night before he was to be crucified, when he warned them of his coming death. They were anxious and fearful. If Jesus meant by this counselor or helper an Arab prophet to be born more than five hundred years later in a foreign land, what possible counsel or help could that offer the disciples? Moreover, John 14:16–17 brings out several qualities of the Counselor that suggest no reference to Muhammad. Jesus calls the coming one a spirit whom the world would not see. He would remain with them forever. As a spirit, he would be in the disciples, as no mortal man could be. The world would not know the coming one, but only those who believed and accepted him. He is identified with the Holy Spirit in John 14:26. In addition, Jesus promised that the Spirit would be coming in a very short time. Finally, we see in the Acts of the Apostles that these prophecies were fulfilled just ten days after Jesus' ascension, on the day of Pentecost.[21] Muslims have ignored or rewritten history in order to find a way to fit in their *a priori* conviction that Christ predicted the coming of Muhammad.

It would be helpful to show a Muslim how Jesus is the culmination of history with no further need of another prophet (Matt. 28:20; Eph. 2:20; Heb. 3:3) or further revelation (John 20:30–31; Rev. 22:18–19). Jesus was a prophet, not just for the children of Israel, but for all people (Matt. 28:19; Acts 1:8).

Jesus' Crucifixion

Christ's dying on the cross is a scandal in Islam. It remains one of the chief reasons why Muslims deny the Christian faith. The Qur'an says, "They neither killed nor crucified him; it had only the appearance of it." Rather, Jesus was "lifted up to God" (Surah 4:157, 158). The qur'anic text speaks mysteriously of the death of Christ, but Muslim commentators have understood this to refer to the death of Christ at the end of time. A Shi'ite tradition adds, "They did not kill his soul, his person." Generally, Islamic interpretation has always been of a docetic type, asserting that there was a "substitution" for Christ on the cross, after which he was taken up to God, not resurrected.[22]

Three passages in the Qur'an seem to teach that Jesus did die: Surahs 3:55, 5:117, and 19:33, which says, "Peace on me the day I was born, and the day I die, and the day I shall be raised alive!" But the verses commonly used by Muslims to accuse Christians of disbelief are Surah 4:156–58:

> And because of their disbelief and of their speaking against Mary a tremendous calumny; And because of their saying: We slew the Messiah Jesus son of Mary, Allah's messenger—They slew him not nor crucified, but it appeared so unto them; and lo! those who disagree concerning it are in doubt thereof; they have no knowledge thereof save pursuit

> of a conjecture; they slew him not for certain, But Allah took him up unto Himself. Allah was ever Mighty, Wise.

The suggestion that verse 157, which mentions "those who disagree concerning it," speaks of the various parties in the Christological disputes within Christendom, is doubtful. It probably refers simply to the great difference that Muhammad observed between Jews and Christians.[23] In the *Hadith* of the Prophet, the denial of the death of Jesus on the cross is elaborated. Since the Qur'an both affirms and denies the death of Jesus, this *Hadith* attempts to harmonize its teaching by saying that, although Jesus died for a few hours, he was not crucified.[24]

Muslims believe that a plot was devised to crucify Jesus, and that an actual crucifixion took place, but that it was not Jesus who was crucified. Someone else was crucified in his place, possibly Judas. God came and rescued Jesus from his enemies and raised him up to heaven.[25] In Muslim tradition we find:

> And they spat upon Him and put thorns upon Him; and they erected the wood to crucify Him upon it. And when they came to crucify Him upon the tree, the earth was darkened, and God sent angels, and they descended between them and between Jesus; and God cast the Likeness of Jesus upon him who had betrayed Him, and whose name was Judas. And they crucified him in His stead, and they thought that they crucified Jesus. Then God made Jesus to die for three hours, and then raised Him up to heaven; and this is the meaning of the Koran verse: "Verily, I will cause Thee to die, and raise Thee unto Me, and purify Thee above those who misbelieve."[26]

Muslims have put forward a variety of views as to whether the Qur'an teaches that Jesus actually died on the cross. These include theories of Jesus being taken up by God before crucifixion, of Judas appearing like Jesus and being crucified in his place, of Jesus dying for a few hours and then being taken up by God, and of Jesus swooning on the cross but never really dying there.

From the Muslim perspective, the matter of Christ's crucifixion places a huge gulf between Islam and Christianity. This Christian doctrine cannot be metaphysically harmonized, as can other doctrines, such as the person of Christ or the Trinity. Probably the most difficult concept in Christianity for a Muslim to understand is the meaning of the crucifixion and the doctrine of redemption.[27]

The qur'anic denial of the crucifixion is one expression of its emphasis upon the triumphant and transcendent sovereignty of God. As arbiter of the destinies of all living creatures, God would not allow his prophet-servant to be defeated or humiliated by his enemies.[28] The denial that Jesus died on the cross is primarily a denial that the crucifixion was a Jewish victory. Because there is no Islamic conception of sacrifice, the Qur'an never speaks of the Atonement or the saving work of Jesus.[29] Muslims vigorously deny any notion of substitutionary atonement. But to the Christian, Christ's substitutionary death on the cross is the foundation of the faith whereby the incarnation of God's eternal love is manifest in the defeat of sin and evil.

These are some questions that Muslims ask, showing that the crucifixion of Christ is incomprehensible to them:

> Does the crucifixion of Jesus as conceived by the Christian churches befit the Justice, the Mercy, the Power, and Wisdom of God? Was God the Most Merciful, the Most Forgiving and the Most High unable to forgive men's sins except by inflicting this cruel and most humiliating alleged crucifixion on one who was not only innocent but also dedicated to His service and cause in a most remarkable way? Is this the application of God's mercy and forgiveness or the reflection of His justice and love?[30]

Muslims reject the Christian concept of the Atonement not only because the Qur'an does not speak of it, but because it seems irrational and does not fit in with their conception of God and man. There are two major beliefs about God that relate to this. First, God is almighty—he does whatever he pleases and is answerable to no one. Second, God is merciful—he forgives whomever he pleases. Therefore, since the will of God is so dominating and arbitrary, there is no necessity for any atonement. God has no need to satisfy his own justice, as Christians believe.[31] Muslims also reject Christ's death because, in their view, prophets do not suffer or sin.[32] God will protect them and uphold their honor.

It is remarkable that the Qur'an nowhere comments on the Christian interpretation of the significance of Christ's death. This leads one to conclude that Muhammad did not have accurate information concerning the orthodox Christian faith.[33] As we have seen, Muhammad's first wife, Khadija, came from an Ebionite Christian background that hated sacrifices and denied Jesus' deity.

To help Muslims understand the cross of Christ, it seems necessary to build up to it from the Old Testament. If possible, use illustrations from prophets they are familiar with, like Adam, Noah, Abraham, Jacob, Moses, David, Jonah, and John the Baptist. The prophecies, types, and sacrifices in the lives of these prophets point to the coming substitutionary atonement of Jesus on a cross. Combine that with a proper understanding of the nature and character of God as holy, just, and loving. God's character makes the Atonement necessary. Our own sinfulness, in the light of God's holiness, demonstrates that only the holy Messiah was worthy to pay the price for our sin by his death. Yet he demonstrated his divine power and righteousness by his resurrection from the dead to deliver us from condemnation and death. Thus, the Cross and the Resurrection were necessary for salvation from the penalty of sin.

Jesus' Return

The prophet Muhammad referred to the place of Christ within Islam by speaking of Christ's second coming at the end of the world to establish peace. So Islamic eschatology has the same important figure of Christ as does Christianity, but his role is not identical.[34] Muslim commentators teach that when Jesus returns, he will die, showing his human frailty.[35] This contradicts the New Testament passage that says, "For we know that since Christ was raised from the dead, he cannot die again; death no longer has mastery over him" (Rom. 6:9).

The Muslim view of Jesus' role in the future is found in the *Hadith* compiled by al-Bukhari:

> Narrated by Abu Huraira: Allah's Messenger (PBUH) said: "By Him (Allah) in Whose Hands my soul is, surely (Jesus) son of Mary, will shortly descend amongst you (Muslims) and will judge mankind justly by the law of the Qur'an (as a just ruler) and will break the Cross and kill the pigs and abolish the *Jizya* (a tax levied upon the non-Muslims who are under the protection of a Muslim government. The *Jizya* tax will not be accepted by Jesus and all mankind will be required to embrace Islam with no other alternative). Then there will be abundance of money and nobody will accept charitable gifts." (Sahih Al-Bukhari, Vol. 3, Hadith No. 425).[36]

The biblical view of Jesus' return has something in common with this description, namely, that he will return as our judge and that everyone will submit to God. Jesus said, "Moreover, the Father judges no one, but has entrusted all judgment to the Son, that all may honor the Son just as they honor the Father. He who does not honor the Son does not honor the Father, who sent him" (John 5:22–23). Clearly, Jesus is speaking of his divine authority as our judge. Our submission to Jesus' lordship is portrayed by Paul: "Therefore God exalted him to the highest place and gave him the name that is above every name, that at the name of Jesus every knee should bow, in heaven and on earth and under the earth, and every tongue confess that Jesus Christ is Lord, to the glory of God the Father" (Phil. 2:9–11).

Conclusion

In some circles it is common to speak of Islam as "a Christian heresy," but for the Muslim the heresy is Christianity itself. Islam claims that historic Christianity has misconstrued the mission of Jesus. Islam sees itself as correcting Christian distortion of Jesus and of God. The Christian sees Islam as taking away the very heart of its understanding of both. This is due to the *jahiliyyah* (ignorance) that most Muslims have of what Christians really believe. They have been content to believe whatever confirms their prejudgment of Christianity. The partial truth that Muslims have of Christ blinds them to the full truth, so that it ends up becoming an untruth.[37]

Despite differences between Islam and Christianity, Muslims believe that the Islamic conception of Jesus provides a firm basis for understanding Christianity if Muslims look to their own traditional sources, rather than to modern Christian attacks on Islam. Then, too, Christians will gain an appreciation for Islam, with its high respect for Jesus as one of the greatest prophets who brought the spiritual way.[38] It is true that by studying the Islamic conception of Jesus, Christians will gain a better understanding of Islam. However, the Islamic conception of Christ destroys all the basics of the Christian faith, leaving no Christian faith at all. Christianity is empty without Christ being the revelation of God, the Savior of sinners by his substitutionary atonement, and the One before whom every knee shall bow and every tongue confess that Jesus Christ is Lord.

The life, message, death, and resurrection of Jesus are the heart of the gospel—and some of the most vigorously denied aspects of the Christian faith. In order to convert Muslims to Christ, these truths must be presented to them in a clear and winsome way.

For Reflection/Action

1. In witnessing to a Muslim, how would you deal with the issue of Jesus as the Son of God, if it came up?
2. How would you respond to a Muslim who says that Jesus predicted the coming of Muhammad?
3. How can we present Jesus' crucifixion to Muslims with clarity, so that its necessity and importance are understood?

CHAPTER SEVEN

Human Nature and the Effects of Sin

Human Nature

Man's Weakness and Forgetfulness of God

In Islam, a person's goal is to achieve integration of all aspects of life by means of the realization of the one God, called *tawhid*. Therefore, achieving *tawhid* or oneness is the essence of that faith (or conviction: *iman*) which is the basis of Islam. Man suffers from forgetfulness of God, so that although he may confess one God, he actually lives as if there were many gods. Islam's aim is to make people whole again, in order that they may be pure. Each person is to be God's vicegerent (*khalifah*) on earth, reflecting the divine names and qualities. God is one, and so people must become whole in order to reflect the One.[1]

The Islamic view of men and women sees them as having two natures, a soul and a body. Human nature is weak (Surah 4:28), easily led astray, and covetous (Surah 4:32), so it is necessary to set limits to human freedom of action. These limits are the law. As creatures under law, human beings are perfectible, but not perfect. One does not achieve perfection because one is weak and forgetful of God. In general, Islam explains the evil of people and society as coming from our inherent feebleness, rather than from our active rebellion. What results from forgetfulness can be countered by reminder. Our problem is one of sins rather than sin, of lapses rather than self-assertion. The aim of communal allegiance is to discipline and educate people to deal with human frailty. Therefore, "salvation" is largely a communal effort. "The achievement of *Islam* presupposes and requires the community."[2]

Fate and Moral Responsibility

Submission to the will of God, a fundamental principle of Islam, may be exemplified by a humble Muslim, but it often leads to passive acquiescence in things as they are or to fatalism in moral and ethical matters. The concept of submission gets exaggerated to the point where it effectively blocks progress and hinders reform. For example, many of the balcony railings of apartment buildings in Teheran, Iran, were built low, and it was fairly common for small children to climb over them and accidentally fall to their death. Nothing was being done to change this situation. It was thought that the death of these children was the will of Allah and should just be accepted. This fatalistic worldview, combined with an exaggerated view of the omnipotence of Allah, "leads to fatalism in moral and ethical matters, and an almost complete lack of any sense of moral responsibility. God is the source of all things, and nothing can happen (the Muslim argues) except by His direct will. Consequently He is the source of evil as well as good, and every action of man is in accordance with a pre-ordained plan. So the sinner can always say, 'God made me so, He ordained it so, I was but walking in the path He ordered.' "[3] This lack of a sense of responsibility for one's actions is seen in what is expected when a Muslim man and woman are alone together. It is thought that it is beyond a person's control to keep from committing adultery in such a situation. Therefore, Muslim women must always be under the protection of a male family member and should generally stay at home.

The Rejection of Original Sin

The Qur'an teaches that the human race was given an innately pure nature called *fitrah*. However, we were created weak, though not separated from God by that weakness. All people (except for prophets of God) commit sinful acts, but this is not due to a radically sinful nature. People sin because of their forgetfulness of God. Furthermore, people can, by their own actions, free themselves from their bondage to sin. God has dealt with sin by mercifully sending the Qur'an to man. He commands Muslims to continue dealing with sin by *da'wah*, calling all people to the path of Allah.[4]

Christians see man as made in the image of God, being a faithful and adequate representation of God with psychosomatic unity, true knowledge, righteousness, and holiness (Eph. 4:24). This image of God still exists in us, but it was partially lost when Adam and Eve fell from righteousness and communion with God into sin and separation from God. This original sin still pervades the whole human race and manifests itself in actual sins in all people.

The Christian witness that the rebellion of Adam and Eve has tragically distorted man, and that sinfulness pervades us individually and collectively, is quite contrary to Islam. Islam teaches that although Adam disobeyed Allah, he repented and was forgiven, and was even given guidance for mankind. People are not born sinners, and the doctrine of the sinfulness of every person has no basis in Islam.[5] Therefore, Islam has no place for a doctrine of redemption. This crucial Christian doctrine is not even mentioned in Islam.

The Qur'an tells us that Satan enticed Adam: " 'O Adam, shall I show you the tree of life and power eternal?' Adam ate of the tree and committed a transgression and an evil deed. But God corrected him and he atoned and was rightly guided." Therefore, Adam committed a misdeed, that of thinking evil to be good, of ethical misjudgment. "Adam is the author of the first human mistake in ethical perception, committed with good intention, under enthusiasm for the good. It was not a fall but a discovery that the good is possible to confuse with the evil: . . . This is a decisive advance in man's self-perfecting, in his realizing of God's command to do good and avoid evil."[6] Muslims reject the Christian belief in original sin, the belief that all men are by nature sinful, in rebellion against God. They ask, "How is it possible that the sin of one man, a personal act which is purely moral, became the responsibility of another, or of all men? Also, how could the punishment of one man be made applicable to all men?"[7]

The concept of original sin is totally foreign to the Muslim. "It is heard to mean that somehow there is a reach of man's evil which is beyond the range of God's creative goodness and that the Christian gospel is darkly sinister in its view of the creation. On the contrary, sin only matters because good matters."[8] "Original" has reference to the fact that self-centeredness permeates the whole of the human personality, and that sin does not refer simply to evil acts of the body or external deeds that break God's revealed law. In fact, Jesus points to sins of the spirit, the pride of piety, and the degeneracy of the mind as being greater sins than external infractions of the law and sins of the flesh.[9]

In order to help a Muslim understand how we have fallen in sin with Adam, which has affected our whole nature, it is helpful to show how God made a covenant with Adam, which he broke. Being the representative head of the human race, his broken relationship with God affected all his descendants. Therefore, God provided a covenant of grace for his people, by which we may be saved from our sin.

The Prophets and Sin

Although the Qur'an teaches that Adam was the first sinner (Surah 2:35), Muslims believe that all of the prophets were sinless, including Adam. This is especially asserted in regard to Muhammad, even though the Qur'an, *Sunnah,* and history speak otherwise. Muslims believe that a prophet of God must possess the quality of inerrancy (*ismah*), that is, freedom from error in the transmission of God's revelation. But they would also say that this means that the prophet must not commit sin. Sin and opposition to the claims of the religious call and its propagation are impossible in a prophet, for they would contradict his religious mission. This would destroy the confidence of the people in his calling and destroy the purpose of the religious call itself. The Qur'an refers to the inerrancy of the prophets: "And We chose them and guided them unto a straight path" (Surah 6:88); "He revealeth unto none His secret, save unto every messenger whom He hath chosen, and then He maketh a guard to go before him and a guard behind him, that He may know that they have indeed conveyed the messages of their Lord. He surroundeth all their doings, and He keepeth count of all things" (Surah 72:26–28).[10]

Evangelical Christians believe that the entire Bible is inerrant in the original autographs, for what the authors wrote was inspired by the Holy Spirit (2 Tim. 3:16; 2 Peter 1:20–21; John 14:26; 16:13). Although God guided the lives of the prophets and apostles, especially in the writing of the Scriptures, this does not mean that these men were sinless. The Scriptures often mention the sins of the prophets and apostles. Only Jesus is shown to be sinless. Even though Muslims assert that all of the prophets were sinless, the Qur'an records their transgressions of the moral law and repentance, such as Adam's sin of eating from the forbidden tree (Surah 7:11–27), David's adultery (Surah 38:18–25), Solomon's repentance (Surah 38:31–36), Job's turning in repentance (Surah 38:42–45), and Muhammad's prayer for forgiveness of sin (Surah 47:19).[11] Nothing casting any doubt on the sinlessness of Jesus is mentioned.

The Muslim Concept of Sin

The Source of Sin

For the Muslim, sin comes from such things as ignorance, bad social contacts and companions, incorrect knowledge, bad habits, laziness, lack of judgment, and invisible influences that have an hypnotic effect.[12] As we have already seen, Allah has predetermined what people will do; he leads people astray, and he tests them.

By contrast, Christians understand sin to proceed from the heart and mind, from one's own evil desire. A sinful act is the expression of a depraved and perverse heart, mind, disposition, and will. All men are depraved by nature. Satan sometimes is the source of temptation, but we are responsible for our actions.

Great and Small Sins

After the death of Muhammad, one of the major debates among Muslim *'ulama* (legal experts) had to do with sin and its consequences: Is it possible to sin and yet remain a Muslim? What is the significance of sin if one can sin and still be submitting to Allah? In order to avoid the logical consequences of equating sin with rebellion (which is apostasy, which should be punished by death), one group argued for a distinction between big sins and little sins.[13] This argument prevailed.

The Qur'an is silent on the nature of sin, and says almost nothing about its origin, result, or remedy. Its concept of sin is the doing of that which is forbidden, *haram*, or the omission of duties that are obligatory, *fard* or *wajib*. It regards sin as the willful violation of a known law. Sins committed in ignorance are not really crimes against God. Muslim commentators disagree in distinguishing between great and small sins. Some list seven great sins (*kebira*): idolatry, murder, false charges of adultery, wasting the substance of orphans, usury, desertion from *jihad*, and disobedience to parents. Others list seventeen or even seven hundred great sins. To the Muslim, all sins except the great sins are regarded with utter carelessness and no pangs of conscience. Lighter offenses, such as lying, deception, anger, and lust will be "easily forgiven."[14] Committing little sins will not exclude you from the community of the faithful. Avoiding the great sins will cause Allah to remit your evil deeds and allow you to enter paradise (Surah 4:31). The greatest and unforgivable sin is that of *shirk*, associating partners with Allah. Another great sin is to say that the revelations received by Muhammad were lies.

Islam minimizes the awfulness of sin. This is a reflection of the Muslim view that Allah is not absolutely unchangeable or eternally just. A Muslim would never say that Allah is not just, but when compared to the God of the Bible, he is not. Allah leads people astray. He allows his prophets things that are ordinarily forbidden and wrong. Even ordinary believers are allowed to do what is really not right, because they are believers. Nothing is right or wrong by nature, but becomes so by the arbitrary decree of the Almighty. What Allah forbids is sin, even if what is forbidden seems right and lawful to the human conscience. What Allah permits is not sin and cannot be sin at the time he allows it, even though it may have been sin before or after.[15]

An initial and fundamental problem in evangelizing Muslims is their lack of consciousness of sin. This comes in large measure from their view of Allah's character and from their model, the life of Muhammad. There is no comparison between the moral and ethical life of Jesus and that of Muhammad, even according to the Qur'an and *Hadith*.

To the Muslim, there is no distinction between the ceremonial law and the moral law. It is as great an offence to pray with unwashed hands as it is to tell a lie. This lack of distinction is most evident in the *Hadith* of the Prophet: "The prophet, upon whom be prayers and peace, said, One dirhem of usury which a man eats, knowing it to be so, is more grievous than thirty-six fornications; and whosoever has been so nourished is worthy of hell-fire."[16] An Ethiopian convert from Islam in Canada told one of the authors how there was a serious conflict between Muslims in his village in Ethiopia over the proper way to have water drip from your hands when doing ablutions. His best friend, family, and village ostracized him when he confessed to his friend that he had drunk a small amount of wine at a social function. He was not allowed into the mosque. Their refusal to extend grace and forgiveness was one of the factors that led him to Christ.

Actually, according to the Qur'an and tradition, all sin is really a matter of minor importance. Although everyone is concerned to avoid hell and make it into heaven, God readily forgives sin. Besides, in Islam you do not have a guarantee of attaining heaven, even if you are sinless. Muhammad himself is said not to have been assured of a place in heaven. On the other hand, many Muslims believe that after suffering in hell for a time for their sins, they will go to paradise. It is the repetition of the *shahada*, "There is no god but Allah, and Muhammad is the Apostle of Allah," that makes one a true believer. All other considerations are less important.[17] Repetition of this sentence is said to combat the enemies within, reaffirm the divine unity, and integrate the human soul with its center. *Subhanan Allah* (Glory to God) and *Allahu Akbar* (God is the Most Great) are often repeated in prayer; their repetition is said to wipe out sins. Doing good deeds also brings forgiveness for sins. For example, according to a *Hadith* reported by al-Bukhari, Muhammad related that a man found a very thirsty dog. So the man went down into a well to get the dog a drink by filling his shoes with water. "Then Allah was grateful to him and forgave him his sins."[18]

Sin's Consequences and Remedy

Human depravity and the true nature of sin itself have no place in the Qur'an. It is not enough just to use the word *sin*. Both Islam and Christianity use the same word, but, for a Christian, the Muslim's definition of sin is inaccurate and therefore inadequate. The reason for the discrepancy is that Christians see Islam as having an inaccurate and inadequate concept of God. If you don't know how holy God is, you can't know how sinful man is, and the result is a religion without salvation. This is the fundamental difference between Islam and Christianity. In Islam, man makes himself acceptable to God, but in Christianity, God makes man righteous and acceptable through Jesus' substitutionary atonement. It is difficult for the average Muslim to perceive of sin as wrong done to the holy love of God. Allah is perceived as totally "other" or transcendent. He is an arbitrary being who does what he likes and favors "whom he pleases." Man is simply the slave of Allah. Even man's offenses have been predetermined. In accordance with its minimizing of sin, Islam does not emphasize, as does Christianity, the consequences of sin or the hostility of evil to the purposes of God. As a result, the crucifixion of Christ is unnecessary in Islam.

A Muslim would agree that God sees our hearts, and that he judges us more by our intentions than by our actions. In the Muslim view,

> a person who does a very good thing for the wrong reason may be judged severely and the man who we look on as a terribly wicked man, may do something wrong but with the right intentions and be declared with little or no guilt at all. He who does a wrong thing, has one strike against him. He who intends to do what is right but doesn't do it will be counted as if he did the right. If he does the good, it will be multiplied ten times. God has a divine justice that we cannot with our finite minds understand. If God looks at something and calls it "just," it is just and good, even if it looks wrong to us.[19]

We can find the biblical response to this in 1 Samuel 15:1–29, Matthew 21:28–32, Isaiah 1:11–20, and Micah 6:6–8.

Muslims know nothing of the sanctifying power of the Holy Spirit at work in the believer to produce a holy life that is pleasing to God. Islam offers nothing to transform a sinner into a saint. Muslims simply rely on individual effort and collective discipline through knowledge to produce a changed life. But there is no power there to change the heart. As Christians, we need to show how man has a great need for grace, forgiveness, and the new birth in Christ. Sin is more than just an outward breaking of the law. God knows how we have violated his holiness in our hearts. Because of God's justice, there is condemnation and a penalty where his laws have been broken. In the Christian perspective, this is where there is an unmistakable need for grace. God offers it to us on conditions that deal justly with the holiness we have offended.[20] Only God in Christ, being sinless, could bear our sin and pay the penalty we deserve by death on a cross. Then the wrath of God against sin is satisfied. We are justified (made right with God) through faith in Jesus Christ and his substitutionary atonement on the cross. As Robert Lowry writes in his hymn, "What can wash away my sin? Nothing but the blood of Jesus." As the apostle John says, "The blood of Jesus, his Son, purifies us from all sin" (1 John 1:7). Not only did Jesus die for us, but he rose again from the dead and lives today. Through his resurrection, we, too, are able to live by faith. Without his resurrection, there is no faith and no Christianity. We would still be dead in sin (1 Cor. 15:14, 17).

Righteousness

Since "there is no one righteous, not even one" (Rom. 3:10), what are we to do? Muslims attempt to establish their own righteousness before God by their good works, which they hope will balance out their bad deeds and omissions. By saying extra prayers, observing extra fasts besides Ramadan, repeating the ninety-nine most beautiful names of Allah, giving alms, and doing other good works, a Muslim hopes to receive Allah's mercy and forgiveness, but still has no guarantee of it. But the Bible gives us the answer to man's dilemma. We can be made right with God and have assurance of eternal life.

"But now a righteousness from God, apart from law, has been made known, to which the Law and the Prophets testify. This righteousness from God comes through faith in Jesus Christ to all who believe" (Rom. 3:21–22). The biblical concept of receiving the righteousness of Christ as a free gift by faith is totally foreign to Muslims. A helpful passage to share with a Muslim is Paul's prayer for the Israelites, which may be applied in a similar way to Muslims:

> Brothers, my heart's desire and prayer to God for [Muslims] is that they may be saved. For I can testify about them that they are zealous for God, but their zeal is not based on knowledge. Since they did not know the righteousness that comes from God and sought to establish their own, they did not submit to God's righteousness. Christ is the end of the law so that there may be righteousness for everyone who believes. (Rom. 10:1–4)

Although Muslims are zealous for God, their zeal is not based on knowledge. Such zeal characterized the Pharisees in Jesus' day. They sought to establish their own righteousness through keeping the law. However, they failed, as all still do today. This passage tells us what a true Muslim ("one who submits") should be: one who submits to God's righteousness in Christ by faith.

Abraham, too, was declared righteous by his faith. "Abraham believed God, and it was credited to him as righteousness" (Rom. 4:3, quoting Gen. 15:6). It was not a matter of his having achieved something that made him acceptable to God. Paul further explains the meaning of these words: "The words 'it was credited to him' were written not for him alone, but also for us, to whom God will credit righteousness—for us who believe in him who raised Jesus our Lord from the dead. He was delivered over to death for our sins and was raised to life for our justification" (Rom. 4:23–25). So our righteousness comes only from God, by our believing that he sent Jesus to die and rise again for our salvation from our sins.

For Reflection/Action

1. How are the different views of God in the Qur'an and the Bible reflected in how he deals with sin in Islam and Christianity, respectively?
2. Prepare an outline of a Bible study designed to bring a Muslim to a personal conviction of his sin.

3. Some Muslims may already recognize their sin, but without understanding its serious consequences for their relationship with God. How can you help them see that there is no solution apart from the work of Christ on the cross?

CHAPTER EIGHT

Living One's Faith in the World

Our Role in the World

Muslims understand that the purpose of our existence is to be God's *khalifah* (vicegerent), having been entrusted with the responsibility of fulfilling the divine will. That divine will is partially fulfilled in nature as natural law, but part of it is to be fulfilled by us as moral law. In this way, we are distinct from all other creatures. Only humans act freely, having the capacity for responsible moral action to fulfill the moral part of the divine will.[1] By worshiping God in full submission to his will, we are fulfilling the purpose for our creation and existence. Our obligation to serve God is felt by us to be normal because it fulfills our natural inclination to do so. People have a natural state of being called *fitrah*, which is the pattern according to which God has created all things. Everything fits into the pattern for which it was created in accordance with the law of God. Submission to this *fitrah* brings harmony, because what is inherent in one's true nature is realized. Opposition to God's pattern brings discord, because of the realization of what is contrary to one's true nature. God and man have made a covenant with each other by man's acknowledgment of the truth of God's lordship. Therefore, if we are guided rightly in this life, we will remember our covenant and live in such a way that our worship, acts of piety, life, and death will all be for the sake of God alone.[2]

The key to salvation for a Muslim is that God is one. What saves is the purity or totality of this belief, which implies the loss of self. *Tawhid* (oneness) is to be expressed in all aspects of both individual and collective life. In Islam, man does not need salvation in the Christian sense, but divine guidance. *Da'wah* is the call to follow this divine guidance (*hidayah*) in order to recover one's true rationality, innocence, and dignity as God's *khalifah* on earth.[3]

In contrast to Islam's view of man's role in the world, Christians know that God made us to bring praise and glory to himself for his good pleasure (Isa. 43:7; Ps. 86:9; Rev. 15:4). We are able to do that because he has created us in his image (Gen. 1:26–27), distinguishing us from all other creatures. We are able to have fellowship with God through the redemption accomplished by Christ on our behalf. Having been made new creatures in Christ, we are able to do everything for the glory of God as God's Spirit works through us. Man was called by God to have dominion over the earth and to subdue it. Therefore, God calls us to glorify him through holiness in all aspects of our lives. God is sovereign over his creation, and works through us to establish his kingdom. That kingdom is established as the created order is redeemed and re-created in the work of Christ.

David Shenk expresses the difference between the Muslim and the Christian views of God's acts and will for us as follows:

> Communication with our Muslim friends concerning our commitment to the Kingdom of God is a basis for fruitful dialogue. However, in that witness we experience pain, for we quickly recognize that both the nature of the Kingdom and its implementation are vastly different from a Quranic or a Biblical perspective. The *hijra* and the cross are opposite to one another as the means through which the Kingdom is established. Islam and the Christian faith therefore move in opposite directions in their understanding of how God acts in history and how he brings about his will on earth.[4]

Living One's Faith in the World: the Islamic State

Shari'a

Islam's creative center is *tawhid*, the witness that there is no god but Allah. This means that Allah is the ultimate cause of all existence and action, and that men are free and responsible to actualize the will of Allah. This understanding means that religion is civilization, and that civilization is religion. Islam is a total system of values, belief, and conduct. All knowledge is to be classified from an Islamic point of view.[5]

The *Shari'a* is the road that leads to God, guaranteeing a harmonious life in this world and happiness in the hereafter. It contains the divine will that is applied to every situation in life. Since it considers every aspect of human action, it sanctifies all of life and gives religious significance to what appear to be the most mundane activities. In Islam, there is little or no distinction between law and religion. For the Muslim, law is an integral part of revelation, so that political, social, and economic life are integrated into an all-encompassing religious worldview. The *Shari'a* integrates man and society to realize unity (*tawhid*) in human life.

The concept of law in Islam is completely authoritarian. The *Shari'a* is the constitution of the community and the will of Allah, as revealed through the Prophet. Since Allah is the head and legislator of the community, to violate or neglect the law is not only an infringement of the social order, but also an act of religious disobedience—a sin requiring a religious penalty.

God's rule demands man's submission. But in Islam, certain external conditions are necessary in order for man to submit fully. "Man is perfectible but the conditions of his perfectibility are environmental, circumstantial and thus also political."[6] In Islam, there are no inward conditions of regeneration or radical transformation. Devotional practice is indispensable, but the outworking of Islam is far from being only a religious matter. For a Muslim to be what he really should be requires the Islamic political order. The faith shapes and controls the state, and the state is the instrument of faith. Presupposed in Islam is government that enables obedience. "Man in Islam can only truly be himself when the appropriate Islamic conditions in the state are realized around him."[7]

This calls for an Islamic state. "The Islamic state today is the state which has instituted 'a Muslim government which believes in Allah and the Last Day, which applies laws for Muslims stemming from the Islamic *Shari'a* and which develops to meet the developments of the times.' "[8] The objective of an Islamic state is "Islamicity," which requires obedience to the teachings of Islam in all its various aspects. To do this, it must establish *al-din* (the faith) and secure the interests of the ruled. Establishing the faith is the justification for the existence of the Islamic state. Anyone who does not commit himself to this objective is considered a rebel against the state.[9] A government that fails to uphold these objectives of the faith and the interests of the ruled is an illegal government which Muslims are not bound to obey or serve.

Knowing the Will of God

A common question that Muslims ask (as do Christians) is, "How can I know the will of God?" A Muslim knows the will of God through the *Shari'a*, which is the codification of the teaching of the Qur'an; the *Hadith*, the tradition of the actions and sayings of Muhammad; the consensus of the *'ulama*, the Islamic scholars; and *qiyas*, analogical reasoning. On a more personal basis, Muslims know the will of Allah through the help of others more qualified to explain the Qur'an to them, such as their imam. Since God is not personal to Muslims, they do not have the enlightenment and leading of the Holy Spirit. Sufis would find the will of God as do other Muslims, but with the inner light and reflection on the attributes of God. But the *Shari'a* will not help a person decide whom to marry, which job to take, or what school to go to.

For the Christian, knowing the will of God and his leading in everyday decisions of life is based on a personal relationship with the living God through the Holy Spirit. The Spirit leads us through the Word of God, prayer, circumstances, and God's people in the church. A Muslim cannot know the will of God until he is known by God in a personal way. Through general revelation, Muslims know something of the will of God. Their conscience teaches them right from wrong. Numerous truths of the Bible are also found in the Qur'an. But this is not enough to know God's will and bring glory to him through their lives.

Political Thought

When Muhammad began his mission in Medina, it was not primarily directed at the individual soul, as it had been in Mecca, but at people in society. Revelation was focused on the outer person, in his dealings with his neighbor and others. The Prophet's example was seen as bringing order to the lusts, appetites, and ambitions of natural man, thus creating a communal whole that was dedicated to the Creator's will. In doing this, Muhammad took into account all the facts of life, including work, commerce, profits, disputes, war, punishment, reward, procreation, marriage, divorce, vengeance, and diplomacy. The Muslim community established in Medina is described in the Qur'an as "the best community established for men."[10]

Beginning in the latter part of the ninth century, Islamic political thought became concerned with finding ways to apply the law of Allah to all of man's activity in his quest for perfection and well-being in this world, and everlasting happiness in the hereafter. With that in mind, Muslim thinkers began to harmonize Islamic laws regarding human conduct with Platonic and Aristotelian conceptions of political life. Distinguished Muslim thinkers, such as al-Farabi and Ibn Sina, regarded the *Shari'a* as the constitution of the ideal Islamic state. They argued that the Islamic state would lead individuals to attain the ultimate perfection and happiness that all seek.[11]

The *falasifa*, the Muslim disciples of Plato and Aristotle, regarded man as a social being who is unable to provide himself with all that is necessary for his needs without the help of his fellow man. So the individual is part of a community that can provide him with practical and intellectual perfection or the highest good. Thus, one can find the complete satisfaction of one's physical, intellectual, and moral needs only through society (*qawm*) and through cooperation with other people to achieve the perfection of one's nature. This leads one to regard society as indispensable to the survival of humanity. Consequently, there is a necessity for political and social organizations, and ultimately the authority of the state, without which society would disintegrate. Because of people's wicked tendencies, they become enemies of one another, making it is impossible for them to live in an orderly manner in association with one another without the authority of the state.[12] In the Islamic state, the twofold happiness of well-being in this world and bliss in the next is guaranteed by the imam who rules. Separation from this state would surely deprive the individual of the opportunity for perfection and of gaining ultimate happiness.[13]

Classical Islamic political thinkers envisioned a perfect society, which has never been realized, as an organized humanity without national boundaries. It would be like a family which had the same Creator and Father. No wars would occur because each person would have the same vision, not of a particular nation, but of humanity; not of a particular king, but of God.[14]

Kenneth Cragg has well summarized this concept of the Islamic state:

> This belief that the political expression and the rule of God can coincide has been the ruling characteristic of Muslim belief about society and the Muslim hope about history. On the negative side, no separation between the realm of religion and the realm of the state is proper or tolerable (though the shape of the connection is variable and debatable). Islam exists to be not only a way of devotion, but a form of government. It expects the rule of God, not only over, but as, the kingdom of men. The po-

> tential identity between them was the original keynote and the perpetual ambition of Muslim history.[15]

Islam legislates for man under God. This legislation is thought to be feasible, given certain prerequisites. These are the Islamic state over all, the pattern of habituation (five daily prayers, an annual fast, a pilgrimage, and periodic *zakat*), and the solidarity of the community (*ummah*) of Islam. With these three elements and the reinforcement of the tradition of the Prophet, man is held to be perfectible. There is not the acknowledgement found in Romans, "For what I do is not the good I want to do; no, the evil I do not want to do—this I keep on doing" (Rom. 7:19). Islam "has a confidence that law in revelation, mercy in community, example in tradition, constraint in collective patterns, and the aegis of Islamic rule, together suffice to attain that submission under God which is man's calling and duty."[16]

Living One's Faith in the World: the Kingdom of God

As we have seen, Islam is the visible rule of Allah in the political state. However, Christians deny that visible rule can be equated with the kingdom of God, although throughout church history this has at times been affirmed.

The kingdom of God is one biblical concept that can effectively meet both the religious and the cultural needs of the Muslim. The kingdom of God is comprehensive in its response to the Islamic *al-din* (complete way of life) and *da'wah* (call to recover true rationality, innocence, and dignity as God's vicegerent). But it must be presented from a biblical framework rather than an Islamic one. We begin with a presentation of the ministry of Jesus Christ, as he proclaimed the kingdom of God.[17]

The major theme of Christ's ministry was the coming of the kingdom of God. It is with this message that he began his ministry (Mark 1:15). Bruce Nicholls describes it:

> He conceived of the Kingdom as the universal reign of God in heaven and on earth, in both the spiritual and the created realms. Jesus was aware that he was the bearer of the Kingdom, in him the Kingdom was realized, yet he looked for its consummation at the end time. He saw his mission as the anointed one uniquely sent by the Father to the whole person, to the whole world and to the whole fabric of society.[18]

We can see what Christ had in mind regarding his mission when he indicated that it fulfilled the prophecy of Isaiah (Luke 4:17–19) and also when he replied to the disciples of John the Baptist (Matt. 11:2–6). Jesus taught that his power to forgive sins and perform miracles were signs of his messianic kingship. His lifestyle exemplified his teaching. Jesus traveled about "preaching the gospel of the kingdom and healing every disease and sickness" (Matt. 9:35). The early church had the same vision of the centrality of Christ and the kingdom of God as it spread its message (see, e.g., Acts 28:23).

Jesus had a cosmic concept of the kingdom, as Bruce Nicholls explains:

> His Kingdom was not of this world yet he taught his disciples to pray to the Father, "Thy Kingdom come, thy will be done, on earth as it is in heaven" (Matt. 6:10). In casting out the demons, the Kingdom came upon his hearers (Luke 11:20). In the victory of the Cross the ruler of this world was cast out (John 12:31). Paul expounded the same triumph of Christ over cosmic principalities and powers when he spoke of the Father delivering us from the dominion of darkness and transferring us to the Kingdom of his beloved Son (Col. 1:13).[19]

Jesus spoke of the kingdom as something that is present now and also as something that is yet to come. The kingdom may be entered by those who repent and believe and come as a little child, totally dependent and trusting. The kingdom is present now by grace in the lives of those who have believed, but in the future Jesus will rule as a glorious king with all the splendor of heaven.

As a result of the proclamation of the kingdom, there emerges the church, which is founded on the confession of Peter that Jesus is the Christ (Matt. 16:16–18). The church is the community of the people of God, who are called out together to serve him. It is the body of believers who are neither identical to the kingdom nor independent of it. Where Christ reigns within the visible body of believers, there can be found the kingdom of God. This church goes beyond any culture, but makes an impact upon it.[20] The church is not simply a community in submission to the will of an unknowable God, as in Islam, but an incorporation of the believer into the family of a self-revealing God who loves us unconditionally.

"The Kingdom of God is also a Kingdom of justice because law is an expression of the character of God as holy-love."[21] The law is morally good and is to be loved. But Islam makes the law people's master and teaches obedience to it as the way of "salvation." This abuses the role of law because it makes law autonomous. It is similar to the abuse of Old Testament law found in Judaism. As *din al-fitra* (natural religion), Islam assumes that every person is competent to recognize the law as truth and has the power to keep it. Little or no grace is needed to fulfill its requirements. All men are called to submit and obey.[22]

Christ's teaching regarding the kingdom was totally dissociated from any political understanding of a kingdom (Mark 12:13–17; John 18:36). His idea was of an invisible, spiritual kingdom. But this kingdom is not confined to the sphere of the ethical, based on the principle of love. The whole content of religion is part of the kingdom. The kingdom consists not only of righteousness, but also of life, forgiveness of sin, and communion with God. All that belongs to the kingdom is the result of the work of God, not human works. We are to petition God to bring his kingdom to realization, so that he may set up his reign in us in a way that will be revealed through our actions.[23]

The kingdom is centered in God himself; therefore, Jesus teaches that it is the supreme object of human pursuit. In Matthew 6:33 we see that seeking after the kingdom is opposed to seeking after earthly things, because basically it is to seek after God himself.[24]

Jesus warned against excessive spiritualizing to the point that the external world is seen as totally worthless and outside the direct control of God. Jesus began a work that was aimed at a supernatural renewal of the world to overcome all evil. It involved the renewal of both the physical and the spiritual world.[25] Peter writes, "But in keeping with his promise we are looking forward to a new heaven and a new earth, the home of righteousness" (2 Peter 3:13). Jesus taught believers to be in the world, but not of the world, with its value system and sin.

Jesus made it clear that while the kingdom is now actually coming, a complete separation between good and evil will not be a reality until the end of the age. The church, as the externally organized kingdom, will continue to have the limitations and imperfections of its sinful environment until the day when it will be purified of all evil.[26]

The kingship of God is intended to influence and control the whole of human life, as Jesus taught in the parable of the leaven. Whenever different spheres of human activity, such as science, art, the family, the state, commerce, and industry, come under the controlling influence of righteousness, we can say that there the kingdom of God has been manifested. These different spheres of human activity can be separate from the visible church, but if they truly belong to the kingdom of God, they are a product of the regenerated life of the invisible church.[27]

Explaining the centrality of the kingdom, Geerhardus Vos says,

> The Kingdom . . . proclaims that religion, and religion alone, can act as the supreme unifying, centralizing factor in

the life of man, as that which binds all together and perfects all by leading it to its final goal in the service of God.[28]

Spreading the Vision

A vision statement for the growth of Islam in America says,

> The Prophet established a city state and expanded it through da'wah, defensive wars and preemptive strikes against his enemies. The equivalent of that city state in America would be Islamic organizations and Muslim neighborhoods. We should promote Muslim neighborhoods in all major cities of the U.S. to serve as nuclei and expand them through conversion and migration to the Muslim enclaves. The development of enclaves would give us control over the schools, local politics and help in establishing necessary institutional infrastructure. As these enclaves grow in size through conversion and immigration, the Muslims will have some say in national politics and perhaps even be able to elect Muslims as congressmen and senators. Naturally, at some point in time, we will be able to elect a Muslim as President in the White House. In time, we will be able to do what we cannot even say at this time. Defensive actions in our time, analogous to the defensive actions of the Prophet, would be to respond to the attackers on Islam in literature and the media. Preemptive strikes against the enemies of Islam, analogous to the preemptive strikes of the Prophet, would be ideological exposure of falsehood of secular humanism, secular nationalism, Christianity, Judaism, Hinduism, Buddhism and other religions and cults. However, in many cases mere presentation of the truth of Islam aggressively but rationally will be adequate to defeat the falsehood; Muslims may not need to attack other systems and religions.[29]

The Qur'an states that Islam is to spread through preaching by the use of rational argument. The Muslim is required to respect resistance to Islam at the level of contrary ideas. Forced conversion is prohibited. But if this resistance to Islam puts obstacles in the way of preaching or the free and responsible interchange of ideas, then Islam prescribes that the obstacle be removed by force. If religious resistance uses the sword, then Islam enjoins Muslims to use the same. However, the recourse to violence is justified only to put an end to the violent obstruction, never to force the opposition to convert to Islam.[30]

One of the responsibilities of an Islamic state is "*jihad* (holy war) against those who oppose Islam after calling upon them to embrace it, or to accept protection as non-Muslims, so that the right of Allah is upheld in proclamation of the religion in its entirety."[31]

The Qur'an permits fighting in case of oppression in these words: "Those who are fighting have been granted permission to do so because they have been oppressed, and Allah is indeed able to grant them victory" (Surah 22:39).

This attitude is contrary to that of Jesus and the New Testament. At the time of Jesus and the apostles, there was much oppression of both Israel and the believers in Christ. Jesus' disciples wanted the kingdom to come in its fullness right away, but Jesus told them that it was not yet time for that. First, the gospel of the kingdom had to be preached to the whole world (Matt. 24:14; Acts 1:6–8). Jesus also warned them of the coming of many false Christs and false prophets, who would lead many away from the truth. While we suffer from evil and abuse, we are blessed by God and are to rejoice that we participate in the sufferings of Christ (1 Peter 4:13–14). We are to commit ourselves to our faithful Creator and continue to do good (1 Peter 4:19).

Jesus' ministry in Palestine became a model for how the church should proclaim the kingdom of God. It was a ministry of both word and deed. Bruce Nicholls describes it like this:

> Evangelism and church planting, the prophetic rebuke of social injustice, the compassionate service to the poor and

> oppressed find their unity in the gospel of the Kingdom. Thus service through medicine, education, aid, etc., is not an instrument of proselytization but the evidence of the transforming power of the gospel. Jesus never debated the priority of one aspect of mission over another; he just lived according to his own mandate.[32]

"The Kingdom of God becomes the objective reference point to evaluate, reject, adapt and transform culture in the faithful proclamation of the gospel and the building of the Church."[33] It is the central message of the gospel and should be our message as Christians to Muslims. A Reformed world-and-life view, which captures every thought for Christ and exercises his dominion over all of life, is the most effective answer to the comprehensive view of religion in life that is found in Islam.

For Reflection/Action

1. When a Muslim and a Christian each ask, "How can I know the will of God?" how is their concept of God's will different?
2. Why is the ideal Islamic state an unrealistic, unachievable goal?
3. How is the kingdom of God, as Jesus preached it and demonstrated it, an effective answer to rule by the *Shari'a* (Islamic law)?
4. How can you demonstrate the coming of the kingdom of God to Muslims in a way that would make it clearly visible to them?
5. How does the Christian goal of doing everything for the glory of God differ from the Muslim goal of submitting to the will of Allah? How can you demonstrate these differences to your Muslim friend?

Conclusion to Part 3: Theological Understanding

While Muslims and Christians can affirm and give thanks for those things that unite them, both must confess that there are some important differences between them. The Muslim testifies that the Qur'an is God's final and definitive revelation of his perfect will to mankind. The Christian testifies that Jesus Christ is the living Word of God in human form. For the Muslim, the Qur'an is the criterion of truth, while for the Christian, the total biblical witness, culminating in Jesus the Messiah, is the criterion of truth. These commitments determine what the Muslim and the Christian believe about God, man, salvation, guidance, righteousness, revelation, and judgment.[1]

For the Muslim, man's success and salvation lie in accepting God as his God, as *Ma'bud* (the object of worship, reverence, loyalty, and obedience). Just as the revelation of Christ is the redemptive act of God for Christians, so Islam believes that the revelation of Muhammad is the redemptive act of God. As the revelation of Christ redeemed man from bondage to sin, so the revelation of Muhammad redeemed man from bondage to *shirk* (associationism) and *kufr* (ungodliness or no faith).[2]

Both Islam and Christianity agree that God is merciful and that he loves. The question is, How closely does God choose to identify with our human situation? How does God express his love and mercy? God's mercy is expressed in Islam supremely through the revelation of a perfect law. God's love is supremely expressed in Christianity in the suffering, redemptive love revealed in the life, crucifixion, and resurrection of Jesus the Messiah. These differences are very significant.[3]

The holiness of God and the sinfulness of men are two vital omissions in the qur'anic revelation, from the Christian perspective. These two truths are inseparable and together pose the problem that required as its solution the vicarious sacrifice of the Righteous One in the place of the sinner in order that salvation might be provided for him. If either the holiness of God or the sinfulness of man is reduced or overlooked, the need for salvation by grace disappears and a religion of human good works becomes plausible. This is just what is found in Islam.

Both Muslim and Christian can agree on this: truth is the authoritative revelation from God. But this starting point is also the point of divergence. Is the Word of revelation preeminently a book that descended from heaven with Allah's revealed will, or is it supremely evident in the person of Christ, who is revealed to us through understanding the Bible that was inspired by the Holy Spirit? For the Muslim, the Qur'an is revered as an eternal, uncreated book preserved in heaven and almost worshiped. The Bible-believing Christian trusts in the Bible as God's authoritative, inerrant word, which reveals God supremely in Christ for our salvation.

Part Four

Reaching Muslims

We have presented thus far a framework for understanding Islam. With this background, we can work to reach Muslims with the gospel. Now we turn our attention to actually reaching Muslims. But first we must address the theological basis and motivation given to us by God to bring them the gospel. Otherwise, we may be satisfied with mutual understanding and dialogue. We have been commissioned with an urgent message, upon which depends the eternal destiny of a billion Muslims. After discussing the basis for our mission, we will plunge into the practical aspects of carrying it out. We have found these approaches to be useful in our own ministry as well as in those of others throughout North America.

CHAPTER NINE

The Theological Basis for Muslim Evangelism

The Sovereignty of God

"God, from all eternity, did, by the most wise and holy counsel of his own will, freely, and unchangeably ordain whatsoever comes to pass." (Westminster Confession of Faith, III.1)

> "But the plans of the LORD stand firm forever,
> the purposes of his heart through all generations."
> (Ps. 33:11)

In him we were also chosen, having been predestined according to the plan of him who works out everything in conformity with the purpose of his will." (Eph. 1:11)

What then shall we say? Is God unjust? Not at all! For he says to Moses, "I will have mercy on whom I have mercy, and I will have compassion on whom I have compassion." It does not, therefore, depend on man's desire or effort, but on God's mercy. For the Scripture says to Pharaoh: "I raised you up for this very purpose, that I might display my power in you and that my name might be proclaimed in all the earth." Therefore God has mercy on whom he wants to have mercy, and he hardens whom he wants to harden. (Rom. 9:14–18)

At the heart of witnessing to Muslims is the sovereignty of God. It is the basis of any effort we make among Muslims. Our great God is sovereign in leading us to Muslim friends to whom we can communicate the gospel. He is also sovereign in bringing them to confess his Son as their Lord and Savior. His saving work does not depend on our methods or effort, but on his great mercy on those whom he has chosen. However, this does not mean that we are not involved in God's work of bringing his people to himself. God has decided to use us as his ambassadors to bring the good news to the lost. Christ's love compels us. He has committed to us the ministry of reconciliation (2 Cor. 5:11, 14, 18–20).

The biblical concept of God's sovereignty means at least three important things. First, it means ownership. All things in this world belong to God—the earth, the heavens, and everything else. God owns it all because he is Lord of all. Second, it means authority. God has an absolute and kingly authority to execute his perfect will and require his creatures to carry out his commands. They must obey his will with full submission. His commands express his holy character. They show us his holiness, righteousness, and unconditional love. They are seen more fully in his relationship with us as our Redeemer and Father. Third, God's sovereignty means control. God is the master of his universe. At times he is displeased and angry with it for its sin and rebellion. But it never frustrates or threatens him.[1]

Thus, God's sovereignty in reaching out to Muslims provides our supreme encouragement. If we believe that God owns, controls, and has authority over his creatures, then witnessing to Muslims becomes a privilege, rather than a burden. If you become discouraged because you find that your witness to Muslims is less effective than it is to other groups, be encouraged to know that God will bring into his sheepfold all of his elect. We are not the ones who save, but God alone. We are simply his ambassadors (2 Cor. 5:20) and witnesses (Acts 1:8). If you believe the Bible's teaching on God's sovereignty, then witness to Muslims with boldness, encouragement, and joy. If you have trouble accepting this doctrine, then pray and ask God, the Holy Spirit, to enlighten your understanding.[2]

Salvation Only Through Jesus Christ

Before witnessing to Muslims, one must understand that salvation is attained only through Jesus Christ. It has become popular in certain circles today to think that people in other religions get to heaven by following their own path. One may hear: "They believe in God, too. So won't God have compassion and mercy on them as well? Don't all religions teach us how to do good? Don't Muslims believe in one God and in Jesus as a great prophet who did miracles?" We know that Muslims believe this, but it is an incomplete and distorted view of God and Jesus. As we have seen, the Muslim God does not have the same attributes as the Christian God. The essential role of Jesus as Savior, through his death and resurrection, are missing. God is unknowable in Islam. As Christians, we know he has revealed himself as a person to us. So there are irreconcilable differences between Islam and Christianity.

The Bible is full of claims that salvation comes exclusively through Jesus. He himself says, "I am the gate; whoever enters through me will be saved" (John 10:9). The apostle Peter declares, "Salvation is found in no one else, for there is no other name under heaven given to men by which we must be saved" (Acts 4:12). You may also look at John 3:16–18; 14:5–6; 1 Timothy 2:5–6.

In the context of Christians suffering persecution in Thessalonica, Paul writes to them that "God is just." When Jesus returns, "he will pay back trouble to those who trouble you and give relief to you who are troubled." He goes on to say, "He will punish those who do not know God and do not obey the gospel of our Lord Jesus. They will be punished with everlasting destruction and shut out from the presence of the Lord" (2 Thess. 1:6–10).

Our claim to absolute truth does not lead us to intolerance and unwarranted condemnation of others, but to a love for our neighbor and a burden that others might know and experience the liberating power of God from sin. What we have to share is *good news!* In speaking to people from other faiths, we should listen and learn and agree with them on what we share in common. But we cannot compromise on the truth claims that the gospel makes on all of us. God is the God of all the universe, the Creator of all people, and he has revealed himself to us through Jesus Christ and his Holy Scriptures. He provided for the salvation of all people from sin through Jesus Christ. As Paul says in Romans 3:29–30,

> Is God the God of Jews only? Is he not the God of Gentiles too? Yes, of Gentiles too, since there is only one God, who will justify the circumcised by faith and the uncircumcised through that same faith.

A little earlier Paul writes, "This righteousness from God comes through faith in Jesus Christ to all who believe" (v. 22).

Someone once asked Jesus, "Lord, are only a few people going to be saved?" His answer was "Make every effort to enter through the narrow door, because many, I tell you, will try to enter and will not be able to" (Luke 13:23–24). That door of entrance is through Jesus by faith. Islam is essentially man-centered and works-oriented. In it, human pride is exalted because of the focus on what we do. Islam denies the way of the cross and the need for the death of Jesus to save us from our sins.

In his letter to the Ephesians, Paul reminds them of their state before they became Christians:

> Therefore, remember that formerly you who are Gentiles by birth and called "uncircumcised" by those who call themselves "the circumcision" (that done in the body by the hands of men)—remember that at that time you were separate from Christ, excluded from citizenship in Israel and foreigners to the covenants of the promise, without hope and without God in the world. But now in Christ Je-

> sus you who once were far away have been brought near through the blood of Christ. (Eph. 2:11–13)

Note that Paul says that they were "without hope and without God in the world." What was it that brought them into the new Israel, to be partakers in the covenant promises? It was the blood of Christ. Jesus Christ gave them hope and new life by his sacrificial death on the cross for their sins.

The Cross of Christ

From man's point of view, Islam is a logical, tight, reasonable, achievable religion, by which a person can live. But though it continually speaks of God, it is actually man-centered. It focuses on what we do to submit to God's will in the hope that we can do enough to receive his mercy. As we minister to Muslims, we often sense a spiritual darkness that keeps them from seeing the truth of the gospel. Paul explains why this is so: "The man without the Spirit does not accept the things that come from the Spirit of God, for they are foolishness to him, and he cannot understand them, because they are spiritually discerned" (1 Cor. 2:14). The free gift of salvation by God's grace without works is totally foreign to their minds. That Jesus Christ could be a substitute for the punishment of their sins is contrary to the teaching of Islam, which insists that each person must pay for his own sins. But it is impossible for us to pay for our sins, since God demands absolute holiness. Our good works are only what is already required of us. They do not balance out our guilt. Therefore, we are condemned to eternal death.

God's grace for salvation is found in the cross of Christ. Paul continually preached the cross of Christ during his ministry, for the essence of the gospel is found in what Jesus did on the cross. Paul writes,

> For the message of the cross is foolishness to those who are perishing, but to us who are being saved it is the power of

> God. . . . For since in the wisdom of God the world through its wisdom did not know him, God was pleased through the foolishness of what was preached to save those who believe. Jews demand miraculous signs and Greeks look for wisdom, but we preach Christ crucified: a stumbling block to Jews and foolishness to Gentiles, but to those whom God has called, both Jews and Greeks, Christ the power of God and the wisdom of God. (1 Cor. 1:18, 21–24)

> For I resolved to know nothing while I was with you except Jesus Christ and him crucified. I came to you in weakness and fear, and with much trembling. My message and my preaching were not with wise and persuasive words, but with a demonstration of the Spirit's power, so that your faith might not rest on men's wisdom, but on God's power. (1 Cor. 2:2–5)

If you have any doubts about the scriptural teaching that we are justified before God solely by our faith, I encourage you to study Galatians, particularly chapter 3. There we see that in the preaching of Christ crucified we come to saving faith. At that point, we receive the Spirit, not through any human effort to keep the law. When we truly understand that salvation is totally of God, and not of human effort, then we know that God will be faithful to work through his Word to create faith in the hearts of our hearers.

Prayer for Muslims

Prayer is a privilege that God has given believers. In it we can have an intimacy with him. This privilege must never be neglected or taken for granted. It is only through prayer that we can ever hope to see any spiritual results in the lives of Muslims. It is only the Spirit of God who will move the hearts of people to recognize their sin and need of a Savior, to repent, and to trust only in the work of Christ for their salvation. If it is the work of God, then why must we pray? Because it is in response to our prayers that God acts. God commands us to pray. Jesus said to his disciples, "The harvest is plentiful but the workers are few. Ask the Lord of the harvest, therefore, to send out workers into his harvest field" (Matt. 9:37–38). In the Gospels, we see that Jesus was constantly in prayer. This is to be our lifestyle as well. As the apostle Paul tells the Thessalonians, "Pray continually" (1 Thess. 5:17).

Two attitudes must be kept in mind when we are praying for Muslims and ministering to them: boldness and humility. Our boldness in prayer comes from seeing the power of the kingdom unleashed in people's lives. This power brings forth miracles, healing, justice, and salvation. As Harvie Conn has written, "The human response to the open display of the kingdom of God's power is faith. Jesus adds boldness in prayer to that human response" (Matt. 21:21–22).[3] In prayer, we have the privilege, as children of God, to demand that our Muslim friend be saved. "Prayer's asking is not wishing. It is demanding that people come to Christ because Christ has come to us. It is demanding that the world be changed because Christ has come to change it."[4]

On the other hand, our prayers must be humble. Jesus prayed and taught us to pray with kingdom humility: "Your will be done on earth as it is in heaven." God's will is to be exalted and our willfulness is to be destroyed. This speaks to a constant problem for most Christians: the problem of substituting activity for prayer. "Activity is me-centered, prayer is God-centered."[5] The tendency to be activity-centered is clearly illustrated in Luke's account of Mary and Martha with Jesus (Luke 10:38–42). In humility, one recognizes the power of the Spirit to enable us to do any spiritual good that brings glory to God.

Prayer needs to be present at each step of our mission work. Conn says, "Biblical evangelizing is a two-fold commission: to preach and to pray, to talk to people about God and to talk to God about people."[6] Therefore, pray and do not give up. Even when your Muslim friend can't understand why you don't accept Muhammad as a prophet and why you believe that Jesus is more than a prophet, don't give up praying for him or her. We may not see results in the same way or at the time that we expect, but if we pray in faith, God will answer our prayers.

Finally, especially in light of the group of people for whom we are praying, we ought to follow Paul's request: "Finally, brothers, pray for us that the message of the Lord may spread rapidly and be honored, just as it was with you. And pray that we may be delivered from wicked and evil men, for not everyone has faith. But the Lord is faithful, and he will strengthen and protect you from the evil one" (2 Thess. 3:1–3). As you enter the enemy's territory with the gospel message, there is sure to be spiritual opposition, which at times may be very fierce. Even in the freedom of the U.S. and Canada, threats can be made on your life for your bold witness for Christ. Certainly any converts from Islam will be opposed by family and friends. They may be ostracized and expelled from their home. So let us remember in prayer our brothers and sisters in the Lord who are living under very difficult circumstances because of the Evil One.

Worship

> May the peoples praise you, O God;
> may all the peoples praise you.
> May the nations be glad and sing for joy,
> for you rule the peoples justly
> and guide the nations of the earth. (Ps. 67:3–4)

John Piper says in *Let the Nations Be Glad!* that worship, not missions, is the ultimate goal of the church. "Missions exists because worship doesn't." He continues,

> Worship, therefore, is the fuel and goal of missions. It's the goal of missions because in missions we simply aim to bring the nations into the white-hot enjoyment of God's glory. The goal of missions is the gladness of the peoples in the greatness of God.

Dr. Piper goes on to say, "Passion for God in worship precedes the offer of God in preaching. . . . Missions begins and ends in worship."[7] Therefore, our corporate worship as a gathered body of believers who are focused on God is not peripheral to missions, but foundational to sending us out in mission. Worshiping our God compels us to reach Muslims because we believe they are not worshiping the true God of the Bible. How can we rest in worshiping our Lord, knowing that there are millions of our dear Muslim friends who are not part of this true worship of God?

We see that at the consummation of history there will be a great gathering of all kinds of people to worship the Lord. The apostle John saw this scene to come:

> After this I looked and there before me was a great multitude that no one could count, from every nation, tribe, people and language, standing before the throne and in front of the Lamb. They were wearing white robes and were holding palm branches in their hands. And they cried out in a loud voice:
>
> "Salvation belongs to our God,
> who sits on the throne,
> and to the Lamb." (Rev. 7:9–10)

As a result of reaching out to our Muslims friends, we will eventually see many of them with us. What a glorious scene we have to look forward to, when millions of former Muslims from many nations will be a part of that great gathering.

Missions

The church has turned its back on Muslims because of their resistance to the gospel. However, as we understand the Scriptures, we see that Muslims are to be included in the harvest field. For Jesus said, "I have other sheep that are not of this sheep pen. I must bring them also. They too will listen to my voice, and there shall be one flock and one shepherd" (John 10:16).

Richard P. Bailey, who has ministered to Muslims for many years, both abroad and in the U.S., says, "God is also bringing Muslims into our own neighborhoods from parts of the world where they could never see the resurrection power of Christ demonstrated in the lives of believers. Hundreds have turned to Christ as a result."[8]

Observing that past efforts by Christians to communicate with Muslims have met with limited success, we do not want to be limited ourselves by concepts and approaches used in the past. Since Muslims are not inclined to come to us, we must go to them in ways that reflect the character of our Savior. Therefore, we advocate a concept that pushes beyond the restrictive boundaries that we have inherited from the past.

In being God's voice to Muslims, we must be free of any prejudice or antipathy toward them. We must not view Muslims as our enemies, for we have much in common with them. Because of what we have in common, we can join together in working against secularism and injustice. Seeing people suffer injustice provides an opportunity for Muslims, Christians, and Jews to work together for justice and peace. Even when there are times when Muslims are fiercely opposed to the work of Christians, Jesus has called us to love our enemies and pray for them (Matt. 5:44). For we too were once enemies of Christ, but he loved us and died for us (Rom. 5:8, 10).

Our Lord Jesus said, "For the Son of Man came to seek and to save what was lost" (Luke 19:10). He also said, "It is not the healthy who need a doctor, but the sick. I have not come to call the righteous, but sinners" (Mark 2:17). In light of Jesus' words, we do not want to stay shut up within the walls of our own fellowships, but want rather to obey Jesus' command in Matthew 28:19 and Acts 1:8 to go into the world and make disciples among those who do not yet know him.

The following passages of Scripture provide us with the missionary mandate to take the gospel to Muslims:

> "And this gospel of the kingdom will be preached in the whole world as a testimony to all nations, and then the end will come." (Matt. 24:14)

> "Therefore go and make disciples of all nations." (Matt. 28:19)

> He said to them, "Go into all the world and preach the good news to all creation." (Mark 16:15)

> "Repentance and forgiveness of sins will be preached in his name to all nations, beginning at Jerusalem." (Luke 24:47)

> "My prayer is not that you take them out of the world but that you protect them from the evil one. . . . As you sent me into the world, I have sent them into the world." (John 17:15, 18)

> "My prayer is not for them alone. I pray also for those who will believe in me through their message, that all of them may be one, Father, just as you are in me and I am in you. May they also be in us so that the world may believe that you have sent me." (John 17:20–21)

> "But you will receive power when the Holy Spirit comes on you; and you will be my witnesses in Jerusalem, and in all Judea and Samaria, and to the ends of the earth." (Acts 1:8)

These texts remind us of our calling in God's kingdom, which is to take the gospel of the kingdom to a dying world. We must see ourselves as being in the world for the sake of the lost. It is not the only reason we are here, but it is certainly a major one. This missiological reason makes us forget who we are in terms of our ethnic origin and breaks down our walls of hostility as we reach out to Muslims.

Not only are we sent by Jesus' command to bring the gospel to Muslims, but we feel a compulsion to reach those who have never had the opportunity to hear it. The apostle Paul had such a drive to reach the unreached:

> It has always been my ambition to preach the gospel where Christ was not known, so that I would not be building on someone else's foundation. Rather, as it is written: "Those who were not told about him will see, and those who have not heard will understand." (Rom. 15:20–21)

Almost all Muslims are those among whom Christ is not known as revealed in the Bible. The light of the gospel has been obscured by the deception of a totally transcendent god, a simply human Jesus, and salvation based on our good works and right guidance.

Everyone needs to hear the good news of salvation from the Lord, no matter what their ethnic or religious background may be:

> For there is no difference between Jew and Gentile—the same Lord is Lord of all and richly blesses all who call on him, for, "Everyone who calls on the name of the Lord will be saved."
>
> How, then, can they call on the one they have not believed in? And how can they believe in the one of whom they have not heard? And how can they hear without someone preaching to them? And how can they preach unless they are sent? As it is written, "How beautiful are the feet of those who bring good news!" (Rom. 10:12–15)

Unless there are preachers to bring the good news, how will Muslims hear and believe and be saved? But for them to hear, preachers must be sent. Those who bring good news are sent out by the Lord Jesus himself. He said to his disciples after his resurrection, "As the Father has sent me, I am sending you" (John 20:21). Preachers of good news are also set apart by the Holy Spirit and sent out by the church with prayer (Acts 13:2–3).

Salvation

The Lord was not pleased with the worship being led by the priests in Israel during the prophet Malachi's day (after 433 B.C). He told them that it would be better if they shut the temple doors and did not light useless altar fires. The priests were not truly honoring and worshiping the Lord. The Lord rebuked them:

> "My name will be great among the nations, from the rising to the setting of the sun. In every place incense and pure offerings will be brought to my name, because my name will be great among the nations," says the LORD Almighty. (Mal. 1:11)

God told the unfaithful priests that he had people in other places and in later times who would bring him the love and devotion he demanded. These people are the Christians of today from every tribe and tongue, whose prayers are the incense offered (Rev. 5:8) and whose "sacrifice of praise" is "the fruit of lips that confess his name." Good works and sharing with others are also sacrifices pleasing to God (Heb. 13:15–16), which make the Lord's name great among the nations through its witness (Matt. 5:16).

The priests in Malachi's day thought that those in other nations were without hope because they did not have access to the temple in Jerusalem and the priestly sacrifices. But now even Gentiles are included among the people of God. Peter explains how:

> As you come to him, the living Stone—rejected by men but chosen by God and precious to him—you also, like living stones, are being built into a spiritual house to be a holy priesthood, offering spiritual sacrifices acceptable to God through Jesus Christ. . . . But you are a chosen people, a royal priesthood, a holy nation, a people belonging to God, that you may declare the praises of him who called you out of darkness into his wonderful light. Once you were not a people, but now you are the people of God; once you had not received mercy, but now you have received mercy. (1 Peter 2:4–5, 9–10)

Now those who were not the people of God are his people. Those who had no priesthood are now priests before God, offering spiritual sacrifices that are pleasing to him. So now even the descendants of Ishmael, who had been rejected as the heir of God's promises of blessing (Gal. 4:30), are now included in that blessing. This was declared by the Lord through the prophecy of Isaiah:

> All Kedar's flocks will be gathered to you,
> the rams of Nebaioth will serve you;
> they will be accepted as offerings on my altar,
> and I will adorn my glorious temple. (Isa. 60:7)

Kedar and Nebaioth are the names of two of Ishmael's sons. Here they are described as bringing acceptable sacrificial offerings to the Lord in his temple. So the picture here is that although the son of Hagar had been sent away by Abraham at God's command, his descendants would someday be brought back to a true eternal home prepared for them. In this messianic age, the Gentiles—people from every nation and tongue—are to be brought into the kingdom of God, to enjoy his eternal blessings. The nations will stream toward the mountain of the Lord (Isa. 2:2–3), the new Jerusalem (Rev. 21:24, 26).

God's promised blessing to the Arabs is made specific in the prophecy of Isaiah:

> In that day there will be a highway from Egypt to Assyria. The Assyrians will go to Egypt and the Egyptians to Assyria. The Egyptians and Assyrians will worship together. In that day Israel will be the third, along with Egypt and Assyria, a blessing on the earth. The LORD Almighty will bless them, saying, "Blessed be Egypt my people, Assyria my handiwork, and Israel my inheritance." (Isa. 19:23–25)

God's people from formerly enemy nations will worship together because of their transformed hearts. God will make us all one people who praise his name for ever and ever.

The mission to which we have been called is founded on who Jesus Christ is and what he came to do. Jesus said, "I am the good shepherd. The good shepherd lays down his life for the sheep. . . . I have other sheep that are not of this sheep pen. I must bring them also. They too will listen to my voice, and there shall be one flock and one shepherd" (John 10:11, 16).

From this passage we glean four points:

1. Christ is seeking those who are his from every nation.
2. He will find them and bring them to himself.
3. His message to these people is spoken through us.
4. They will listen, understand, and confess Jesus as Lord and Savior.

This means that Christ is our partner in ministry. It is he, not us, who brings Muslims to himself. They have been chosen to be members of his church, under his lordship. As Jesus said earlier, "No one can come to me unless the Father who sent me draws him, and I will raise him up at the last day" (John 6:44).

In John's vision on the island of Patmos, he saw the Lamb, looking as though he had been slain, with the four living creatures and twenty-four elders falling down before the Lamb. And they sang a new song:

> You are worthy to take the scroll
> and to open its seals,
> because you were slain,
> and with your blood you purchased men for God
> from every tribe and language and people and nation.
> You have made them to be a kingdom and priests to serve our God,
> and they will reign on the earth. (Rev. 5:9–10)

Again we see that the purpose of God was to send Jesus, his Son, to purchase people from all nations with his blood, to make them a kingdom and priests who rule in the kingdom of God. If this is God's plan, then he certainly has in mind that millions of Muslims from around the world will come to believe that Jesus died on the cross for their sin. God has chosen us to fulfill his plan by our witness.

Eschatology

Many passages speak of the second coming of Christ as the culmination of the establishment of God's kingdom. Jesus' incarnation and public ministry inaugurated the coming of his kingdom. With his second coming, Jesus will bring in the consummation of his kingdom. We now live in a period of time between the kingdom's inauguration and its consummation. This time is characterized by spiritual warfare until the final victory is won. Satan was defeated by the death and resurrection of Christ, but he continues to fight until all things are placed under the feet of Christ at his return. And so we look in great anticipation to the future return of Christ, with a sure hope of reigning with him and enjoying eternal peace.

Knowing this, we should reach out to the Muslims, who are lost in their sins. They do not know Jesus in his first coming as "Jesus," the one who saves his people from their sin. Our hearts should move us to reach them with the gospel of the kingdom, telling them loudly and clearly that "Jesus is coming again, not as a Muslim," but as King and Lord to judge the living and the dead. In other words, we are saying to them that the Day of Judgment is coming. We spent a year in our Meetings for Better Understanding (see chapters 10 and 12) with Muslims, discussing the Day of Judgment and the second coming of Christ. We discovered that their eschatological understanding is totally different from our biblical eschatology. Muslims simply look forward to the day when Jesus will return to establish Islam and then die. Jesus is not seen as our Judge, Lord, and King, who rules forever. Muslims look forward to a paradise of earthly pleasures (wine, women, and song), not entering the presence of God and enjoying him forever. This is a very important reason for witnessing to Muslims. We see how true this is, as Anthony Hoekema writes:

> The expectation of Christ's Second Advent is a most important aspect of the New Testament eschatology—so much so, in fact, that the faith of the New Testament church is dominated by this expectation. Every book of the New Testament points us to the return of Christ and urges us to live a godly life and always be ready for that return. This note is sounded repeatedly in the Gospels. We are taught that the Son of Man will come with his angels in the glory of his Father (Matthew 16:27). Jesus told the high priest that the latter would see the Son of Man sitting at the right hand of power and coming with the clouds of heaven (Mark 14:62). Frequently Jesus told his hearers to watch for his return, since he would be coming at an unexpected hour (Matthew 24:42, 44; Luke 12:40). He spoke of the blessedness of those servants whom he would find faithful at his coming (Luke 12:37, 43).[9]

As we anticipate Christ's return, we must think of our Muslim friends who have not yet heard the gospel. Our anticipation should motivate us day and night to be involved in starting an outreach to Muslims with the good news of the Savior who is coming again. "And this gospel of the kingdom will be preached in the whole world as a testimony to all nations, and then the end will come" (Matt. 24:14).

For Reflection/Action

1. Does God plan to bring blessing to the descendants of Ishmael? If so, what implications does this have for our ministry?
2. Knowing that the crucifixion of Jesus is such a stumbling block for Muslims, how should we present the cross of Christ to them?

CHAPTER TEN

How to Reach Muslims

Finding Your Muslim Friends

To meet Muslims, you need to make yourself available. If your daily schedule is too full, it will be hard to find the time it takes to relate to Muslims you don't already know. We often set our agenda, only to find that God has another one in mind. Take time to see where God is at work. Join in with God's agenda, making time for his divine appointment. Our tendency is to get caught up in human endeavors rather than God's work. Our model should be to do as Jesus did: "Jesus gave [the Jews] this answer: 'I tell you the truth, the Son can do nothing by himself; he can do only what he sees his Father doing, because whatever the Father does the Son also does'" (John 5:19).

If you plan to set up an organized outreach to Muslims, first study the demographics of your community. Find out where Muslims live and work, what type of Muslims they are, where the mosques and Islamic schools are, and what the felt needs of the Muslim community are. This will be of invaluable benefit in getting started. Below are some suggestions to get you going.

Mosques

Many mosques cater to particular ethnic groups or attract those who follow the leadership of the imam of the mosque. Some mosques have a mixture of African-Americans and immigrants from traditionally Islamic countries, while others will be principally African-American or Palestinian or Pakistani. Some mosques are listed in the yellow pages of the phone book under "Churches." First-generation mosques may often be found meeting in such places as a gymnasium, a former mattress showroom, or a closed factory. More and more cities have newly constructed mosques with traditional Islamic architecture, even including minarets.

Muslim Businesses

Some larger cities have Muslim green pages, similar to the yellow pages, listing all types of businesses run by Muslims. These can range from medical offices and bookstores to *halal* meat markets, bakeries, and restaurants. These green pages will also list mosques, Islamic centers, and Islamic schools. Muslims can be found running convenience stores and gas stations, sidewalk food carts, or incense and jewelry stands.

International Students and Scholars

Practically all colleges and universities in North America, except those where you have to be a Christian to be accepted, will have some Muslim students. Many larger universities have an organized Muslim Student Association, which has as one of its purposes the propagation of Islam. The Muslim Student Association's Friday prayer meetings on major university campuses will usually have a wide variety of students from many countries.

Communities

In some cities, immigrants from certain countries (e.g., Lebanese, Pakistanis, or Albanians) live in close proximity to each other in a section of the city. Often there are associations, publications, and schools for these immigrant groups, which help to preserve their home culture and Islamic way of life. Large communities of Arabs may be found in Detroit, Michigan, of Turks in Newark, New Jersey, and of Iranians in Los Angeles, California.

Names

Islamic names are distinctive and may be easily identified in phone books, school directories, and apartment complexes. Looking for Muslim names will help you locate Muslims in your community. Most Muslim names come from Arabic. Turkish names are usually distinctive from the Arabic ones, with a different vocalization (e.g., Mehmet for Muhammad).

Methods for Reaching Muslims

There are a wide variety of means that may be used to bring the gospel to Muslims. You will need to determine which methods are best suited to your gifts, resources, and target audience. Our own experience has been primarily in friendship, prayer, and team evangelism, small group and one-on-one Bible studies, hospitality, use of a variety of media, correspondence courses, and Meetings for Better Understanding. These methods have proved to be effective in reaching Muslims for Christ. This does not mean that other methods are not also useful. The best approach is to combine various methods. Most of these methods may be used not only in North America, but throughout the Muslim world. In some countries, there are restrictions on particular approaches.

1. Bible Correspondence Courses

Bible courses may be advertised to Muslims through letters sent in the mail, personal contacts, fliers, and advertisements in newspapers and on the radio. This provides a list of Muslims showing some interest in knowing more about Christ. The most effective means of getting them interested in following through with a Bible correspondence course is through initial friendship and showing the *Jesus* film. A Bible course allows you to go into more depth and lead a person to Christ. Courses are written for a specifically Muslim audience. Each lesson is completed by the student and returned by mail to the coordinator of the course for grading and comments. This approach has been quite successful in Islamic countries, especially when students have been followed up with personal visits. It has been used only to a limited extent in the U.S. The most difficult part has been to follow up those showing initial interest. Unless this is done, those beginning the course will forget and ignore what they started.

2. Bookroom or Book Table

In a Muslim-populated area, a bookroom or reading room may be set up with a Muslim decor. Bible verses in Arabic calligraphy may be hung from the walls. The staff may wear clothing that has appeal to Muslims. Tables with culturally appropriate Christian literature may be set up on the sidewalk and inside. For hospitality and to encourage discussion, tea and coffee may be served. The *Jesus* film can be shown in several languages and can be scheduled several times a week.[1]

Another variation of this method is to set up a book table in the student center of a major university. Display Christian books and booklets in various languages from Islamic countries to attract Muslim international students into discussions. This approach has also been used at Islamic book fairs, where one pays for space to set up one's display.

3. Children's Bible Club in the Home

This is a strategic ministry because researchers have found that in the U.S. more than 85 percent of those who receive Christ do so before they reach the age of fifteen. Half of the Muslim population in the world is under the age of fifteen. Invite the children of your Muslim neighbors to a weekly Bible club meeting in your home or yard. Activities could include arts and crafts, field trips, Bible stories, memory verses, songs, and refreshments. Often parents will want to be involved in some way. This kind of ministry opens doors to ministering to the children's parents as well. This may work especially well in the summer or could be done on weekends during the school year.

4. Church-Mosque Relationships

Christians involved in outreach may wish to visit Muslim leaders and mosques informally, so that they can become acquainted with each other and build meaningful relationships as human beings. Community issues of common concern may be jointly addressed, such as the drug and crime problem, graffiti, and racial and ethnic conflicts. A church and a mosque could set up a joint project to clean up the neighborhood park together. In Fremont, California, Saint Paul's United Methodist Church and the Islamic Society of the East Bay constructed a church and a mosque side by side on the same property. They named their common access road "Peace Terrace" to be an example to the world.

5. Counseling

Occasionally Christians in a leadership position, such as an administrator, professor, physician, pastor, or lawyer, or even as neighbors or colleagues at work, will have the opportunity to give counsel to Muslims. This may occur when there are marriage problems, immigration questions, health problems, or employment problems. As Christians, we can show real concern, care, and love in helping them with their problem from a Christian perspective. These times are often ones of great emotional turmoil and anxiety. Our patience and trust in God, a God who answers prayer, can be a great witness.

Mostapha and Fatima came as immigrants to live in a large Pennsylvania city. They had been married for over eighteen years, but their marriage was plagued with problems. Over time they became friends with a godly Christian family. They shared their problems with their American friends. The sovereign Lord led them and their American friends to meet with me (one of the authors). They shared their family problem with my wife and me for three hours. It seemed that there was no solution. I asked Mostapha to forgive his wife. He said, "I cannot forgive her." I asked, "Why?" He said, "I do not know." I said to him, "I know. You cannot forgive because you are not forgiven yet." And I asked him, "Would you like to be forgiven now?" Mostapha said, "Yes. How?" I explained the gospel to him. Mostapha and Fatima were ready to pray to God, asking for his forgiveness. My wife and I led them in doing that by standing and holding hands and praying together. Mostapha was crying like a child, as he was praying after me with Fatima. They prayed the sinner's prayer and they surrendered their lives to the Lord Jesus that night. The American friends who were there were stunned and amazed at how the Lord led all of us that evening to come to this point of forgiveness. The couple's relationship started to improve day by day. Mostapha took the initiative to say "I love you" to Fatima for the first time after eighteen years of marriage. On Valentine's Day, he brought her flowers with a card for the first time in their lives. This is the power of the gospel in the area of forgiveness.

6. Debates

In this form of outreach, the Islamic and Christian communities are invited to a lecture room or hall to hear two knowledgeable persons debate the merits of a chosen topic in relation to Islam and Christianity. After each speaker has made his initial presentation, an opportunity is given for response.

This approach must be carried out with much prayer and sensitivity in order not to cause unnecessary offense. An argument can be won, but the battle lost, when the message is not communicated with love and winsomeness. A Christian speaker must be well versed in Islamic apologetics and in the Bible.

This approach has been used with some success in London at "Speaker's Corner" in Hyde Park. In this situation, the crowd that gathers responds to the speaker directly at intervals throughout his presentation. A formal rebuttal is not given by another speaker, but comes from those in the crowd. It is best if the speaker has an assistant with him from another ethnic background to be a backup with responses and give the main speaker a break. A team of coworkers should be in the crowd to assist in following up individuals who show interest. This form of outreach has been used more as a form of preevangelism, causing Muslims to develop doubts and question their faith.

A danger in debating is that Muslims will often rally a large group from their community to the debate, greatly outnumbering the Christians. Usually when people leave a Christian-Muslim debate, both sides think that their side won. Often the debates are videotaped, edited in the Muslims' favor, and distributed in the Muslim community to motivate Islamic *da'wah*. In attacking the "sacred cows" of Islam, the boasts of some may be silenced, but that probably will not win people to your side. The positive—the power of the gospel—should be emphasized.[2] One needs to ask, "Is the debate leading to more or less contact between Muslims and Christians after it is over?"

Debate is sometimes used in the New Testament, such as by Stephen with the Jews in Jerusalem (Acts 6:9–10), by Apollos with the Jews in Achaia (Acts 18:27–28), and by Paul with the philosophers in the marketplace at Athens (Acts 17:18), in the synagogue and lecture hall of Tyrannus in Ephesus (Acts 19:8–10), and while under house arrest in Rome (Acts 28:23). Jesus, too, confronted the Pharisees (Matt. 23:13–33) and the money changers in the temple (Mark 11:15–18). Debate can work in the right context. But it can also lead to acts of violence, such as was experienced by Stephen in Acts 6–7.[3]

7. Dialogue

"Dialogue involves two individuals or groups empathetically listening to each other with respect and frankly witnessing to their own faith."[4] Although dialogue can be somewhat similar to debate, it is less confrontational. Areas shared in common and differences are examined by both sides. For some, especially in ecumenical circles, dialogue may lead to syncretism. For others, it is closer to the approach of Meetings for Better Understanding, where both sides inform each other of where one stands. Dialogue requires humility, respect, openness to new insights, and trust. It "corrects stereotypes and fosters understanding, communication, cooperation, and witness. Furthermore, it does not require the abandonment of belief in the uniqueness of one's own faith since dialogue involves authentic witness."[5] In engaging in dialogue, one needs to beware of the attempts of some to use the opportunity to "win the day" rather than simply promote mutual understanding.

8. E-mail Chat Rooms

Christians interested in religious discussion may enter Muslim chat rooms on the Internet. Friendly discussion with Muslims from around the world may lead to fruitful results in sharing the gospel as well as learning about Islam. In using e-mail, one can speak without the face-to-face anxiety. You can be sure that your message is heard because of the immediate response. Here is an example of someone using this method:

> I know that dedat2's upbringing is somewhat Christian although I do not think his family was very serious about Christianity. In the chat rooms in front of everyone, dedat2 is reasonably obnoxious. He likes to rant about mistakes in the Bible and ridicule the Bible at every opportunity. However one day I convinced him to come into a private chat room with me. This is a room where no one

can see your messages except you and the other person in the room with you. Well miracle of all miracles, dedat2 became cordial and polite. His attacks on the Bible it seemed to me were a defense from others who insult Islam and Muhammad. We spoke of many topics in the Bible, as I am sure he was trying to convince me that the Qur'an was right. Until we got around to Isaiah 53. He said that he was not familiar with it and that he would research it. A few days later he contacted me and said that he also felt that chapter 53 could be about Jesus. But Muhammad says that Jesus was not crucified and why would he lie? I did not know how to respond to this question. I told him that the Bible has been trustworthy for me up to now and that there is no reason to doubt it. At that point, one of us had to leave so we agreed to pray about it.[6]

9. Friendship Evangelism

When Christians take time to do things with Muslims, their Muslim friends can experience Christ in them and have an opportunity to talk about who Christ is. Friendship builds trust, which in turn provides open doors for witness. See more on this in chapter 11.

10. Hospitality and Family Evangelism

Using this method, Christians invite Muslim families or singles into their homes to eat together, so that Muslims can experience Christ's love in the family. This is biblical evangelism in action (Luke 14:12–14; Rom. 12:13b). Sharing a meal together is one of the best ways to create bonding in relationships. Your Muslim guest may be invited to participate in your family devotions. Hosting a Muslim student overnight for an international student conference is a great way to develop strong ties with your guest. Children in your home often help to develop warmth and rapport with your guest.

11. House Churches

Muslim families that have begun to trust Christ and to feed on God's Word need to be encouraged and nurtured through worship with other believers. Families that do not have access to compatible traditional fellowships are taught to worship together in homes. Ideally, these house churches should have from five to twelve people. Having twenty-five people in one home may be too overwhelming for one host each week. Also, because of the cultural emphasis on hospitality, too much time may be taken up with that, as opposed to worship, in a larger group. House churches are often mentioned in the New Testament (Acts 18:7; Rom. 16:5; 1 Cor. 16:19; Col. 4:15; Philem. 2).

12. International Dinners

Plan an ethnic dinner that focuses on a particular Muslim country or part of the world, hosted in a larger home or a church hall. Invite international students and/or immigrants from that country, as well as from other places, to attend. If you are focusing on Turkey, invite students from the Turkish Student Association at your local university. Encourage believers to attend as well, with the understanding that they are there to serve, befriend the international guests, and host the tables. If possible, recruit cooks from the ethnic group you are focusing on to help plan the menu and cook the meal. Plan a program of music and/or folk dance from the theme country after the meal. Then have a speaker give a low-key, culturally sensitive gospel message. Preferably the speaker should be someone who has been to your theme country. If not, he should be familiar with speaking to Muslims. Make response cards available on the tables for follow-up. On one side of the room, set up a book table with Christian literature in English and their language that is appropriate for Muslims.

13. Mail Evangelism

Many Muslims can be effectively reached with portions of Scripture through the mail. An offer of a Bible correspondence course could be included. Muslim names can be identified in telephone directories and university student directories. The names could be distributed to interested persons in various churches or prayer groups. Along with the names, a packet of culturally appealing gospel material with a cover letter is given to those doing the mailing. Each envelope should be individually addressed and stamped with stamps, rather than a postage machine. Regular prayer should be offered for those receiving the mailing. A return post office box address should be included for a response and possible follow-up of those showing interest in receiving more literature. For more details on this form of ministry, read Bill Dennett's book, *Sharing the Good News with Muslims*, or contact Turkish World Outreach.

14. Media Evangelism

Literature, tapes, films, and radio can have a powerful impact in helping to bring Muslims to faith in Christ. "Further Ministry Resources" at the back of this book lists many places where these resources are available. Dr. James M. Boice's expository sermon tapes have been used with great benefit by Church Without Walls (available from the Alliance of Confessing Evangelicals, 1716 Spruce St., Philadelphia, PA 19103). Although Muslims will watch Christian television shows, such programs generally do not appeal to the heart of a Muslim culturally, methodologically, or spiritually. Since so many Christian television programs seem like secular entertainment, Muslims can be confused about what true Christianity really is. Many Muslims listen to Christian radio programs, but need personal follow-up to help answer their questions and lead them to Christ. Follow-up is also needed after the distribution of tracts and pamphlets. Here is an example from an Operation Mobilization (OM) team in Lebanon:

After openly sharing and distributing gospel literature in the marketplace in a town that had not been visited by OM for over two decades, a man said to the team,

> "When you are finished, please bring your people to my restaurant. I would like to feed you." After their hunger had been satisfied, their host surprised them by pulling a tattered Gospel tract from a drawer in his counter. "When I was 12 years old," he explained, "someone gave me this tract. I have been waiting for 21 years for someone to come and tell me more about this Jesus." I'm sure there were some tears of joy shed in that restaurant as this team had the privilege of leading this hungry soul to the Savior he had been seeking.[7]

15. Meetings for Better Understanding

Christian leaders can arrange to have meetings held at mosques and churches. The typical meeting includes an oral presentation by a Muslim and by a Christian on a preselected topic. Some refreshments are served after the initial presentations, which are followed by a period of discussion to learn further, correct each other's misconceptions, and gain a better understanding of each other's faith. A fuller description of this method is given in chapter 13.

16. One-on-one Evangelism

In this method, individual Christians share God's Word with individual Muslims to help them see themselves as sinners who need to be saved and understand the way that God has provided for them to be saved. Often this form of evangelism will be with casual contacts, such as with a fellow traveler on an airplane, someone you meet on the job, or with a street vendor. After initial introductions and the subject of conversation turns to religion, one may ask nonthreatening, thought-provoking questions, such as, "Do you know God?" or "Do you know for sure that you will enter paradise?" Do not say anything that denigrates Islam, Muhammad, or the Qur'an. Asking questions elicits more positive response than making statements. Listen carefully before speaking. If you have appropriate literature available, leave something with the person, such as the Gospel of Luke in their native language or a tract written for Muslims. Dr. William McElwee Miller has written several excellent tracts (available from Fellowship of Faith for Muslims).

17. Prayer Evangelism[8]

Prayer is an essential component of evangelizing Muslims. They are in the grip of a strong deceit of Satan, which necessitates spiritual warfare. The spiritual battle will only be won through prayer for your Muslim contacts, for Muslim countries and leaders, for unity and spiritual growth among those reaching out to Muslims, and for your own close walk with the Lord. Begin praying for specific people and their needs. Let those people know that you are praying for their needs. Then see how God answers prayer. God works through our prayers. All our other efforts will prove fruitless unless they are covered with prayer.

18. Preaching

Bringing the Word of God to Muslims through expository preaching must not be taken for granted or overlooked. Preaching with power and conviction is one of the primary means prescribed by God for the conversion of the lost. Paul instructed Timothy to "devote yourself to the public reading of Scripture, to preaching and to teaching" (1 Tim. 4:13). He was to "preach the Word; be prepared in season and out of season" (2 Tim. 4:2). Muslims respond to good preaching, just as others do. But it must be based on the Bible, rather than simply using a Scripture passage as a jumping-off point to tell a string of stories to build one's self-esteem. Reverence and respect must be shown in all aspects of the service. Occasionally, when a preacher has built a good relationship with a Muslim community, there may be an opportunity even to preach in a mosque.

Some preachers have seen God's blessing come upon Muslims through itinerant crusade evangelism. The major difficulty with this is conserving the harvest through follow-up of those who respond. Those who invited the Muslims or local churches that are given the names of those who respond must disciple them and incorporate them into a fellowship of believers. Otherwise, the pressures are usually too great for the one who received the Word with joy to bear fruit (Luke 8:13).

19. Prison Ministry

The growth of Islam in the African-American community has taken place to a great extent in prisons. One way to reach the African-American Muslim is to have a ministry in the prisons through Bible studies, seminars, and visitation. Good literature can be distributed among the inmates and donated to the prison library. Prison Fellowship is involved in this type of ministry. New Orleans Baptist Theological Seminary now has an extension in a prison in Louisiana where fifty students are enrolled and twenty recently graduated. As an example of what could be done, the twenty congregations in the prison of over five thousand men could be trained to reach the numerous Muslim inmates.

20. Reconciliation Ministry

Due to the centuries of animosity and conflict between Christians and Muslims, a ministry of reconciliation can have a powerful impact on the Muslim community. In 1996 a group marched along the trail of the Crusades through Turkey, bringing a message of reconciliation and asking for forgiveness from the atrocities of the Crusaders. It has been warmly received and given wide publicity. Such ministry is needed in places such as the Balkans, the Philippines, Nigeria, and the Sudan. In the U.S., reconciliation could have a powerful impact on white Christians and black Muslims. Such a ministry requires appreciating the injustice felt, even if it is thought to be overblown; really listening to the others' perceptions, hurts, and needs without interruption, self-explanation, or defense; bringing those who have been artificially kept apart together for interaction and getting to know each other; and forgiveness by pardoning and being willing to be pardoned.[9]

21. Refugee Ministry

Many of the places of conflict in the world where the U.S. has been involved are Muslim countries. Often refugees from those conflicts come to North America. In the 1970s many came from Lebanon and Palestine, and in the 1980s from Afghanistan and Ethiopia. In recent years, there have been Somalis, Algerians, Iranians, and Kurds. World Relief looks for churches to sponsor refugee families. This ministry includes helping a family get settled with an apartment, household goods and furniture, finding or providing English lessons, and providing job counseling, acculturation, and friendship. Through the tangible help provided by Christians and the relationships built, many opportunities for witness become available to the refugee family.

22. Small Group Bible and Qur'an Studies

Christians can meet with interested Muslims to study passages related to preselected topics. These studies have the advantage of allowing informal discussion during the presentations. The Bible and the Qur'an are studied with open minds and spirits. The Bible study leader should have full assurance of his faith and thorough knowledge of the Bible. This is discussed more in chapter 13 and in appendix 2.

23. Door-to-Door Surveys

In this method, Muslim names are identified from a Cole telephone directory, which lists names by street address. These people are then visited by going door-to-door and using a survey to ask questions regarding their faith. The survey can be used in connection with a training program in which the visitor is seeking to learn more about Islam. After stating who you are and what your purpose is, those visiting are often invited into the home for discussions. A frustration with this approach is that people are often not at home.

24. Team Evangelism

Since Islam emphasizes community, it is important that Christians also demonstrate a strong community and family spirit when witnessing to them. Western Christians tend to be overly individualistic. Work as a team to show them that the church is not as individualistic as North American society, but rather is a community and has a collective mind. Organize a team to reach out to Muslims; have team meetings at least monthly for prayer, sharing, organizing, and encouragement. Try to include persons from various racial and ethnic backgrounds on the same team. When Muslims see persons from only one culture reaching out to them, they may infer that Christianity as an individualistic religion. Also, the misconception often coming from the African-American community is that Christianity is the white man's religion. An integrated team will help to dampen that perception.

Principles of Conduct for Visiting a Mosque

Visiting a mosque can be a great way to meet Muslims and learn more about their religion and culture. It can also be a key means of getting Meetings for Better Understanding started and for establishing personal friendships. But following these guidelines should help make your visit a success:

1. Go in Pairs

Do not go alone to a mosque. Jesus gave us the principle of going in pairs when he sent out the seventy-two disciples ahead of him to every place where he was going to go (Luke 10:1). Having another person along helps with encouragement, accountability, support in the other's weaknesses, prayer, and stronger witness.

2. Call Ahead

If a group of Christians is going to visit a mosque, it is courteous to call the imam first, so that the mosque can be prepared for your visit.

3. Follow Their Ethical Code

Be aware of Islam's ethical code regarding how men and women are to relate to each other. For more on this, see chapter 3.

4. Show Humility and Respect

Humility and respect are required behavior at the mosque because it is the sacred place of worship for Muslims. It is also the place of honor for the community. When asking questions, don't come with the approach that Islam is a false religion, but with the attitude that you have come to learn. Show respect to those who are older than you and to those in leadership positions. Respect their point of view, even if you disagree with it.

5. Be a Careful Listener

Being a careful listener is much better than talking, especially if you are visiting the mosque for the first time.

6. Don't Be Argumentative

Show yourself as Christ's disciple, not as an invader who is coming to prove that their religion is false. Do not become argumentative, but listen and speak in love.

7. Be in Prayer

Be in prayer wholeheartedly as you listen or as you speak. Also pray with your team before arriving at the mosque and after you have left.

8. Focus on One Person

In your conversation, focus on one person at a time. If possible, stay with that person for the whole visit. You will want to do this in order to establish a meaningful relationship. If you return to the mosque, try to find the same person to continue the relationship. When going to the mosque as a team, each team member should stay with a Muslim as long as it takes to make friends with him or her. Ten people should not be talking to two or three Muslims; rather, ten team members should talk with ten Muslims.

9. Relate to People Your Own Age

Culturally speaking, it fits well if you find a Muslim of a similar age to befriend. The age factor is important in order to relate more as peers. The younger person feels obligated to listen to the older person because of their longer life experience and out of respect.

10. Use Titles

Use titles when you address your team leader in the context of the mosque, such as pastor, doctor, elder, etc. This indicates to the Muslim mind that this man is qualified to speak about the Christian faith on his team's behalf. It also indicates that as a team you have confidence in this man to be your leader. The same thing should be done when addressing the Muslim leader or teacher. He should be addressed as imam, sheikh, or teacher, such as Imam Warith Deen Muhammad.

11. Follow Their Cultural Codes

When visiting a mosque, follow Islamic cultural codes. Take off your shoes at the door. Usually you will see the place where others have put theirs. Women should wear a head covering, such as a scarf, upon entering. Women should also wear a longer skirt or dress and have their arms covered. Women are not allowed to speak in the mosque during prayer time. Sit behind the rows of Muslims as they go through their prayer ritual. Do not sit cross-legged or point the bottom of your foot at others. Do not put your Bible or Qur'an on the floor or even hold it below your waist.

12. Do Not Join Muslims in Prayer

When the Muslims pray, do not line up with them to stand and bow in prayer. Sit behind the congregation. Do not suppose that you can be a witness to them by following them in the prostrations of prayer and simply praying a Christian prayer while using their outward form. They will mistakenly infer that you are interested in Islam. In some situations, particularly in a Muslim country, that could be dangerous. For if they think that they see you becoming a Muslim, but then backing off from it, your life may be threatened for apostasy.

13. Eating Meals

Occasionally you will be invited to eat a meal with your new Muslim friends at the mosque. You may find that you should eat in the way that they do—for example, eating with your hands, instead of using utensils. Eat with gratitude to our God by praying before eating and commenting on his provision. Also remember the needy and poor who have none, by mentioning them in your prayer or in comments as you see all the food. Your Muslim friends will identify with this.

14. Making Future Contact

If your new friend asks for your address, give that of your leader or church, where the message can be passed on to you. You don't want to be in a situation where your leader is not informed of what is going on in the relationships being formed. This can be important, as sometimes weaker Christians may be invited to a Muslim setting where they may not know how to handle the situation and may be put under quite a bit of pressure. In one situation, a single male Christian was invited to a Muslim home and introduced to an eligible single woman. He felt under much pressure during that visit to convert to Islam and take an interest in the woman.

15. Establish the Friendship

Some team members may be inclined to invite their new friends to dinner right after their first visit to the mosque. It is better not to do this, however, until you have further established the friendship. Before you invite your Muslim guest, speak with your team leader for his advice and prayers. In all cases, maintain good communication with the team leader.

16. Keep Accountability

The team leader should be experienced in ministry to Muslims. Team members should share with their leader what they felt and experienced during the mosque visit for integration, evaluation, prayer, and follow-up.

17. Understand Their Religious Vocabulary

In your conversation with Muslims at the mosque, be aware of their religious vocabulary. For instance, Muslims use such words as

God's *grace*, *faith*, *salvation*, *justification*, *peace*, *joy*, and *holiness of God*. However, the Muslim meaning of these words is different from our biblical understanding of them. For example, when a Muslim speaks of grace, he has in mind material and spiritual blessings that you can earn for yourself. However, biblical grace is unmerited favor—a free gift from God to sinners. Do not be misled by their religious words, which sometimes give you the feeling that their understanding is the same as ours.

18. Keep an Open Door of Friendship

In your conversation, try to keep the door of friendship open all the time. Therefore, when you sense that you are not getting anywhere in the relationship because of differences, suggest to your friend that you postpone the conversation until the next time you meet.

19. Establish Equal Opportunity

If necessary, remind the Muslim with whom you are conversing that you need equal time to speak about your Christian faith. Some Muslims in one-on-one conversation dominate the whole conversation by denying the Christian an opportunity to speak. You should set the rules. For example, listen to him for about fifteen minutes and then ask him to listen to you for an equal amount of time. This procedure will help both of you to have a meaningful and civilized conversation about your faith.

20. Speak God's Word in Response

As you listen to your Muslim friend's conversation at the mosque, take note of his points. As your turn to speak comes, first correct his misunderstanding of your faith. The best way to do that is to quote the Bible a great deal and let the Word of God convict his heart and mind, because it has the power to do so.

21. Distinguish the Bible from Western Culture

Make sure you present biblical Christianity, not your cultural Christianity. Muslims think that the West is Christian. They say that Christianity is not working. They point out the decline of American morality, increased violence, broken families, and other societal ills. They say, "Islam is the remedy for all of this. If America were an Islamic country, you would not see these problems." They forget that even their Muslim nations have the same problems (though often to a lesser degree), but keep them secret. Your responsibility is to make a sharp distinction between Western culture and the teaching of the Bible. Give Muslims the biblical view of life by pointing them to Christ and his lordship. This gives credibility to our faith.

Developing Your Strategy for Muslim Evangelism

In order to develop your own strategy for reaching Muslims with the gospel, it would be worth your while to work on a plan of action with your partners in ministry. To help you think through the process, you will want to develop a strategy around stated goals. Some possible goals would be:

1. Changing attitudes within the church toward ministry to Muslims.
2. Training harvesters or disciple makers.
3. Finding Muslims who are open to hearing the gospel (that is, the "man of peace," Luke 10:6).
4. Meeting felt needs of Muslims.
5. Discipling converts from Islam.
6. Planting house churches with former Muslims.
7. Developing culturally appropriate literature and media for use in Muslim evangelism.

After determining what your goals are, make a chart similar to the one on the next page to plan your strategy. Make a new chart for each goal you have set.

GOAL: TRAINING HARVESTERS OR DISCIPLE-MAKERS

STEPS TO ACHIEVE GOAL	RESPONSIBLE PERSON	TIME TO BE DONE	NECESSARY RESOURCES	EXPECTED RESULT
Call interested people to organize a task force.				
Build community on the team.				
Offer a Muslim awareness seminar; make contact with Muslims.				
Form a team for outreach. Work in pairs. Organize a prayer team. Organize a research team.				
Tools: • resources to help us understand Islam and witnessing/discipling • resources to use with Muslims for evangelism/discipleship				
Short-term, intense summer missions outreach				
Ongoing in-service training/accountability/evaluation/prayer				

For Reflection/Action

1. What do you need to do to adjust your schedule to meet with Muslims?
2. Write down some goals for reaching Muslims in your area.
3. Develop a strategy for reaching those goals using the format outlined above.
4. Make plans with your partners in ministry to visit a local mosque.

CHAPTER ELEVEN

Guidelines for Friendship Evangelism[1]

Know Your Audience

> Paul then stood up in the meeting of the Areopagus and said: "Men of Athens! I see that in every way you are very religious. For as I walked around and looked carefully at your objects of worship, I even found an altar with this inscription: TO AN UNKNOWN GOD. Now what you worship as something unknown I am going to proclaim to you. (Acts 17:22–23)

After introducing yourself, tell your Muslim acquaintance about your family, your job, your living situation, and other appropriate things. If you have visited their native country, speak of the positive things you experienced there. Try to find some common interests or points of contact to which you can both relate. This may be in the areas of hospitality, morality, and zeal for one's religion. Spend a lot of time, especially at the beginning of a relationship, asking open-ended questions, so that you can learn as much as possible about the background of the person to whom you are witnessing. In this way you can address the needs, fears, and hopes of the person most appropriately. In return, he will listen attentively. However, do not ask too many questions, since many Muslims consider that impolite. Rather, share about yourself. This will make them feel comfortable about speaking about themselves.

At some point in getting to know your new friend, ask questions about what he believes. In return, he may ask about what you believe. Ask questions that cannot be answered with yes or no, but require explanation. For example, you might ask, "What is your religious background?" or "What is your concept of God?" or "How does Islam deal with the issue of forgiveness?" You may want to ask something about Islam, even if you already know what kind of answer to expect. This will help you know the person better and know more of the specifics of his background.

Be a good listener. Pay attention not only to the words your friend is saying, but also to his body language and facial expressions. Respond in such a way that he will know that you understand what he is saying. Take your time to build the relationship. Approach him with respect, grace, and gentleness. Be patient with a slow talker or with someone struggling with English as a second language. Eye contact is not considered good manners in Muslim culture. Look down, particularly when speaking to someone of the opposite gender. Demonstrated humility is highly esteemed.

Make sure that you understand what he means by the words he uses. His understanding of religious terms such as *God*, *sin*, and *salvation* may be very different from how you understand them in a biblical framework. Some study of Islam will help you immensely to better understand their thinking. However, remember that each person is unique and may not hold consistently to the tenets or worldview of Islam.

Develop a Friendship and Establish Trust

> The alien living with you must be treated as one of your native-born. Love him as yourself, for you were aliens in Egypt. I am the LORD your God. (Lev. 19:34)

> "The Son of Man came eating and drinking, and they say, 'Here is a glutton and a drunkard, a friend of tax col-

> lectors and "sinners." ' But wisdom is proved right by her actions." (Matt. 11:19)

In a suburb of a large Pennsylvania city, a Christian woman named Nancy had a knock at her door. Upon opening the door, she met a Muslim professor with his family, who were house hunting. They had just looked at a nearby house and wanted to meet some of the neighbors. The Lord led them to Nancy's door. She gave them a warm welcome, which so impressed them that they decided to buy that neighboring house, even though they had seen better houses in the area. They told her, "We bought this house because of you!" She said, "Because of me? What did I do?" They said, "When we knocked on your door, you welcomed us, and we felt that you would be a good, friendly neighbor, whom we could trust." Now Nancy is a close friend with the family, and her Christian life is a real witness to them. This shows that in being kind and caring to Muslims, you can gain their trust and witness to them.

Consider establishing a close friendship initially with just one or two Muslims. A great deal of time and energy is needed to develop a close, trusting friendship in which you can freely share much of your life in Christ. Normally this would mean that men should develop close friendships with men, and women with women. Pray to the Lord about leading you to the right person to establish a friendship. Often internationals expect more from a friendship than many Americans do. Internationals are used to deeper relationships that involve much time.

Make sure that your actions back up your verbal witness. You can be sure that your friend will be watching your life and attitudes carefully to see if they are consistent with your words. Charles Kraft tells us,

> At least with respect to life-affecting messages, the communicator is a major part of the message he delivers. For effectiveness, there needs to be congruence between the communicator's behavior and his statements. Can love, for example, be learned from an unloving person? Or faith

> from a doubting person? Or joy from a complaining person? Or wisdom from a fool? The answer is, Only occasionally—and then only when the receptor engages in a disproportionate amount of adjustment and reinterpretation to make the message come out differently at his end.[2]

Internationals, colleagues, and neighbors may wonder why you are taking an interest in them. They will be trying to discern your motives. Your "free gospel smells tainted to people whose trust and respect [you] have not earned." Your "love for the people" must not be simply intellectual.[3] Remember, Muslims are made in God's image. Your consistent lifestyle of love will earn you the right to be trusted and heard. Love them as Jesus has loved you.

Spend time together in various contexts that will help to firmly establish the friendship. Eat meals together. Play sports, play chess, or go on an outing. Let your friend know that you are thinking of him by making phone calls or sending a note in the mail. Try to understand him in terms of his religion, history, culture, and family life.

Often it is not appropriate to raise the subject of religion early in the relationship, unless your friend does so. It may depend on how you met. If you are doing something together at an event sponsored by a Christian group, the subject of religion may come up more naturally. It should become apparent fairly soon that you are a Christian, as your friend sees how you spend your time, knows who your friends are, and understands what is most important to you. Show him that you seek to live a godly life.

Pray for Your Friend Regularly

> Pray continually. (1 Thess. 5:17)

> Devote yourselves to prayer, being watchful and thankful. And pray for us, too, that God may open a door for our message, so that we may proclaim the mystery of Christ,

> for which I am in chains. Pray that I may proclaim it clearly, as I should. (Col. 4:2–4)

> Again, I tell you that if two of you on earth agree about anything you ask for, it will be done for you by my Father in heaven. For where two or three come together in my name, there am I with them. (Matt. 18:19–20)

Prayer is essential to winning your Muslim friend to Christ. You are engaged in spiritual warfare. Often there are demonic powers at work in the life of a Muslim, who under the outer shell of Islam may have an animistic worldview. Our spiritual battle is "against the powers of this dark world and against the spiritual forces of evil in the heavenly realms" (Eph. 6:12).

Pray often for your friend and his needs. Let him know that you are praying for him, and ask how you can pray for him.

You may want to pray with your friend by asking his permission first. Rarely will a Muslim reject someone praying for their personal needs. Avoid a preaching style in prayer, but make it known that you have a relationship with a living God who cares for each of us. Praying before meals is appropriate, but first you probably should explain what you are doing. We are to give thanks to God for all good things.

Pray that God would give you opportunities to explain the gospel clearly to your friend. Pray not only for good opportunities, but that what you say will make the good news of God's grace plain to him.

Meet together with others to pray for your friend. Jesus is with any group of believers who agree together and pray in his name. God will answer your prayer. Make a regular time in your schedule to pray for each other's non-Christian friends.

Share the Gospel Naturally and Biblically

> Then Philip ran up to the chariot and heard the man reading Isaiah the prophet. "Do you understand what you are reading?" Philip asked.

> "How can I," he said, "unless someone explains it to me?" So he invited Philip to come up and sit with him. (Acts 8:30–31)

> So he [Paul] reasoned in the synagogue with the Jews and the God-fearing Greeks, as well as in the marketplace day by day with those who happened to be there. (Acts 17:17)

> I have become all things to all men so that by all possible means I might save some. (1 Cor. 9:22)

As a Christian walking with the Lord, you will find that conversation naturally leads to the subject of Jesus Christ. This issue should not be forced into the conversation, but pray that the Lord would provide the right opportunity to respond appropriately in a way that would make an opening for witness to Christ. Remember to be sensitive to the needs of your friend, and look for clues to what may be behind his questions.

As your relationship develops, at the appropriate time say something like this: "Sometime I'd like an opportunity to share some principles with you that will help you understand what it means to have a personal relationship with God." Ask the interest question: "Could I share those principles with you?" This allows your friend to respond. In sharing the gospel, go as far as the interest of your friend will let you. Do not press ahead when you note that your friend has lost interest in what you are saying. You can often tell if his interest is there by the look in his eyes, by his response, or if he follows with any questions or related comments. Pressing too hard with your witness may jeopardize future opportunities to speak with that person. He may think that you are pushy and not interested in him as a person and a friend. The Holy Spirit is the one who moves a person along to be able to receive spiritual truth. Everybody wants an opportunity to be heard. So intersperse your witness to the Lord with questions that bring out where the other person is in his thinking, or pause to give him an opportunity to respond. Be honest with him as you answer his questions about the Christian faith.

Some who witness to Muslims find it useful to ask them questions that lead them to see the inadequacies or inconsistencies of their faith. For example, you might ask your friend if he has any assurance that he will go to paradise. Is the Black Stone in the Ka'aba in Mecca not similar to an idol, since all Muslims bow down to it in prayer and kiss it during the *hajj*? If the Qur'an is an eternal book in heaven, how is it not also a god? When asking such questions, carefully avoid adopting a prideful and demeaning attitude. Rather, in love help Muslims to question their presuppositions.

Avoid getting to the point of your message too fast. A common mistake made by Christians who witness to Muslims is to say something like "Jesus is God" near the beginning of a discussion. Yes, he is, but saying so right away throws up many obstacles to further fruitful discussion. A Muslim will understand us to say we are deifying a mere man—associating partners with Allah, which is the unforgivable sin. Notice how Jesus revealed his deity. He used creative and effective ways without directly saying it in so many words. After his resurrection, Jesus revealed his identity to the two disciples on the road to Emmaus by pointing to the fulfillment of prophecy throughout the Old Testament (Luke 24:13–35). At other times, he spoke of himself as the Bread of Life, the Good Shepherd, the Vine, the Door, the Way, the Truth, the Life, our Judge, and the Son of Man. Your Muslim friend needs to understand that we are not deifying a man, but rather that God became incarnate in Jesus. God alone is the object of our worship. His decision to identify himself with us through Jesus because of his love for us does not diminish his deity.[4]

Share your testimony with your friend. Tell him what the Lord means to you personally. This can have a greater impact than the presentation of abstract concepts alone, because it shows the reality of the living God at work and provides an apologetic that is difficult to refute (John 4:39). Your personal testimony will demonstrate that your faith is relational rather than just a system of doctrine, as in Islam. He will respect what you share out of your everyday experience.

Jesus should be the focus of your witness. Explain who he is and what claims he made. Explain the significance of Christ's death and resurrection. At this point, you may want to refer to Abraham's offer of his son as a sacrifice, for which God provided a ram as a substitute. This event is celebrated annually by Muslims. Tie in Jesus' being the Lamb of God, who was sacrificed to take away the sins of the world. When you get an opportunity to study the Bible with your friend, it is important to study parts of the Gospels that deal with the message and mission of Jesus. However, some other doctrines also need to be covered in your witness, such as the nature of God and the nature of (fallen) man. Your friend's views will be quite different from your biblical understanding.

Attacking your friend's religion will not endear you to him. Usually it will be counterproductive. You could win an argument, but lose the friendship. Islam is very important to him. Find out what makes it important to him. Investigate his religion to learn to appreciate what it has to contribute. This will win you his respect. Make it clear that our relationship with God is not a fearful one, in which we rely on our own efforts, but a confident and trusting one, in which we rely on God's mercy and grace to us, based on what Christ did for us.

Distinguish carefully between Christianity and American culture. Most internationals think that the U.S. is a Christian nation and assume that nearly everybody is a Christian. So the negative things they experience in the United States are sometimes associated with Christianity, such as a low state of morality. Even some Americans speak of the U.S. as a Christian country. Clearly explain what distinguishes a person who has true faith and follows the Lord from his heart. Include in this the distinction between a genuine believer and a mere churchgoer.

Introduce your Muslim friend to other Christians. Collective witness and love is important to help your friend see that Christianity has an impact on many people and is not just your personal faith. Other people's witness can often have an impact in a way that yours may not have. So do not be jealous or exclusive in your friendship with the person to whom you are witnessing. It has been said that a Muslim usually needs to have a significant relationship with at least twenty Christians before he will begin to understand the gospel. Our unity and love as a community of believers will have a great impact on a Muslim. Note John 13:34–35 and John 17:20–23. The seed of the gospel will grow in the soil of how believers relate to each other as seen by the world.[5]

Invite your friend to Christian events at which he will feel comfortable. Explain what a speaker may have said at a Christian meeting. Make sure that a Scripture passage is clear to your friend. Be sure to let your friend know what kind of event you are bringing him to. Do not bring him to an event with an evangelistic message without telling him that that is what he should expect to hear. Otherwise, he may be offended and feel that he has been used as an object of proselytization.

A church service is probably not one of the first things to which you should bring your friend. A foreign-born Muslim will not understand that we worship God in church. He will be confused and troubled by our wearing of shoes in church, by men and women sitting together (and sometimes even touching one another), by the crossing of our legs, by our feet being put next to the Bible in the pew rack, by people setting the Bible on the floor, and by our sitting to pray. Muslims often have trouble understanding what is going on and what is being said. A better way to introduce your friend to Christian fellowship would be to invite him to a small Bible discussion group. After some orientation, you may want to invite him to church with you.

Give good Christian literature to your friend that addresses his needs at the point he is at on his way to Christ. At an appropriate time, give him a New Testament or Bible. Internationals often like to have one in their native language. Some like to have a diglot version, with English and their native language in parallel columns. Give them a modern language version. These are available from the Bible societies listed under "Further Ministry Resources" at the back of this book.

Identify as much as possible with your Muslim friends, demonstrating interest in their subculture and identity. One way to do this is to eat like they do when you are with them—using a piece of pita bread or your fingers, as the case may be, and eating their national foods. You can also learn greetings and common phrases in their language. Be sure to show an interest in, and pray for, their problems.

Show Hospitality to Your Muslim Friends

> But no stranger had to spend the night in the street,
> for my door was always open to the traveler. (Job 31:32)

> Do not forget to entertain strangers, for by so doing some people have entertained angels without knowing it. (Heb. 13:2)

> Practice hospitality. (Rom. 12:13)

It is exciting to think about what God may do through your hosting of international Muslim students in your home. Many may not have any other opportunity to be in an American/Canadian home while they are here in North America.

It would be best to host a small group, individual, or couple in your home at least twice during the school year. That would give you the opportunity to have a greater impact on your guests. You might even want to have the second or following dinners in the home of another family or individual with whom you have teamed up to host students. Holidays, such as Thanksgiving, Christmas, and Easter are great times to host international students because they have a break from studies and the holiday provides a natural opportunity to talk about its significance in relation to the Christian faith.

Pray for the students whom you invite to your home. Pray that they would be comfortable in your home, that they would experience Christian love, and that there would be an opportunity to speak of the Lord sometime during their visit.

Make sure that arrangements to get to your home are very clear. Some newly arrived students do not know how to get around the city very well yet. Others may not really understand your English clearly on the phone. In some cultures, people may say that they understand in order to be polite, but they really don't understand. So have them repeat the instructions back to you if you doubt they understood them. You are strongly encouraged to send them a postcard with directions and confirming when you are expecting them. Make sure they have your name, address, and phone number. If they need a ride to your home, you may find it helpful to work with another believer with a car to assist you in hosting and transporting the students. These arrangements should be made clear, too.

When inviting your guests to dinner, be sensitive to whether there are certain foods they do not eat, and do not serve such foods. Muslims do not eat shellfish, pork, or anything with a pork product. Some Muslims will only eat meat that is *halal*—that has been killed in the Islamic way, in the name of Allah. Often an international student will not recognize the food you have prepared or know how to eat it. So you can give some explanation. They may also be uncomfortable using a knife and fork. Often what makes a big hit is to serve a dish that is typical of their part of the world. Or explain to them that what you have prepared is a typical American dish. Some internationals like to cook and would be glad to show you how to cook one of their native dishes at a second get-together.

You may want to bring in spiritual issues during your visit by having a devotional reading or Bible reading after the meal. When giving thanks to the Lord before the meal, you could give a brief explanation of what you are doing and pray for your visitors as well as thanking God for the food. Possibly during a second visit, you could show the *Jesus* movie to your guests on video. Another possibility would be to play the *International Opinion Game*.[6] This is a good game, in which each person in turn picks a card that has questions to help you get to know each other and stimulate discussion. There are different categories of questions, one of which deals with values and spiritual issues.

Follow up the students' visit with a phone call or card to indicate your continued interest in them. If possible, continue a friendship that can be a context for ministry to them.

Meet Their Needs

> Jesus answered her, "If you knew the gift of God and who it is that asks you for a drink, you would have asked him and he would have given you living water." . . . "Everyone who drinks this water will be thirsty again, but whoever drinks the water I give him will never thirst. Indeed, the water I give him will become in him a spring of water welling up to eternal life." (John 4:10, 13–14)

> Then Peter said, "Silver or gold I do not have, but what I have I give you. In the name of Jesus Christ of Nazareth, walk." (Acts 3:6)

> Some men came carrying a paralytic on a mat and tried to take him into the house to lay him before Jesus. . . . When Jesus saw their faith, he said, "Friend, your sins are forgiven." . . . He said to the paralyzed man, "I tell you, get up, take your mat and go home." (Luke 5:18, 20, 24)

Everybody has needs. They seem to be limitless at times. Meeting the felt needs of your target group can be a way to gain a real entry into their lives and hearts. Some of those needs may be met by helping with spoken English, correcting grammar on a school paper, providing transportation, finding a doctor for a sick child, coping with culture shock or loneliness, being part of a community, or finding an apartment or job. Although needs like these are worthy, many times felt needs do not correspond with real needs. Felt needs can even blind Muslims to their real needs. We need to help them see what their real needs are and point them to the solution.

The Scripture verses above show us that the Samaritan woman, the lame beggar, and the paralyzed man each were looking for a particular need to be met, but Jesus and Peter saw their real need and met it first. Then their physical or material needs were met. This teaches us the priority of meeting the deep spiritual needs of people over their other needs, although the two are often intricately interconnected. Often a solution in the spiritual realm brings solutions to more mundane needs.

Our lives need to show how Jesus can meet real needs. As we pray for our friends, let them know that we are praying for them; as they see answers to those prayers, they will see how Jesus can meet their needs. Many Muslims have fears and insecurities about their future, death, and whether Allah will accept them into heaven. The assurance we have should be made evident. Explain to them that our assurance is based on our faithful God's promises in his Word.

Dawood (David), from the Sudan, used to train Muslims in his homeland to kill Christians. God allowed him to leave his country and go to another Arab country. While he was there, he got sick. A group of caring Christians prayed for him to be healed. Mercifully, God healed him. It became important for him to know something about this God who could heal in answer to prayer. The Christians who prayed for him welcomed him to their Bible study. As they were teaching him the Bible, the Holy Spirit convicted him of his sin. Dawood gave his life to Christ and was baptized. This is the power of the gospel demonstrated through God's healing. It shows how God can use people like us to meet real needs, both physical and spiritual.

Encourage a Response to Christ

> When the people heard this, they were cut to the heart and said to Peter and the other apostles, "Brothers, what shall we do?"
>
> Peter replied, "Repent and be baptized, every one of you, in the name of Jesus Christ for the forgiveness of your sins. And you will receive the gift of the Holy Spirit. The promise is for you and your children and for all who are far off—for all whom the Lord our God will call."
>
> With many other words he warned them; and he pleaded with them, "Save yourselves from this corrupt generation." (Acts 2:37–40)

Do not pressure your friend to become a Christian. Be careful not to mistake courtesy for spiritual interest. Pressure to become a Christian may cause him to reject your friendship. Do make sure that your friend knows how to become a Christian, so that at the appropriate time he may do so. In an appropriate context, invite him to receive Christ as Lord and Savior. But do not pressure your Muslim friend to make a commitment to Christ, especially in front of other Muslims. He will not do it. There would be too much peer pressure in such a situation. What others think is very important to Muslims.

Be sure to explain the cost of becoming a Christian. For many Muslims, it could cost them their relationships with family members, their jobs, their friends, and even endanger their lives. Some of the same costs are there for immigrants and even for native-born Americans. On the other hand, at the appropriate time also let them know the danger of not committing one's life to the Lord.

If your friend is ready to respond to God's grace in the gospel, offer to pray with him or her in a prayer of repentance for sin, acceptance of Christ's death as a substitutionary atonement for sin, new life in Christ's resurrection, and receiving of God's Spirit in one's life. Ask that Jesus Christ would become his Lord and Savior.

He may want to repeat a prayer after you or pray a prayer on his own after you coach him on what to pray.

It is important to follow up on your friend's commitment to Christ, to make sure he understands the gospel, has assurance of his faith, and has been incorporated into the church, where he can grow spiritually. Baptism of the new believer serves this purpose and is commanded by Christ. In baptism, the new believer publicly identifies himself as a disciple of Jesus Christ.

Why There May Not Be a Ready Response to Christ

> Then Agrippa said to Paul, "Do you think that in such a short time you can persuade me to be a Christian?"
>
> Paul replied, "Short time or long—I pray God that not only you but all who are listening to me today may become what I am, except for these chains." (Acts 26:28–29)

Family pressure and job security are important factors that may keep your Muslim friend from making a commitment to Christ, especially among foreign-born Muslims who plan to return to their home country. People are often rejected or disowned by their families for becoming Christians. Others lose their jobs, have difficulty getting a job, or jeopardize their opportunity for advancement by becoming a Christian.

Severe persecution faces some who become Christians, especially those from predominately Muslim countries where it is illegal to change one's religion from Islam. In some cases, the penalty may be death, according to the *Shari'a* (Islamic law).

The leadership ambitions of students who come here may cause them to refuse the gospel. They may realize that as a Christian they would not be able to attain a position of privilege and power. This may be especially true in totalitarian societies.

Christianity has often been identified as a Western religion. People in third world nations still connect Christianity with colonialism and imperialism. America's strong support for Israel is incomprehensible to those from the Arab world. Because of these associations, Christianity is often rejected by internationals. Confusion is also made between Americanism and Christianity. This confusion is found not only among international students, but also among American Christians. Some people assume that Westerners are Christians just because they grew up that way. Some African-Americans (especially Black Muslims) think of Christianity as the white man's religion, not realizing that Christianity has been in Africa among blacks since the first century (Acts 8:26–39; 13:1). Indeed, there are more Christians in the non-Western world today than in the West.

Christianity is sometimes identified with being narrow, irrational, bigoted, racist, or the cause of much fighting in the world. These views are a distortion of true Christianity, but they may be true of particular Christians. Muslims often identify Christianity with the Crusades of the Middle Ages. Believing that America is a Christian nation, they identify Christianity with loose morality, such as premarital and extramarital sex, the gay lifestyle, frequent divorce, consumption of alcohol, and the spread of AIDS. Their thought would be, "Who would want to convert to a religion that leads to that kind of life?"

Disillusionment with Christianity because of previous encounters with nominal Christians causes some to reject the faith. When they see "Christians" getting drunk on campus and sleeping with members of the opposite sex, they become disillusioned with Christian moral standards. Racial and ethnic discrimination has also been a source of deep hurt.

Some internationals have been forewarned to beware of Christians when they come to North America. Especially those who are government-sponsored students and scholars may have been warned to keep their thinking in line with the government's ideological policy. This is especially true for those coming from nations with totalitarian governments and strict Islamic ideology. Some of these students' activities are watched by government spies.

Initial curiosity about the Christian faith may be expressed by attendance at Christian activities and Bible studies, but it may change to rejection after that curiosity is satisfied. When Christian doctrines such as the Trinity, the sinfulness of humanity, and Christ's deity, death, and resurrection are made known, some Muslims find them too hard to reconcile with their Islamic belief system.

Continue the Friendship

Love never fails. (1 Cor. 13:8)

Even if your friend is not interested in Christianity, continue your friendship. Demonstrate that your friendship is not dependent on him or her becoming a Christian. Show that you have love for him or her as a person.

Do not lose hope or give up on your friend becoming a Christian. Often the work of the Holy Spirit takes a long time from our perspective. George Muller prayed daily for the conversion to Christ of five of his friends. The first was converted after eighteen months, the second after five years, the third after eleven years, the fourth shortly before his death (after about fifty-four years), and the fifth a few years later.[7] God answers in his own time when we pray according to the mind of Christ. One point of advice is that when a friend is not responsive to the gospel after repeated attempts to speak of it, you may better use your time and energy with those who are responsive and are hungry for spiritual truth. That doesn't mean that you don't continue the friendship or prayer, but you should redirect the major portion of your energy toward other people. However, this takes much discernment and needs guidance by the Holy Spirit. From a study made by missionaries in Iran, it was estimated that it usually takes at least six months of contact with Christians before a Muslim receives Christ.

Even if your friend does not become a Christian while in the U.S., he may become one after returning to his own country. You may be able to help get him in contact with Christians in his home country. This friend may also introduce you to some of his international friends who are looking for a friend and/or are interested in the Christian faith. Finally, those internationals who do not respond to the gospel often return to their countries to take important positions in which they can determine policies favorable to Christianity. They may also influence the level of persecution and oppression that Christians suffer in their country. That may depend on their perception of Christianity from your friendship.

Cautions

> You know that everyone in the province of Asia has deserted me, including Phygelus and Hermogenes. (2 Tim. 1:15)
>
> Alexander the metalworker did me a great deal of harm. The Lord will repay him for what he has done. You too should be on your guard against him, because he strongly opposed our message. (2 Tim. 4:14–15)
>
> But avoid foolish controversies and genealogies and arguments and quarrels about the law, because these are unprofitable and useless. (Titus 3:9)
>
> A righteous man is cautious in friendship. (Prov. 12:26)

There are several reasons for being cautious about developing friendships with Muslims. First, be careful about being used. Someone may become dependent on you to give them a ride to the mall, to help them write their papers, or to attend a Christian conference without having to pay anything. One student ran up a large long-distance phone bill, making calls to the Middle East in the home of his host during a Christmas conference. (When asked about it, the student did pay for the calls.)

At times one needs to beware of a Muslim's motives for developing a friendship with you. When I (Bruce McDowell) and my wife, Susan, were dating before getting married, I arranged for her to tutor the wife of an Afghan air force colonel in English. The family had recently come to Philadelphia as refugees. After several tutoring sessions, the Afghan woman began to speak about her husband and how she was getting too old to have more children. She suggested that Susan would be a good second wife. Then Susan noticed that after a meal, eaten on the oriental carpeted floor, the wife and children left the room, leaving Susan and the Afghan man to talk. He asked if she could give him driving lessons. At that point, Susan realized that it was time to go.

Beware when there doesn't appear to be any reciprocal giving of themselves in the relationship. Often this can be difficult to judge because students, refugees, or recent immigrants may not be in much of a position to be reciprocal. Be careful of the use of your time. Evaluate whether taking your friend to the mall would be a real act of love and an opportunity to build your friendship or just a time for him to have his need met. Keep in mind that the Qur'an teaches, "Let not the believers take disbelievers for their friends in preference to believers. Whoso doth that hath no connection with Allah unless (it be) that ye but guard yourselves against them, taking (as it were) security" (Surah 3:28). However, this verse is interpreted as referring to those who are enemies of Islam, which could be a Christian if you are seen as opposing Islam.

One day I (one of the authors) received a phone call at my office from a man with a foreign accent who claimed to be a convert from Islam. He said he had come from Utah and wondered if I could help him. We arranged a time to meet, but he never showed up. Subsequently I found out that he had been at the local seminary and had also contacted a couple of others in the area who minister to Muslims. He asked a number of probing questions that seemed a little odd. When I asked about his background, things did not seem to fit together. Maybe that is why he did not show up for our appointment. Beware of spies. This man seemed to be gathering information on Christian activity among Muslims. The governments of some Muslim countries have informants among their students to keep them from straying from Islam or getting involved with radical groups. Beware of divulging information about Christian activity, particularly anything that is aimed at reaching Muslims. Do not print in church bulletins or put on church bulletin boards the names of Christian workers in Muslim countries. If you do have their name posted, do not indicate the country where they serve. Their names have been known to turn up on lists in the countries where they serve. Consequently, they may be expelled from their country of service.

As mentioned before, do not let your discussions with Muslims become arguments. This will be fruitless. You will leave with a sense of broken trust. Arguments will make it difficult to continue the relationship at a level at which your friend will really listen to you. Maintain your cool and wait for the appropriate time to speak. If you are repeatedly denied an opportunity to speak, and the other person remains argumentative, this may be an indication that it is time to find the person of peace who is open to hearing the truth.

Testimonies of Friendship

The power of the gospel is demonstrated by loving a Muslim. Amina came to America as an immigrant. A religious lady by nature and family background, she was looking to go to the mosque as usual. She asked one of her countrymen and his wife to give her a ride to the mosque, which was in a large city in Pennsylvania. The husband said he would do so, but he did not do it. Amina felt very strongly that the man and his wife were not true Muslims because they did not keep their word. Since Amina did not drive, she went for a walk. The sovereign Lord led her to walk by a church building. Out of curiosity, she knocked on the church door. A Christian woman was in the building and opened the door for her with a big smile. Amina was amazed at that. After she was invited in and befriended, she was invited to attend a Bible study and the Sunday service. She attended both consistently. Then she was put in contact with me (one of the authors). As I was talking with her on the phone, I introduced her to Christ. She gave her life to the Lord Jesus right then. Later I preached at the service in which I witnessed her water baptism. She is now a member at that church and is trying to reach her sons for Jesus. I asked her why she became a Christian. She responded, "I was touched by the love of the lady who opened the church door for me." This demonstrates the power of the gospel in showing love to people like Amina.

Hussein, a Muslim immigrant living in Georgia, divorced from an American, non-Christian wife, was left with his two sons. As he shared the story of his struggles with a pastor (an associate of one of the authors), the pastor offered, "I can help you." Hussein started to bring his two children to the pastor's home after school. The pastor and his wife took care of them. They fed them physically and spiritually and helped them in their homework. Sometimes they kept them for the weekend. One day, as the pastor was sharing the gospel with the older boy, he asked, "How can I become a Christian?" The pastor explained it to him, and he gave his life to Jesus Christ that night. Meanwhile, the younger brother was watching the *Jesus* movie in the living room with the pastor's wife. After the film ended, the pastor invited the younger brother to study the Bible with him. That same evening, the younger brother also committed his life to Christ. They were so joyful about it that they immediately told their father. The pastor thought that the father would be upset. But it was the opposite. After a while, their father noticed that the boys' behavior had changed for the better. Their grades in school also improved dramatically. After a year or so, they were baptized. I (one of the authors) baptized the older brother. The two brothers became members of the church where this pastor ministered.

I asked Hussein, "Why do you allow your children to be Christians?" He replied, "Well, they are free to choose. It's much better for them to be a Christian and live a godly life than to live ungodly lives and shoot someone for five dollars." Hussein called his parents overseas after his sons' baptism, and told them what happened. They were very upset and asked him, "Why did you not take them to the mosque?" He said, "I did for several years, but the mosque did not offer them what the church offered." Yes, this is the power of the gospel in caring for someone in their time of need.

As you read these stories and others in this book, we encourage you to remember three facts: (1) God is sovereign over the affairs of men. (2) The gospel has great power. (3) We are not to underestimate our great God and what he can do in bringing Muslims to himself. Therefore, our responsibility in all of this is to trust the Lord and witness to our Muslim friends faithfully, believing that God will bring his chosen ones among them to himself. Thus, if you are witnessing without seeing fruit, do not get discouraged. The word of God does not return to him empty, but will accomplish what he desires and achieve the purpose for which he sent it (Isa. 55:11). These are testimonies of what God has done. Will he not do such things again?

For Reflection/Action

1. Put the above principles into practice by inviting a Muslim to your home for a meal.
2. Are there any significant differences between friendship evangelism with a Muslim and with anyone else? What would be the key rule of thumb?
3. What factors may be different in sharing the gospel with someone from another country and with someone from the U.S./Canada?
4. Think of a Muslim friend with whom you have a desire to share the gospel. What have you done to develop your friendship? How have you sought to share your faith? What approaches seemed to work and not to work?
5. Find two other people who have a friend to whom they would like to witness; meet together to pray for each other's friends.

CHAPTER TWELVE

Meetings for Better Understanding

Philosophy of Ministry

Meetings for Better Understanding provide an opportunity for the Muslim and Christian communities to share their spiritual beliefs in an effort to understand one another better. Bible-believing Christians who love Muslims sit together with them at a table in a mosque or a church to seek better understanding of the things of God in a friendly and civilized way. We need to be more open to hearing each other. In the past, Muslims and Christians accused each other of many bad things. Each one's attitude was one of hatred and conflict at every level. Muslims and Christians would rarely sit down together and try to understand each other or find common ground from a theological perspective. As Muslims and Christians sit together, they can learn how the others live and think. They can gain a better understanding of each other's religious expression. Rather than holding to stereotypes of one another, they will be able to see each other as people with many common concerns. Sitting at a table together opens each one up to accept and understand how the other thinks, theologically and socially.

In our day, when so much communication is impersonal through the mass media, images, sound bites, and cyberspace, it is still most effective to communicate face-to-face. By creating a friendly personal environment, one can communicate one's message with respect, understanding, and honesty. The format of "Muslims and Christians at the Table" provides just that environment.

At such a gathering, Christian and Muslim speakers present their views from the Bible and the Qur'an, respectively. These meetings are not debates. One should avoid argument, which is not productive. Therefore, we do not encourage any criticism of the Qur'an or Muhammad at these meetings. We can, however, point to the contrasts between the two faiths.

These meetings are not dialogues, as some define them, in that the aim is not for either side to compromise its message or mix the two faiths. This is not to be done because the two religions are not equal; their two books are not equal. One of them is very false (although containing some truths), and the other one is very true. The gospel presents the absolute and truthful God.

Therefore, the reasonable approach to Muslims is to hold Meetings for Better Understanding, where the two communities come together to discuss topics of mutual interest. For example, we discuss the unity of God in the Scriptures and the unity of God in the Qur'an. When we give them the chance to tell their story, we ask them to give us the same chance to tell our story. When they hear a radically different message of Christ from what they know in Islam, we trust that the Holy Spirit will bring them to conviction. We have seen very encouraging results from this. We have done this among Pakistanis, Arabs, African-American Muslims, and other nationalities. This strategy built a sense of community among us.

The same concept of meeting together for mutual understanding is used by different world governments and the United Nations to solve conflicts among nations. People are tired of wars, conflicts, and militant approaches. Through meeting together, many mutual agreements have been made, avoiding conflict. Muslims and Christians can do the same thing by discussing their religious differences. The idea here is not necessarily to agree with each other, but simply to communicate the gospel to our Muslim friends who are open to sitting with us to learn and understand. The gospel has its own power to change their minds and open their hearts to say yes to Jesus, who reveals himself to us in the Holy Scriptures. Meeting once will encourage the participants to meet again and again to learn from each other. They will see that they have the mutual duty to be involved in the process of seeking better understanding.

Such table talk provides a means for Muslims and Christians to discover their responsibilities toward God and each other. They will each be seeking the truth and how they can live what they preach. Their meeting with each other becomes a channel to understand their role in life as people living for God alone, submitting to his will, and glorifying him in every area of their life. In such a setting, if one person becomes abusive and violent, the rest of the group will make him feel ashamed of himself. Both sides will want to demonstrate their good behavior to the other. So this type of meeting prevents violence and disruption. It builds bridges between both parties, rather than walls, as in the past.

In a Meeting for Better Understanding, Muslims and Christians make every effort to present their religious views in a way that the other party can most easily understand. Of course, this makes them study, pray, and even fast, seeking God's blessing of intervention on their behalf. This is particularly true for the Christians, who know that spiritual understanding is the work of God. Through the years, ministries to Muslims that have used this approach have found that it leads them to intensive preparation, study, and prayer—and it has borne fruit. Muslims have responded that they have learned from, and were touched by, Christians who did this. In some cases, they have asked Christians to pray for them and asked to study the Word of God more often. As Christians have done that, our great God has shown his power and mercy by saving Muslims from their sins. They have become brothers and sisters in Christ.

Guidelines for Meetings

In order to insure that the Meetings for Better Understanding are properly conducted, we offer the following guidelines:

1. The purpose of the meetings is to develop better understanding between the Christian and Muslim communities.
2. Each speaker has thirty minutes to speak on the topic and will speak only on that topic.
3. A thirty-minute question-and-answer period is held after both speakers have presented their messages. Questions are to be kept on the topic and are not to be statements of the views of the questioners. Questions can be directed to one or both of the speakers. Each speaker may follow up on the answer of the other speaker once. Other questions that are of personal interest, but are not related to the topic, may be discussed in individual conversations after the formal sessions.
4. The meetings is moderated to insure that the above guidelines are followed. The moderator for each meeting is to be chosen by the group that hosts the meeting.
5. There will be ample time after the formal meeting for people attending the meeting to meet personally with members of the other faith. Refreshments may be served either before or after the question-and-answer session.
6. Meetings can vary in frequency, but once a month is common.
7. Topics are classified as theological or social, and it is common to alternate between the two classes from meeting to meeting.

Topics for Meetings

During meetings, Muslims explain their understanding of what the Qur'an teaches about the topic, and Christians explain their understanding of what the Bible teaches about it. There are two categories of topics:

Theological and doctrinal topics:

1. The unity of God.
2. Who is Jesus Christ?
3. The Bible and the Qur'an, their inspiration and origins.
4. Man's relationship to God.
5. What is sin, and how is it to be dealt with?
6. What is a prophet, and who are the prophets?
7. Adam and Christ—similarities and differences.
8. The attributes of God.
9. Prayer and fasting.
10. Law and grace.
11. What is faith?
12. Images in religion.
13. What are the requirements of paradise/heaven?
14. What constitutes a true believer?
15. Worship—what and how?
16. What is repentance?
17. The Day of Judgment.
18. What is the church/*ummah?*
19. The death of Christ on the cross.

Social topics—"Christian living" and "Islamic living":

1. Religion in daily life.
2. Morality.
3. Family life: husband-wife-child relationships.
4. Marriage, divorce, and remarriage.
5. How do race and color affect religion?
6. The role of men and women in life, according to religion.
7. Human rights.
8. How to raise your teenagers in a secular culture.

9. Principles of friendship and neighborhood responsibility.
10. How to live out your religion in American culture.
11. What the Bible and the Qur'an teach about slavery.
12. The unity of the human race.
13. Why is there so much corruption in the world today?
14. How can Christians and Muslims work together for good?
15. Hospitality.
16. Goodness, godliness.
17. Honesty.

The Biblical Basis for Meetings

The ministry of Jesus provides a model for "meetings for better understanding." Several passages in the gospel of Luke lead us to use this model with our Muslim friends and neighbors. The idea is to build theological, social, and cultural bridges with them.

Our Muslim friends have been coming to the mosque to bow down to Allah as his slaves. Actually, they are not able to serve Allah on their own. Therefore, they need to know that God's eternal Son offers them new life as God's own children. As they receive his free gift of this new life, they will be able to serve him.

> He [Jesus] went to Nazareth, where he had been brought up, and on the Sabbath day he went into the synagogue, as was his custom. And he stood up to read. The scroll of the prophet Isaiah was handed to him. Unrolling it, he found the place where it is written:
>
> "The Spirit of the Lord is on me,
> because he has anointed me
> to preach good news to the poor.
> He has sent me to proclaim freedom for the prisoners
> and recovery of sight for the blind,

> to release the oppressed,
> to proclaim the year of the Lord's favor." (Luke 4:16–19)

Here Jesus goes to the synagogue, the Jewish place of worship, and teaches about himself, using the prophecy of Isaiah 61:1–2. In a similar way, we can honor Jesus Christ by using this model in the mosque, the Muslim place of worship, to teach them about the Christ of the Bible, who reveals himself to us in his Word. Thus, the Lord Jesus Christ should be your main focus in the mosque.

> On a Sabbath Jesus was teaching in one of the synagogues, and a woman was there who had been crippled by a spirit for eighteen years. She was bent over and could not straighten up at all. When Jesus saw her, he called her forward and said to her, "Woman, you are set free from your infirmity." Then he put his hands on her, and immediately she straightened up and praised God. (Luke 13:10–13)

Again, our Lord went to one of the synagogues to teach, heal, and demonstrate his divine power among the people of the law. We believe that Muslims also need the healing power and teaching of Jesus. Therefore, going to the mosque is a critical avenue for ministry to Muslims. As they are touched by Christ's healing power, they become more open to his gospel. Our experience with them through the years confirms that.

One spring I (one of the authors) was interrupted by a phone call at about noon. On the line was a Muslim friend who was working on his Ph.D. in Islamics at a university in the United States. He was calling from London, where his father had just arrived from the Sudan for a very critical operation. As he was talking with his father about me, the father asked him to call me right away and ask me to pray for him. I agreed to do so, but I asked him why he, a Muslim who prayed five times a day, was asking me, a Christian, to pray for him. His reply was, "Because *your God* hears and answers prayer." I told him that I would pray immediately after I hung up the phone, but my friend demanded that I pray right then and there on the phone. "Don't worry about the cost. The Sudanese government will pay the bill! Just pray!" I prayed for more than ten minutes. Later, when his father successfully recovered from his surgery, my friend thanked me profusely. Indeed, the Sudanese government did pay the bill, but it was Jesus who healed. Muslims need this Jesus who forgives sin and heals.

> One day as he [Jesus] was teaching, Pharisees and teachers of the law, who had come from every village of Galilee and from Judea and Jerusalem, were sitting there. And the power of the Lord was present for him to heal the sick. Some men came carrying a paralytic on a mat and tried to take him into the house to lay him before Jesus. When they could not find a way to do this because of the crowd, they went up on the roof and lowered him on his mat through the tiles into the middle of the crowd, right in front of Jesus.
>
> When Jesus saw their faith, he said, "Friend, your sins are forgiven."
>
> The Pharisees and the teachers of the law began thinking to themselves, "Who is this fellow who speaks blasphemy? Who can forgive sins but God alone?"
>
> Jesus knew what they were thinking and asked, "Why are you thinking these things in your hearts? Which is easier: to say, 'Your sins are forgiven,' or to say, 'Get up and walk'? But that you may know that the Son of Man has authority on earth to forgive sins. . . ." He said to the paralyzed man, "I tell you, get up, take your mat and go home." Immediately he stood up in front of them, took what he had been lying on and went home praising God. Everyone was amazed and gave praise to God. They were filled with awe and said, "We have seen remarkable things today." (Luke 5:17–26)

Here Jesus is dealing with Jewish leaders and teachers who opposed his authority to heal and forgive sins. They accused him of blasphemy. In the same manner, Muslim leaders and teachers sometimes get angry at us as we teach them the whole counsel of God, especially the lordship of Christ. At times, discussions between Muslims and Christians can become very tense and the two groups will have to agree to disagree. But when God comes and touches Muslim hearts in conversion, their response is different. They, like the observers of Jesus' miracle, say, "We have seen remarkable things today." Then they join us in singing praises for his marvelous deeds.

So then, it is fitting for us to go to mosques and to Muslim homes to meet them and present Christ, who heals and forgives sins.

Practical Suggestions for Establishing Meetings

One mission group that had begun to meet with a Muslim group at a Pakistani mosque was told by the mosque leadership that it was not beneficial to meet with them. The mission group immediately met to think things through and see what they could learn. It became clear to them that there was an important group of people at the mosque who had influence besides the imam. The imam was the first and usual point of contact. Now they realized that they needed to include the other leaders right from the start. They also realized that just because they communicated with the imam, there was no guarantee that what they said would be adequately communicated to others. The other leaders had questions. They wanted to know why they should meet with the Christian group and what benefit they would have in doing so.

The mission group also realized that trying to arrange meetings on an indefinite schedule would give the meetings a low priority on both mosque and church calendars, as well as on people's personal schedules. It was recognized that meetings needed to be set up with a definite commitment from all parties on a monthly basis throughout the year or at least within the limitations of seasonal events.

Accordingly, the mission group produced a summary document that could be left with the Muslims to introduce them to the concept of Meetings for Better Understanding. The document describes the meeting format, gives several reasons why they should consider meeting with Christians, and provides a detailed list of both theological and social topics to be addressed (as listed above). It is clearly stated that meetings should ordinarily be held once a month. Several copies of the document were provided, so that they could be passed on to other mosque leaders.[1]

One Christian group had a series of monthly dialogues with Muslims at a Southern university. Two hundred people were regularly attending. Then one month the Christians invited a convert from Islam to give his testimony at the meeting. That resulted in a great outcry and such a disruption from the Muslim participants, that the police had to be called. After that, the meetings could no longer continue. This shows that one must be very sensitive in dealing with Muslims. In a Meeting for Better Understanding, one should not be offensive by trying to win them over with one-upmanship. Using the testimony of a convert is an offensive tactic. Simply present the Word of God and let it do its work (Isa. 55:11; Heb. 4:12).

How should one deal with the widely different understandings, backgrounds, and attitudes of different Muslims? In our experience, this can be a big problem, and we decided not to bring different groups together. For example, if we are meeting with the Ahmadiyya Pakistani, we meet with them separately, and do not tell them that we are also meeting with an African-American mosque. We have found it best to be discreet. If you are meeting with Shi'ites, stay with them, and don't give them your secret. And if you are meeting with Sunnis, stay with the Sunnis. You have to meet with specific groups separately.

How does nationality affect the ministry? Is there is any reason to stick with Muslims from a particular country? We found out that Egyptians and Sudanese can work together, as can Syrians, Lebanese, and Saudi Arabians. There is conflict, but not that much. But when you bring all these nationalities together, plus the African-American Muslims, then you can expect trouble.

Is there a preferred way of witnessing to Muslims: in large groups, small groups, or individually? To start your ministry with a large group of Christians witnessing to a large group of Muslims gives you the advantage of showing them that Christianity is community minded, not an individualistic religion. This is important for Muslims to see, since Western society has become so extremely individualistic. Large groups also indicate that Christianity is a religion for all of God's people. Small groups do this also. With individuals, you are building a relationship one-on-one. All three of these approaches—large groups, small groups, and individuals—are very important. It depends on your circumstances and the opportunities that you have.

Testimony of God's Blessing

One Sunday afternoon I (one of the authors) was preaching in a mosque in a large Southern city through a previous agreement between Bible-believing Christians and God-fearing Muslims. My topic was "God's Image in Man." I used material from James M. Boice's book *Foundations of the Christian Faith* in my presentation. Two Muslims in the audience, one an engineer and the other a medical doctor, publicly asked me some questions for clarification. The sovereign Lord led these two men to accept him as Lord and Savior as they were eating dinner at the mosque with me. This demonstrates the power of the gospel in teaching the Word of God faithfully. It can even be done in a mosque.

Ali, a Pakistani engineer living for many years in a Midwestern city, showed interest in attending a church after attending a

Meeting for Better Understanding. As he was listening to the gospel at that meeting, he saw the difference between biblical teaching and Islamic teaching. He mentioned that he did not believe in his imam's teaching and asked if he could attend a church service. One member of the Christian team at the Meeting for Better Understanding was a pastor. Ali was introduced to the pastor and expressed his desire to attend a church service. We don't know for sure if he actually attended or not, but at least he saw the difference between the gospel and Islam. Again, this shows the power of the Word of God.

How Meetings for Better Understanding Are Being Used

The concept of Meetings for Better Understanding has been used in a variety of places. One coworker began using it in Orlando, Florida. As a result, over four hundred Muslims were showing up every month. The concept has been used by campus ministry staff at a major university in Pennsylvania through the Muslim Student Association. In recent years, Meetings for Better Understanding have been taking place regularly in Atlanta, Chicago, Houston, Norfolk, Pasadena, and Philadelphia, where they first began. Overseas, the concept has been used in Liberia, where it began with six mosques. It has also been used effectively in Egypt with small groups. This approach is particularly effective in the West, but it can work well in Muslim countries, too, because it is not threatening.

In one Midwestern city, Muslims and Christians found that they were able to have some great discussions together in a relaxed and enjoyable atmosphere at a summer picnic. An added benefit of the picnic was that it attracted more women. The Meetings for Better Understanding have been attended mostly by men. Through the picnic, Christian women were able to make friends with Muslim women.

Muslim Motives for Agreeing to Meetings for Better Understanding

In his booklet *Bridgebuilding Between Christian and Muslim—A Seminar at Warner Pacific College*, Jamal Badawi gives an Islamic perspective on why Muslims and Christians should meet together:

> I would like first to express my thanks and appreciation to those who arranged this seminar, and I do hope that we leave it with *a better understanding of each other and with more positive attitudes*. With nearly one billion followers each Islam and Christianity are major religions that influence the thinking and values of over 40 percent of the world population. While there are theological differences, some of which might be significant, there are nonetheless other important areas of belief that are shared by both communities: belief in Allah, or God; belief in revelation, in prophets, in the Holy Books of Allah; in life hereafter and in a divinely inspired moral code organizing and regulating human life during our earthly journey to eternity.
>
> For the Muslim, constructive dialogue is not only permitted, it is commendable. In the Qur'an we read "Say, 'O people of the book' (a term which particularly refers to Jews and Christians) 'come to common terms as between us and you: that we worship none but Allah; that we associate no partners with Him (in His powers and divine attributes); that we erect not from among ourselves lords and patrons other than Allah.' If then they turn back say you 'Bear witness that we are Muslims.' (Bowing) to the will of God." (al-i-Imran; 3:64)
>
> The methodology of that dialogue is also explained in the Qur'an; "Invite (all) to the way of your Lord with wisdom and beautiful exhortation, and argue with them in ways that are best." (al-Nahl; 16:125) A prerequisite for any constructive dialogue is that both communities should

> not learn about each other through sources that are unsympathetic, critical, or even hostile: they should rather try to formulate an honest idea as to how the other faith is seen in its own authentic scriptures and as practiced by those who are truly committed to it. This need is even more significant in the case of the Muslim-Christian dialogue. The average Christian has heard of or has read about Islam mostly through writers who have had colonial or missionary motives, which might have given a certain slant to their interpretation of Islam to the western mind.[2]

Muhammad A. Nubee explains why North American Muslims are open for dialogue with Christians in his introduction to the booklet *Christian-Muslim Dialogue:*

> *Muslim-Christian Dialogue* also makes clear the Islamic point of view in these matters and shows how the Qur'an, revealed to the Prophet Muhammad some 600 years after the life of Jesus, peace be upon both of them, corrects the errors that crept (knowingly or unknowingly) into the message that Jesus brought. This book should prove to be a very valuable asset to both Muslims and Christians, particularly given the interest in dialogues between the two faiths. God willing, this book will be an effective tool for Muslims in our efforts to invite Christians to Islam. Conversely, Christians should become more aware of what in fact the Bible says and what Jesus [PBUH] actually taught, as a result of studying this book. Indeed, as a Muslim the hope is that the Non-Muslim will accept the Truth and bear witness to the Oneness of Allah and that Muhammad is His slave, servant and Messenger.[3]

It is clear from these extended quotations that the primary goal of Muslims in their dialogue with Christians is to invite the latter to become Muslims. In their eyes, becoming a Muslim is not so much conversion as reversion to one's original state. According to Islam, all men and women are born Muslims, but are made Christians or pagans by their parents and circumstances.

Christians may be intimidated by such an aggressive approach by Muslims. Yet, Samuel Zwemer, in his book *The Moslem Christ*, encourages Christians to be diligent in using opportunities to witness to Muslims:

> We must become Moslems to the Moslems if we would gain them for Christ. We must do this in the Pauline sense, without compromise, but with self-sacrificing sympathy and unselfish love. The nearest way to the Moslem heart can often be found better by subjective than by objective study. The barrier may be in the heart of the missionary as well as in the heart of the Moslem. He should cultivate sympathy to the highest degree and an appreciation of all the great fundamental truths which we hold in common with Moslems. He should show the superiority of Christianity both in doctrine and life by admitting the excellencies of doctrine and life in Mohammedanism, but showing immediately how Christianity far surpasses them. Many Moslems are at heart dissatisfied with Muhammad as an ideal of character. Therefore, while the missionary should be careful not to offend needlessly, he should boldly challenge a comparison between the life of Muhammad and the life of Jesus Christ, even as known to Moslems from their own books.
>
> Compromise in this regard will not win the respect of Moslems. They glorify their prophet, why should we not glorify ours? A loving and yet bold presentation of the distinctive truths of our religion and of the surpassing grandeur and beauty of the character of Jesus Christ will never alienate a Moslem heart. The heart of the gospel and that which possesses the greatest power of appeal to Mo-

hammedans, as to every sinner, is the union between God's mercy and God's justice manifested in the Cross of Christ.[4]

Qur'anic References Used as Points of Contact

Meaningful Meetings for Better Understanding may begin by referring your Muslim friends to relevant qur'anic references on the subject.

1. A Formula

> O people of the Book! Let us come together upon *a formula* which is common between us—that we shall not serve anyone but God, that we shall associate none with him. (Surah 3:64)

We see in this verse a challenge and an invitation to Christians to seek through Meetings for Better Understanding to understand and find the "formula" or agreement mentioned in this verse. By referring to this qur'anic verse, Christians can challenge their Muslim friends to hold Meetings for Better Understanding on a monthly basis for two to five years to find the "formula." If monthly meetings continue for five years, the Muslims will hear the gospel sixty times. If each meeting lasts for three hours, they will have over 180 hours of exposure to the gospel over those five years. So many hours of exposure cannot help but have an impact on the hearers.

In the Church Without Walls ministry, we see these meetings as the principle means of communicating the gospel to Muslims. We make every effort to keep Muslims coming to these meetings, so that they might continue to hear the gospel, and that the Holy Spirit might use it in their hearts. Even when the Holy Spirit does not choose to use his word in Muslim hearts, we rejoice that these Muslims heard the gospel for a time. We may never see the results, but God may use this exposure to the gospel many years in the future.

2. Compete in Goodness

> If God so willed, he would have made all of you one community, but he has not done so that he may test you in what he has given you; so compete in goodness. To God shall you all return and he will tell you the Truth about what you have been disputing. (Surah 5:48)

With this verse, you can strengthen your challenge to Muslims to strive with Christians to continue meeting for a long period of time as you together seek God and his truth. The Christian understands that he has been drawn close to God. The Muslim also believes that he has been drawn close to God. This conviction facilitates the Muslim's tolerance of, and patience with, Christians, whom he sees as ignorant people. He is often, then, willing to make every effort to bring us into the fold of Islam. We should welcome these efforts as opportunities to share the gospel with him.

3. Rebelliousness Among Themselves

> God raised up prophets who gave good tidings and warning and God also sent down with them the Book in truth, that it may decide among people in regard to what they differed. But people did not differ in it (i.e. with regard to the Truth) except those to whom it had been given (and that only) after clear signs had come to them; (and this they did) out of (sheer) rebelliousness among themselves. (Surah 2:213)

According to the teaching of the Qur'an, there was originally a unified humanity which, due to its own rebelliousness, became divided. Some Muslim scholars see this divided state as fostered by various versions of the "one Book" that were introduced by different prophets. Why prophetic revelations should act as a force for disunity does not seem to be explained, except to say that it is a mystery that God could overcome if he so willed. The fact that

God does not so will is explained as providing an opportunity for the various religions to compete with each other in goodness, as stated in the previously quoted surah.

Again, this verse could be used to encourage Muslims to meet with Christians for learning, relearning, and reacting to foster competition in godliness and acting justly. This provides yet another door for the gospel, as Christians meet with Muslims and teach the whole counsel of God. It raises specific questions about what this "unified" humanity was like, what the "one book" is like, why the Qur'an mentions four books (the Torah of Moses, the Psalms of David, the Gospel of Jesus, and the Qur'an of Muhammad), and which of them is the right book. This verse also opens up questions about man's rebellion, why God allowed division among men, and what his plan is for the human race. Answering such questions can take many meetings and allow for continued sharing of the good news of Jesus.

4. Common Ground of Belief

> And argue not with the People of the Scripture unless it be in (a way) that is better, save with such of them as do wrong; and say: We believe in that which hath been revealed unto us and revealed unto you; our God and your God is One, and unto Him we surrender. In like manner We have revealed unto thee the Scripture, and those unto whom We gave the Scripture aforetime will believe therein. And none deny our revelations save the disbelievers. (Surah 29:46–47)

Muslims try to find common ground of belief as stated in the latter part of verse 46. Yusuf 'Ali comments: "Mere disputations are futile. In order to achieve our purpose as true standard-bearers of Allah, we shall have to find true common grounds of belief, as stated in the latter part of this verse, and also to show by our [Muslim] urbanity, kindness, sincerity, truth, and genuine anxiety for the good of others, that we are not cranks or merely seeking selfish or questionable aims."[5] Muslims are trying to be kind to the People of the Book as indicated by this commentary. If this is the case, then this is one of the reasons why Muslims should seek to meet with Christians for better understanding of the things of God. This is the ideal of Islam, which verses 46–47 teach. They have here a reason to share their beliefs with others. We quote this passage as a point of contact, encouraging them to meet with us.

5. Reason with Them in the Better Way

> Call unto the way of thy Lord with wisdom and fair exhortation, and reason with them in the better way. Lo! thy Lord is best aware of him who strayeth from His way, and He is Best Aware of those who go aright. (Surah 16:125)

Here we have an injunction for Muslims to call nonbelievers to the way of the Lord with wisdom and winsomeness. Muhammad Asad translates "reason with them in the better way" as "argue with them in the most kindly manner." He comments on this by referring to Surah 29:46 (noted above) and saying, "This stress on kindness and tact and, hence, on the use of reason alone in all religious discussions with adherents of other creeds is fully in tune with the basic, categorical injunction, 'There shall be no coercion in matters of faith' (2:256)."[6]

6. Repel Evil with Goodness

> The good deed and the evil deed are not alike. Repel the evil deed with one which is better, then lo! he, between whom and thee there was enmity (will become) as though he was a bosom friend. (Surah 41:34)

Muhammad Asad comments that "repel the evil deed with one which is better" "relates to scurrilous objections to, and hostile criticism of, the Qur'an" and refers back to *ayah* 26, which speaks of those who are bent on denying the truth.[7] Wahiduddin Khan[8] expounds this verse in this way:

> So revolutionary is this idea, that even an enemy is to be treated as a friend. One should consider even one's enemy as a potential friend and respond to his mistreatment with goodness. Therefore, according to the Quran, we do not have the right to call anyone kafir which is the situation that emerges when the Muslims see non-Muslims as the 'other.' To call people kafir just because they do not claim to be Muslim is to violate God's injunctions. *Kafir* literally means *munkir* as translated by Shah Abdul Qadir. *Munkir* is someone who rejects or conceals the truth. If the message has never been presented to a people then they cannot be called *munkir* let alone *kafir*. Therefore, all races and peoples of the world should be viewed as human beings who are potential allies; allies of Muslims against unbelief. And they should be presented with the theory as well as practice of Islam.[9]

So we find that Muslims are to treat non-Muslims with goodness as a friend, even if they do not accept Islam. They are allies against unbelief. In fact, they ought to meet with Christians to present Islam.

The main idea behind the concept of Meetings for Better Understanding is to encourage face-to-face contact between groups of Muslims and Christians to learn from each other. North America affords a tremendous amount of freedom, compared to most Muslim countries. May this fact bring us to our knees, to plead with God to preserve our liberty and empower us to proclaim the gospel before that liberty is taken from us.

Church Without Walls has seen God work mightily through Meetings for Better Understanding. Through them, Christians and

Muslims have built friendships, shared needs and family problems, shared meals, cried together, loaned money to each other, and been drawn close. Through God's grace, the ice has been broken and has melted, as our relationships with Muslims have become warm and personal.

For Reflection/Action

1. How does the approach of Meetings for Better Understanding avoid some of the pitfalls of some other approaches, such as debates?
2. Why does this approach to reaching Muslims have a powerful impact on many at one time?
3. When visiting a mosque, as suggested in chapter 10, work on developing relationships with mosque leaders, with the goal of organizing Meetings for Better Understanding.

CHAPTER THIRTEEN

Studying the Bible with Muslims

The Power of the Word

As the spiritual descendants of those who rediscovered biblical truths in the Reformation, we are convinced that the Bible is the very Word of God and has the power to transform lives. In order for a person to come to a personal knowledge of the one true and living God, he must have an encounter with the message of the Bible. One of the best ways for this to happen with a Muslim is for him to study the Bible himself. We see the value of Bible study in 2 Timothy 3:15–16: "You have known the holy Scriptures, which are able to make you wise for salvation through faith in Christ Jesus. All Scripture is God-breathed and is useful for teaching, rebuking, correcting and training in righteousness." The Word is necessary for knowing the way of salvation and living for God.

The Word also has the power to open the eyes of the spiritually blind. This happened as Jesus spoke to the two men on the road to Emmaus after his resurrection:

> And beginning with Moses and all the Prophets, he explained to them what was said in all the Scriptures concerning himself. . . .
>
> When he was at the table with them, he took bread, gave thanks, broke it and began to give it to them. Then their eyes were opened and they recognized him, and he

> disappeared from their sight. They asked each other, "Were not our hearts burning within us while he talked with us on the road and opened the Scriptures to us?" (Luke 24:27, 30–32)

Finally, the Word brings conviction of sin and repentance. "For the word of God is living and active. Sharper than any double-edged sword, it penetrates even to dividing soul and spirit, joints and marrow; it judges the thoughts and attitudes of the heart" (Heb. 4:12). We have seen repeatedly how God's Word has a tremendous impact in turning people to the Lord.

Knowing the power of the Word affects our presentation of the gospel. Any Muslim we meet will have certain presuppositions with which he interprets our gospel presentation. These presuppositions will cause him to reject our evidential arguments for the truth of the gospel, even though they appear very appealing and logical to us. Unless we challenge the Muslim's presuppositions, we cannot expect him to arrive at our conclusions. He would be going in the opposite direction. Therefore, as Thomas A. Thomas says, "Unless the non-Christian changes his presuppositions, he will never trust Christ as his personal Saviour from sin. Only the Holy Spirit, as He works through our faithful presentation of the Word of God to the sinner, can change the sinner's presuppositions and bring him to the Saviour. We are completely dependent on Him."[1] This is affirmed by Scripture. "Salvation comes from the LORD" (Jonah 2:9). Only the Spirit of God can open the eyes of the nonbeliever to understand spiritual truth (1 Cor. 2:12). "The man without the Spirit does not accept the things that come from the Spirit of God, for they are foolishness to him, and he cannot understand them, because they are spiritually discerned" (1 Cor. 2:14). We must affirm our presupposition that the Bible is the Word of God and present what God has spoken. A presuppositional presentation of the gospel is most effective and consistent with our assumption that unregenerate people are unable to comprehend God's truth apart from the work of God's Spirit in their hearts.

Forms for Presenting the Gospel

Stories, proverbs, parables, poetry, and illustrations often have a greater impact in your witness than using straight propositional truth, because stories are used to communicate concepts in many parts of the Muslim world. Stories tend to stick in the mind longer than linear forms of thought. This difference in the form of communication is illustrated in the New Testament, where Romans is more linear in thought, and 1 John and parts of Hebrews often return to a common theme. Note also how Jesus taught with parables and illustrations from everyday life. This concrete form of thinking fits the Eastern mind better than the abstract thinking of the Western mind. Some examples of parables that can impact the Muslim mind are those of the wedding feast (Luke 14:7–14), the lost sheep, the lost coin, the lost son (Luke 15), Lazarus and the rich man (Luke 16:19–31), the Pharisee and tax collector (Luke 18:9–14), the unmerciful servant (Matt. 18:21–35), and the two sons (Matt. 21:28–32). Jesus' teaching on his being the Good Shepherd is also powerful (John 10:1–21).

Language

People understand and accept the gospel most readily when it is given to them in their mother tongue. If at all possible, give a Muslim immigrant or international student a Bible or Christian literature in his own language. That way it is more likely to be read. Then he sees that God speaks his language—not just Arabic, as in Islam. Several places to obtain such resources are listed in the back under "Further Ministry Resources."

In order to make your presentation of the gospel to Muslims culturally relevant, it is helpful to use qur'anic terminology—as long as it is given biblical content. Examples would be to say *Ibrahim* for Abraham, *Musa* for Moses, and *Allah* for God. *Allah* is just the Arabic word for God, and is used in the Arabic translation of the Bible. *'Isa* may be used for Jesus, but it too needs to be redefined as the biblical Jesus. *Yesua,* for Jesus, retains the theological meaning of Jesus' name ("Savior"). *'Isa* is found only in the Qur'an and has no real meaning apart from referring to the prophet of Christianity. Numerous theological terms in Arabic that you may want to use will also need to be given a biblical definition. In a country like Malaysia, it is illegal for a non-Muslim to use qur'anic language because the authorities are trying to prevent Christians from using this method of evangelizing Muslims.

Leading Cross-cultural Bible Studies

There may be a variety of reasons why a Muslim would want to study the Bible. It may be a matter of curiosity. It could be due to the friendship and love demonstrated to him or her by Christians. Some may have an academic interest in knowing about the Bible and what Christians believe. Others may want to know more about the Bible in order to be more effective in *da'wah,* winning Christians to Islam. Finally, some recognize a spiritual void in their lives and want to find out if Christians know something that they don't know.

The following guidelines are provided to direct you in effectively leading cross-cultural Bible studies.

1. Establish a good friendship with the student or students with whom you will study. Building trust in a relationship is critical for what you say to be accepted as truth.
2. Meet one-on-one, with a couple, or with a small group to go through the studies. Meeting with one or two people will make it possible for the leader to address the specific problems, misunderstandings, or questions that the student has. The larger the group, the less personal it becomes. Also, Muslim peer pressure not to show any responsiveness to the gospel may hinder open communication of what someone is really thinking.

3. If the studies are used with a group, it is important for the group leader to spend some time individually with the group members to deal with any problems or questions they may have. This provides an opportunity for questions to be raised that individuals may have been either embarrassed or fearful to raise within the group. Unless the group members know each other well and trust each other, they may be afraid to say what they really think. Anything they say may someday be used against them. Often one Muslim will be watching out for another to ensure that he remains faithful to Islam. Students from some countries, like Malaysia, have spies among them to ensure that students remain faithful to Islam. Their activities are monitored. In a group situation, it is helpful to have at least one other Christian, if not several others, to help bring some balance in the discussion, rather than having only one Christian to answer all the questions. On the other hand, the group may become unbalanced if there are too many Christians in the group, so that the Muslims feel they don't have the freedom to ask questions or say what they really think.
4. Each study may be given out to the students either the week before, so they have a chance to read it over before you meet, or at the time you meet. Which you do depends on your students' willingness to read it beforehand.
5. When using a prepared, written lesson, the leader may either summarize the explanatory and introductory parts of the study or have his students take turns reading parts out loud. When students read aloud, they are helped with their English (for foreign-born Muslims), and the leader learns where the student is having difficulty in his understanding.
6. Many words and concepts found in studying the Bible will be new to the students. The leader will need to be sure that they understand the new vocabulary and concepts. One helpful way of dealing with this is to prepare a vocabulary sheet with definitions written next to words. This will

make the studies progress faster or slower, depending on the English level of the students and how much advance preparation has been done by the leader.

7. You may want to begin and end all of the studies with prayer, or wait until you have reached a certain level of understanding with the students. Praying with the students will show your dependence on God for all things, as well as your spiritual understanding. At the end of each study, you could pray for the application of what has been studied in each person's life as well as for personal needs of people in the group.
8. In a cross-cultural Bible study, you will generally not be able to cover the same amount of prepared material as in a group of people from the same culture. A major obstacle is clear communication and full understanding of one another. Often, people may have very different ideas in mind when they use the same words. This is when understanding each other's culture and worldview is important. How much material you can cover in a study depends on several factors: how thoroughly you discuss the issues, the English level of the students, and whether you summarize and discuss what the students have already read on their own or what has been read aloud in the group. If a discussion goes off on a tangent, the leader must bring it back to the lesson at hand. You may have to take two meetings to cover a prepared lesson if your available time is short. In picking up where you left off from the previous week, review briefly what you covered previously, to get everyone thinking together. Avoid going beyond the prearranged stopping time, even if the discussion is good, as that may discourage them from taking the time to meet again the following week.
9. Try to make the topics and questions used in your studies relevant to where the Muslims are in their stage of life, religious development, and personal struggles. Show how the gospel is relevant to all of life.

Suggested Lesson Topics:

- Introduction to the *Taurat*, *Zabur*, and *Injil* (the Bible)
- Allah's condescension
- Geneology from Adam to Yesua el-Masih
- Who is Allah (God)?
- What does Allah require of us?
- Human nature and sin
- The response of Allah to sin (judgment)
- Yesua el-Masih and the kingdom of Allah
- The authority of Yesua el-Masih
- The mission of Yesua el-Masih
- The cross of Yesua el-Masih
    - Ibrahimic sacrifice of his son as a type (*Eid al-Adha*)
    - Substitution
    - Atonement
    - Victory
- New life and the new *shahada*

Some have found that a chronological approach to presenting Bible themes is effective. This helps the Muslim to understand the flow of redemptive history, which is lacking in the Qur'an.

The Discipleship of New Believers

For most Muslims, coming to faith in Christ is a process. Therefore, it may not always be clear at what point they have made a commitment to following Christ. They will continue to have many questions that they need answered about the faith. Don't be quick to tell others about their conversion. Allow new believers to tell their friends when they are ready to do so. A lot of time will need to be invested in discipling new believers. For the most part, this should initially be done one-on-one.

Muslims who make a commitment to Christ need to be discipled in four key areas: doctrine, devotion, ministry, and character. Although new converts will have learned some doctrine during the evangelism process, it is important that they become well grounded in the biblical doctrine of God, Christ, the Holy Spirit, man, grace, and the Scriptures. They will still have many Islamic ideas in these areas that need correction. Muslims come from a belief system of good works, which gives them no assurance of salvation. At the beginning of the discipling process, they need to have assurance of their salvation, such as is taught in 1 John.

In addition, they need to be taught the means of grace, including the basic devotional practices of Bible reading, Bible study, Bible memorization, prayer, fellowship, and participation in the sacraments of baptism and the Lord's Supper. A good place to start, in reading the Bible together, is with the gospel of Luke, followed by Acts.

Incorporation into a body of believers organized as a church will be important for regular feeding on the Word, encouragement in the faith, and equipping for ministry. At the same time, new believers should be encouraged to keep their ties with their family and community in order to be a witness of salt and light to them. They should also be encouraged to reach out to others with the good news. Instruction on how to give one's testimony that focuses on the Lord will equip them for outreach to others. Finally, there needs to be preparation for spiritual warfare and personal attacks for converting from Islam. This would involve teaching on our equipment for spiritual battle and having a close network of supportive relationships.

Character development comes not only through teaching, but in an accountable mentoring relationship. The convert needs to see how you live in a variety of contexts, such as in the home, playing soccer, on the job, and in ministering. Model the Christian life by doing things together. Discussing issues will be an important part of the process. A common problem among many new believers is a lack of trust between them and other believers. This inhibits unity, community, and growth. Teaching and modeling in this area will be important.

Foreign-born converts should be encouraged to read and memorize Scripture in their mother tongue, so that they can witness to their family and friends from their home country. Otherwise, they will become isolated from believers from their home country and feel uncomfortable when fellowshipping, praying, or witnessing in their native language. If they are unfamiliar with Christian vocabulary in their native language, others will think that when they became Christians, they were actually being Westernized or Americanized.[2]

Contextualized Discipleship

As a believer with a Muslim background is discipled, it will be helpful for him or her to have a new Christian perspective on common Islamic themes and concepts. Conveying Christian concepts in a way that communicates most effectively to Muslims will be very meaningful and life affecting. This process, called contextualization, is the interaction of the text of Scripture with a particular human context. Jesus' incarnation is the ultimate paradigm of contextualization; in his life and teaching, he modeled love for one's neighbor and discipling of the nations. Contextualizing the gospel means addressing the issues and concerns of your audience in the most relevant way possible from God's perspective as seen in Scripture. The apostle Paul addressed the people in the synagogue at Pisidian Antioch, a Jewish audience (Acts 13:16–41), differently than those at the Areopagus in Athens, a Greek audience (Acts 17:22–31). The context will bring questions to the text of Scripture (e.g., Did Jesus really die on the cross?), which the text will address with new questions (e.g., Why did Jesus have to die for our salvation to be accomplished?). But the movement of the interaction will always have to go from the text, which is authoritative, to the context, which is relative and changing. The illumination of the Holy Spirit in the context of the church will lead believers in the process of contextualizing theology and practice. Proper use of contextualization will keep believers from the dangers of syncretism in theology, practices, and ethics. The dialogical interaction of Scripture text with cultural context will condemn all forms of idolatry and will purify, transform, and put under Christ's lordship everything in culture that is compatible with God's law.[3]

The five pillars of Islam are the religious obligations of every Muslim. Here are some contextualized Christian alternatives from the Scriptures. We suggest looking up the definitions of the Arabic terms in the glossary of Islamic terms at the back of the book.

Shahada: A new shahada for the new believer may be found in Jesus' prayer: "Now this is eternal life: that they may know you, the only true God, and Jesus Christ, whom you have sent" (John 17:3). Just as the shahada is a summary of Islam, so this verse is a summary of the gospel. To know God is to be called, justified, forgiven, received, and adopted through Jesus Christ, who came to reveal the Father. In him is eternal life.

Salat: "Pray continually" (1 Thess. 5:17).

"Devote yourselves to prayer, being watchful and thankful" (Col. 4:2).

"Then Jesus told his disciples a parable to show them that they should always pray and not give up" (Luke 18:1).

"And when you pray, do not be like the hypocrites, for they love to pray standing in the synagogues and on the street corners to be seen by men. I tell you the truth, they have received their reward in full. But when you pray, go into your room, close the door and pray to your Father, who is unseen. Then your Father, who sees what is done in secret, will reward you" (Matt. 6:5–6).

Zakat: "On the first day of every week, each one of you should set aside a sum of money in keeping with his income" (1 Cor. 16:2).

"Each man should give what he has decided in his heart to give, not reluctantly or under compulsion, for God loves a cheerful giver" (2 Cor. 9:7).

Ramadan: "When you fast, do not look somber as the hypocrites do, for they disfigure their faces to show men they are fasting. I tell you the truth, they have received their reward in full. But when you fast, put oil on your head and wash your face, so that it will not be obvious to men that you are fasting, but only to your Father, who is unseen; and your Father, who sees what is done in secret, will reward you" (Matt. 6:16–18).

Hajj: "I rejoiced with those who said to me, 'Let us go to the house of the LORD' " (Ps. 122:1). The need to go up to the Temple for sacrifice is no longer necessary, having been fulfilled in Christ. As Christians, we do not make pilgrimages to any holy place, but our whole life is a pilgrimage until we reach our heavenly home. Abraham's life of living in tents in the Promised Land was a type of this Christian pilgrimage (Heb. 11:8–10).

God is everywhere, and he may be worshiped anywhere:

> "This is what the LORD says:
> 'Heaven is my throne, and the earth is my footstool.
> Where is the house you will build for me?
> Where will my resting place be?
> Has not my hand made all these things,
> and so they came into being?' declares the LORD." (Isa. 66:1–2)

Jesus declared, "Believe me, woman, a time is coming when you will worship the Father neither on this mountain nor in Jerusalem. . . . Yet a time is coming and has now come when the true worshipers will worship the Father in spirit and truth, for they are the kind of worshipers the Father seeks (John 4:21, 23).

Numerous other common Islamic ideas have Christian alternatives or points of identification.

Da'wah: "Therefore go and make disciples of all nations, baptizing them in the name of the Father and of the Son and of the

Holy Spirit, and teaching them to obey everything I have commanded you. And surely I am with you always, to the very end of the age" (Matt. 28:19–20).

"But you will receive power when the Holy Spirit comes on you; and you will be my witnesses in Jerusalem, and in all Judea and Samaria, and to the ends of the earth" (Acts 1:8).

Hadith: We have the life and the testimony of faith of the faithful witnesses to the Lord who went before us (Heb. 11). "Therefore, since we are surrounded by such a great cloud of witnesses, let us throw off everything that hinders and the sin that so easily entangles, and let us run with perseverance the race marked out for us" (Heb. 12:1).

Halal: " 'Don't you see that nothing that enters a man from the outside can make him "unclean"? For it doesn't go into his heart but into his stomach, and then out of his body.' (In saying this, Jesus declared all foods 'clean.')

"He went on: 'What comes out of a man is what makes him "unclean" ' " (Mark 7:18–20).

"They forbid people to marry and order them to abstain from certain foods, which God created to be received with thanksgiving by those who believe and who know the truth. For everything God created is good, and nothing is to be rejected if it is received with thanksgiving, because it is consecrated by the word of God and prayer" (1 Tim. 4:3–5).

"Therefore do not let anyone judge you by what you eat or drink, or with regard to a religious festival, a New Moon celebration or a Sabbath day. These are a shadow of the things that were to come; the reality, however, is found in Christ" (Col. 2:16–17).

Haram: "Dear friends, I urge you, as aliens and strangers in the world, to abstain from sinful desires, which war against your soul" (1 Peter 2:11).

"Flee the evil desires of youth, and pursue righteousness, faith, love and peace, along with those who call on the Lord out of a pure heart" (2 Tim. 2:22).

Jihad: "Finally, be strong in the Lord and in his mighty power. Put on the full armor of God so that you can take your stand against the devil's schemes. For our struggle is not against flesh and blood, but against the rulers, against the authorities, against the powers of this dark world and against the spiritual forces of evil in the heavenly realms" (Eph. 6:10–12).

Ka'aba: "You also, like living stones, are being built into a spiritual house to be a holy priesthood, offering spiritual sacrifices acceptable to God through Jesus Christ. For in Scripture it says: 'See, I lay a stone in Zion, a chosen and precious cornerstone, and the one who trusts in him will never be put to shame'" (1 Peter 2:5–6).

"Consequently, you are no longer foreigners and aliens, but fellow citizens with God's people and members of God's household, built on the foundation of the apostles and prophets, with Christ Jesus himself as the chief cornerstone. In him the whole building is joined together and rises to become a holy temple in the Lord. And in him you too are being built together to become a dwelling in which God lives by his Spirit" (Eph. 2:19–22).

Khalifah: After God created man and woman in his own image, he gave them a responsibility. "God blessed them and said to them, 'Be fruitful and increase in number; fill the earth and subdue it. Rule over the fish of the sea and the birds of the air and over every living creature that moves on the ground' " (Gen. 1:28).

Jesus said, "From everyone who has been given much, much will be demanded; and from the one who has been entrusted with much, much more will be asked" (Luke 12:48).

In Jesus' parable of the ten minas, we see the responsibility that we have to make good use of that with which we have been entrusted: "So he called ten of his servants and gave them ten minas.

'Put this money to work,' he said, 'until I come back'" (Luke 19:13).

"We are therefore Christ's ambassadors, as though God were making his appeal through us" (2 Cor. 5:20).

Qibla: We pray in this direction: "Let us fix our eyes on Jesus, the author and perfecter of our faith, who for the joy set before him endured the cross, scorning its shame, and sat down at the right hand of the throne of God" (Heb. 12:2).

Shaheed: "If I give all I possess to the poor and surrender my body to the flames, but have not love, I gain nothing" (1 Cor. 13:3).

"When he [the Lamb] opened the fifth seal, I saw under the altar the souls of those who had been slain because of the word of God and the testimony they had maintained" (Rev. 6:9).

Shari'a: "A new command I give you: Love one another. As I have loved you, so you must love one another" (John 13:34).

"For sin shall not be your master, because you are not under law, but under grace" (Rom. 6:14).

"For what the law was powerless to do in that it was weakened by the sinful nature, God did by sending his own Son in the likeness of sinful man to be a sin offering. And so he condemned sin in sinful man, in order that the righteous requirements of the law might be fully met in us, who do not live according to the sinful nature but according to the Spirit" (Rom. 8:3–4).

> "Blessed are they whose ways are blameless,
> who walk according to the law of the LORD. . . .
> "Great peace have they who love your law,
> and nothing can make them stumble" (Ps. 119:1, 165).

Shirk: "'I tell you the truth, all the sins and blasphemies of men will be forgiven them. But whoever blasphemes against the Holy Spirit will never be forgiven; he is guilty of an eternal sin.'

"He [Jesus] said this because they were saying, 'He has an evil spirit' " (Mark 3:28–30).

Umma: Jesus replied to Peter, "And I tell you that you are Peter, and on this rock I will build my church, and the gates of Hades will not overcome it" (Matt. 16:18).

"This mystery is that through the gospel the Gentiles are heirs together with Israel, members together of one body, and sharers together in the promise in Christ Jesus" (Eph. 3:6).

"For this reason I kneel before the Father, from whom his whole family in heaven and on earth derives its name" (Eph. 3:14–15).

"There is one body and one Spirit—just as you were called to one hope when you were called—one Lord, one faith, one baptism; one God and Father of all, who is over all and through all and in all" (Eph. 4:4–6).

"There is neither Jew nor Greek, slave nor free, male nor female, for you are all one in Christ Jesus" (Gal. 3:28).

Wudu: "Christ loved the church and gave himself up for her to make her holy, cleansing her by the washing with water through the word, and to present her to himself as a radiant church, without stain or wrinkle or any other blemish, but holy and blameless" (Eph. 5:25–27).

"Again Jesus called the crowd to him and said, 'Listen to me, everyone, and understand this. Nothing outside a man can make him "unclean" by going into him. Rather, it is what comes out of a man that makes him "unclean" ' " (Mark 7:14–15).

> "Create in me a pure heart, O God,
> and renew a steadfast spirit within me" (Ps. 51:10).

"In a large house there are articles not only of gold and silver, but also of wood and clay; some are for noble purposes and some for ignoble. If a man cleanses himself from the latter, he will be an instrument for noble purposes, made holy, useful to the Master and prepared to do any good work" (2 Tim. 2:20–21).

"[God] saved us through the washing of rebirth and renewal by the Holy Spirit, whom he poured out on us generously through Jesus Christ our Savior" (Titus 3:5–6).

Zamzam: "Then God opened her [Hagar's] eyes and she saw a well of water. So she went and filled the skin with water and gave the boy a drink" (Gen. 21:19).

"With joy you will draw water from the wells of salvation" (Isa. 12:3).

"Jesus answered, 'Everyone who drinks this water will be thirsty again, but whoever drinks the water I give him will never thirst. Indeed, the water I give him will become in him a spring of water welling up to eternal life' " (John 4:13–14).

For Reflection/Action

1. After developing a friendship with a Muslim in your area, invite him to study the Bible with you.
2. What are the most important biblical themes that you should present to a Muslim when giving him the gospel?
3. How can those themes be presented in a culturally sensitive, contextualized way?
4. Write your own Bible studies for a Muslim group, being particularly sensitive to their worldview and needs. This could vary somewhat with different groups of Muslims, in accordance with their sect and ethnic background.
4. Reflect on the approach to Bible study taken in appendix 2.

CHAPTER FOURTEEN

Where Do We Go from Here?

An Open Door of Opportunity

The North American evangelical church needs to wake up to the mission field around us. With the freedom that we enjoy in North America, we have a great privilege to bring the gospel to Muslims with great openness and little need for fear. The freedom we enjoy is one of the very reasons why millions of Muslim immigrants have come to North America. This massive migration has brought the Muslim mission field to the doorstep of the Western church. God is calling the Western church to reach out to our new Muslim neighbors aggressively and lovingly. God has graciously given us an open door for ministry; let us not lose our opportunity.

Ministry to Muslims in North America is different from such ministry in the Middle East, North Africa, and other predominately Islamic areas in several respects. First, we have the freedom here to tell Muslims the whole gospel without any harassment. We can speak freely and openly. There are no secret police to worry about. Secondly, Muslims are more open here. They are living away from many of the societal and family constraints that would make investigating Christianity a fearful proposition. Also, for immigrants or students, the change in environment makes them open to new ideas. Thirdly, they are willing to meet with you, come to Christian activities, and engage in dialogue. This opportunity for ministry should not be missed by the North American church. This is the right place for Muslim missions.

Vision and Motivation

We must share our experience with Muslims with our churches. We need to encourage them, motivating them to reach out to their Muslim neighbors and to nearby mosques with the gospel.

In order to carry out and maintain effective Muslim evangelism, it is necessary to form interchurch and/or individual church teams. Such teams make the Christian witness more effective, because they demonstrate community, support, and love. Such a team should meet at least monthly to maintain interest and accountability.

The Changing Mission Field

We need a balance between sending missionaries overseas and having home missionaries reach the world that has come to us. Many Christians still think that missions work is just for overseas. North America is a very large mission field. Mission work among Muslims in North America is often more effective than work among them overseas. We are beginning to see a greater vision for reaching Muslims here as more and more mission agencies are assigning workers to minister to the immigrants in North America. Generally they are targeting immigrant and student groups from countries where they have traditionally done missions work. The African-American Muslim community is still largely neglected. African-American churches in particular need to address the concerns of the black community, especially of the young men. They need to have a vision for reaching out to the Muslim community and learn how to answer their arguments with knowledge and persistent love. Carl Ellis says, "According to our experience, American Muslim converts who come to Christ have a keen sensitivity to the issues and concerns which led their former cohorts to reject Christianity and embrace Islam. They also have unique insights into where Islam falls short. If we equip them to address these concerns from a biblical perspective, they would be ideally suited to reach Muslims with the gospel."[1]

Training in Islamics

Training in Islamics is essential for effective evangelism to Muslims. Often well-meaning Christians seriously hurt their own witness, as well as that of others, by unintentional (and unrecognized) gaffes. However, when receiving training in Islamics, one must not forget the ultimate goal. Some people initially have a heart for winning Muslims to Christ, but then get so wrapped up in studying Islam, that they forget that they are to be ambassadors of Christ.

Bible schools and seminaries need to include Islamics as part of their curriculum. They should have at least one course in Islamic theology and history and another on the methodology of Muslim outreach. There is a need to establish institutes of Islamic studies from a Christian perspective. A few schools that have M.A. programs in Islamic studies are Columbia International University in Columbia, South Carolina; Fuller Theological Seminary, School of World Mission in Pasadena, California; Hartford Seminary Foundation in Hartford, Connecticut; and Luther Seminary in Minneapolis, Minnesota. Concordia Theological Seminary in Fort Wayne, Indiana, offers an emphasis on Islam in its missions concentration. Both Southwestern and Southeastern Baptist Theological Seminaries have missions and world religions professors with expertise in Islam. A few other seminaries have adjunct professors who offer courses on Islam, such as New Geneva Seminary in Colorado Springs. Church Without Walls has established the Biblical Institute for Islamic Studies (BIIS) in Philadelphia, Pennsylvania, which has attracted both laypeople and missionary candidates. Several mission agencies have also established training programs in

Muslim evangelism, such as Arab World Ministries (Philadelphia), International Missions, Inc. (New York City), and the Assemblies of God (Springfield, Missouri).

Literature and Media

There is a great need for literature and media that clearly present the gospel to Muslims in an appropriate context. Much that is written for a Western audience and translated into other languages is not culturally appropriate. There is also a great need for good Christian literature that responds to Muslim misunderstanding of the Bible. We need to read some of their literature, which has distorted the biblical truth for their own ends. For example, Jamal Badawi of the Islamic Information Foundation in Canada has written a "Jesus Seminar," which discusses Jesus in the Qur'an and Jesus in the Bible. His use of the Bible is particularly designed to support the false teachings of the Qur'an. Therefore, we need joint efforts to make clear the biblical Jesus in his full majesty and divinity, as he revealed himself to be. Then we need to respond by producing literature that refutes their misunderstanding of the Scriptures and correctly puts forth the truth of the gospel.

House Churches

Finally, house churches need to be planted among Muslim converts. This would fit the needs and cultural context for most of them. We have discovered eight reasons why house churches are effective among Muslim converts:

1. Before their conversion, the Muslim converts may have belonged to a mosque that met in a home. Therefore, they are familiar with using the home for the worship of God.
2. House churches help new converts feel more comfortable and secure in coming out of Islam. Traditional churches

have many things that are foreign to them: pews, art with pictures of people, wearing shoes, crossing one's legs, men and women sitting together, Western dress, organizational structure, and the like. Additionally, many church members may be insensitive to the culture and background of converts from Islam.

3. House churches encourage warm fellowship. This creates a sense of community among new converts that makes up for the loss of the Islamic community and Muslim family members, from whom they are now separated. House churches help new converts to develop new friendships and communities. House churches also provide them with the most encouraging setting for establishing true Christian community. Such community does not exist in Islam.
4. House churches make ideal centers from which converts can reach out to their Muslim friends. A Muslim will be more likely to visit a home than a church building.
5. House churches may be used as centers for training in ministry. They can become a school, a hospital, and a factory to train its people to become more educated, healthy, and productive.
6. In house churches, new converts discover and practice their gifts as they participate in ministry and a variety of activities, since worship in house churches is led by laypeople (i.e., the converts from Islam).
7. A house church made up of former Muslims would probably be quicker to meet members' felt needs than if the new believers were incorporated into existing churches.
8. The house church is the ideal place for the children of converts to grow up in the fear and admonition of the Lord as covenant children.

Our ministry of having Meetings for Better Understanding over a three-year period in a major African-American mosque in a large American city led to thirty-four families leaving the mosque and forming house churches in their homes. It fits the urban setting.

Church planters in the Middle East have found that a statement of faith, such as the Westminster Confession of Faith, helps Muslim converts and seekers to see that the group knows what it stands for. They also appreciate formality in worship, with an order of worship and reverence. These things help them understand that the church is not a group that has subversive intentions.

The Challenge

May the God of the Bible open our minds to accept these proposals and to remember that King Jesus is coming again and that Muslims are dying without hope, apart from Christ (Eph. 2:12).

We would like to leave you with the following challenge: "There is no resource the local North American Church lacks to reach Muslims for Christ. Nothing except the long-term commitment and dedication. . . ."[2] Are you willing to make such a commitment to see the church established in the midst of the Muslim community?

My Commitment to Muslim Ministry

In order to maintain one's motivation, to have prayer support, and to multiply the ministry through the diversity of gifts working together as a body, it is important to team up with others. We call these teams that focus on reaching Muslims "Bridge Teams." Such teams have been organized in cities across the U.S. Usually they meet on a monthly basis for prayer, sharing, training, and planning.

One way to encourage the "Bridge Team" to carry on the ministry is to have an annual weekend retreat. The goals of such a retreat would be to renew the vision for ministry, share ideas and experiences, pray, worship, learn from God's Word, and fellowship with like-minded believers. Reports of God's work in the lives of

Muslims through the ministry can be of great encouragement. Such a retreat can have a unifying effect on the team, particularly when team members come from a variety of churches and ministries. We invite your prayerful participation in joining or forming a team, as indicated below. Making a commitment will encourage you to follow through on your desire.

In response to God, and with an attitude of prayer, I commit myself to one year of ministry with the Bridge Team in order to reach Muslims in our area. This commitment includes:

- Monthly Bridge Team meetings
- Meetings for Better Understanding with a local mosque(s)
- One-on-one relationships with Muslims through friendships and hospitality
- Small group Bible/Qur'an studies (as they emerge out of our relationships)

Name ________________________________

Date _________________________________

For Reflection/Action

1. What part will you play in reaching Muslims with the gospel: praying, giving, witnessing, writing, leading Bible studies, training others, building a vision, planting churches?
2. What further steps do you need to take to prepare yourself for effective ministry to Muslims?

APPENDIX ONE

The Story of a Muslim Immigrant

By S. Adam[1]

Step into the shoes of a Muslim.
Try to hear through his ears.
To see through his eyes.
To feel with his heart.

I'm a Muslim. I live in your city of Chicago. But Chicago, with its rush hour traffic, I-94, cold winter winds, and unsmiling faces, is a long way from where my heart is.

I was born in a village in the beautiful mountains of my country, far away. My mother bore me at home. Into my tiny ear were whispered the words of our creed—"There is no god but Allah, and Muhammad is the prophet of Allah."

My family was a haven of human warmth and closeness. Mother loved all eight of us children so tenderly. She slaved day and night to keep food in our mouths and clothes on our backs. We boys were given special treatment—boys are special. Girls are nothing but trouble. Our sisters had to work hard alongside of Mom, with cooking, housework, washing clothes, and dishes.

Father was quite a bit older than mom. He spent a lot of time away from home—at work and with his friends. He loved to go to the mosque and talk about religion with the other men who would gather there. Sometimes we boys got to go with him, especially on Friday, when all the males of the village turned out for the Friday sermon and prayers. Everyone talked about religion all the time. God was very much a part of our lives.

At an early age, I learned to say my prayers. Five times a day. In my prayers, every muscle of my body joined soul and mind in the worship and praise of God.

Then it was fasting. How I longed to join the grown-ups in this spiritual discipline of fasting. No food and no water from before sunrise to sunset—for a whole month. I wanted to prove I could do it. The first time I tried, I got sick. But I soon was able to join the community in this expression of submission to the will of God. What a joy it was to do it together! What celebrations took place every night at the break of the fast! Ah, those were the days!

I took great pride in my religion. Ours was the true religion. I could feel it in my bones. We believed and walked in submission to the one true God. We believed in all of God's prophets: Adam, Noah, Abraham, Moses, David, Jesus, Muhammad. They had all been given the same message: Turn from your sins and believe in the one true God. It puzzled me that Christians didn't want to accept God's final prophet. Was it because he was an Arab? Didn't they know what a wonderful man he was? He was my one and only hero. He was the world's greatest leader. Out of the deserts of Arabia arose a mighty and glorious nation with Muhammad at its head. No person in history ever excelled or even equaled him.

I yearned to make the pilgrimage to Muhammad's hometown, Mecca, and relive the stories that surrounded his life. In Mecca, Muslims from every country on earth gathered as brothers, equal before God Almighty. No religious elite, no priesthood. As servants, we bowed together in worship before our God.

We shook our heads in sadness as we thought of those who had strayed from the truth, like Christians, who had elevated a mere man and placed him alongside God as an object of worship. The prophet Jesus must have been grieved to see people doing that. And then they worshiped Mary, his mother, as well. God forgive them!

We were taught the names of the holy books that God had sent to mankind: the Torah given to Moses, the Psalms to David, the Gospel to Jesus, and the Qur'an to Muhammad. Of course, the Qur'an, being the final revelation, was the complete and perfect word of God. The other books were no longer trustworthy, as Jews and Christians had tampered with them and changed them.

I loved the Qur'an. The musical tones as it was chanted thrilled my soul. Beautiful. Sublime. The music of heaven. I memorized many chapters from the Qur'an and dreamed of being amongst those who had memorized the whole of it.

Religious duty carried over into our home. We were poor, but we shared gladly the little we had. Royal hospitality was freely given to stranger and friend alike. A feast complete with meat that we could ill afford was spread before our guests time and time again. Our home was a beehive of activity. It seemed that someone was always coming or going.

Our concept of an open home was part of the sense of community that bound our village together. It wasn't "me and you," but "us." Nor was it "each man for himself," but "each for the other." It was like one big, happy family. Sure, there were a few troublemakers, but God had put them there to test us.

Honoring our parents was something we were careful to do. We were also careful to see that we didn't bring shame or dishonor on our family name. We boys watched over our sisters like hawks. They weren't about to bring dishonor on us all by any hint of contact with men. I beat my sister once for getting out of line.

I enjoyed my school days, for the most part. It wasn't too difficult, because the community concept of working together carried over into the education system. Homework and exams were community projects! Teachers turned a blind eye as we worked together at getting the right answers on our exams. Sometimes they joined in! So, with little difficulty, I passed my final exams, and then I was off to the big city for the university.

Well, I didn't like it. The big city, that is. The noise, the crowds, the rush. Technology, industrialization, computers, materialism. My people were turning into machines. They were becoming dehumanized. The Western imperialists and colonists were no longer present in person, but forces far more powerful and subtle from the materialistic West were taking over our country and slowly destroying us. We needed to turn from the worship of this way of life and return to God!

Then there was the TV. With satellite dishes, the evil West invaded our living rooms, bringing sex, violence, sensational news broadcasts, and endless commercials urging us to buy, buy, buy! And I began to be influenced. I wanted pleasure. I wanted the house, the car, the video. I wanted to get ahead.

The prospects in my own country were absolutely nil. Economically, we were on the rocks. Unemployment was sky-high. Housing was impossible to find. There was no future. No hope.

Rumor had it that the U.S. was opening its doors to immigrants. So I made my decision. I'd try to immigrate to the U.S. After filling out forms, interviews with immigration officials, medical exams, and months and months of waiting, I finally got permission to immigrate. Then it was time to say good-bye to my family. My heart nearly broke as I held my aging father and mother tight. My mother wept uncontrollably. She feared for me, going to the corrupt West.

I left my village, trying to imprint on my heart forever the sights, the sounds, the smells. Would I ever return? And then I was off! America—here I come!

I flew into O'Hare International Airport. The sky was gray. Everything looked gray. It was February. It felt cold. Suddenly, my heart was seized with fear and dread. A strange country, cold, unwelcoming. Inside the airport, officials looked at my papers and stamped them. They had no smile for me. I was in America. Is this what I wanted? Had I made some terrible mistake?

The next months were rough. Very rough. Many a night I cried into my pillow. I hated it here. Everyone seemed so cold, so distant. I longed for a smile. A warm handshake. To share a cup of coffee with a friend. To laugh with someone. My heart ached for my family, my village, my country.

I thought my English was pretty good when I left my country, but I quickly discovered that I couldn't cope. People spoke too fast. They used words and expressions I couldn't understand. They were impatient with my attempts to communicate.

I felt like I was completely cut off from everyone around me. So alone. But I had no choice. I had burned my bridges behind me. My country didn't take kindly to anyone who chose to leave its shores and immigrate to another country. I couldn't go back. So I forced myself to put the past behind me. I'd find a job and settle down.

The months passed, and I gradually made a few friends—young men like me, who had left their countries to enter this strange, cold land. How we felt like outsiders. The American way was so foreign to us. So mechanical. So harsh. Human contact was minimal. My neighbors never smiled at me or greeted me. Everyone seemed sealed into their own little world. At the stores and in the offices, people seemed to snap or sneer at me. There was no human warmth. So much was self-service: bank machines, car washes, gas stations. People didn't need people anymore in this land.

The TV was unbelievable! At first I was fascinated. So many channels! But then I began to get sick of the constant diet of violence, cheap sex, and silly game shows. The West itself seemed sick. I read the reports of child molesters, murder, rape. Drugs, abortions, alcohol, and suicides were rampant among young people. In my country, alcohol was forbidden by the religion. Drugs, abortions, and suicides were almost unheard of.

God be praised! Islam had preserved my country from moral bankruptcy. If only salvation through my religion could come to the West. I had heard snatches of religious talk in the West. A couple of times, I watched some TV evangelists, but they reminded me of the TV game show hosts I'd seen.

Once, when I was out on the street, someone shoved a piece of paper at me that was something from a book called Romans. It didn't make too much sense.

But, out of curiosity, I decided to visit a church one Sunday. I arrived early and stood at the side as people walked in. No one removed his shoes at the door. Didn't they consider this a holy place? Most of the women looked like they were trying to enter a Miss America pageant. They laughed and carried on in a most immodest way. And they even seated themselves with the men! The young people that arrived at the church door looked like they wanted to be a million miles away from there.

No one took any notice of me, and those who glanced my way seemed cold and distant. There was a coldness about the whole place. During the service, everyone seemed bored. Some were whispering and joking around. A few were even chewing gum. These people didn't seem to know the God I knew. A God of power and might. The God of the Day of Judgment. The Supreme and Eternal, Merciful and Compassionate, Creator and Provider. Truly these Christians had strayed far from the true path.

After the church service, I rushed out of that place and headed to the mosque at Elston and Pulaski Avenues. Inside I found peace and quiet. I greeted the older and younger men sitting there. Some were bowing in prayer. I washed carefully—my hands, my feet, my face. I began to feel clean, inside and out. I began to say my prayers. My heart was filled with gratitude that I was a Muslim. I felt so bound to all the ancient prophets and especially to the prophet of the vast deserts of Arabia. I felt bound to the millions of people who bowed with me in saying the same prayers. I felt bound to the Creator of the universe. Yes, I was glad to be a Muslim.

But deep within I felt a stirring . . . just what had the preacher meant in church when he spoke of the love that Jesus Christ alone gives? Did such love really exist? I guess I had yet to see it in this sad, cold land.

For Reflection/Action

1. If you met this Muslim, how would you reach out to him? What were some of the felt needs of this Muslim immigrant?

2. How might you present your faith to him?
3. What opportunity was missed by those in the church that he visited? What could have been done differently?
4. How does this story lead you to pray for the church? For Muslims in North America?

APPENDIX TWO

A Bible Study Case Study

Bruce McDowell's Bible Study with Rahman

Rahman, a Muslim from Indonesia, was a Ph.D. student in comparative religion at a large university and president of its chapter of the Muslim Student Association.

Over several years, Rahman had attended various activities of the international student ministry that I (Bruce McDowell) was directing, including small group Bible studies, conferences, retreats, films, and international dinners. So we had already been friends for a couple of years before we began a Bible study together. Our meetings took place in his apartment on the university campus. We were only able to cover the introduction and first chapter (of nine) of my Bible study series, because of extensive discussions on many tangents.

To initiate the Bible studies, I met with Rahman for lunch to renew our friendship. During our lunch conversation, we discussed a number of religious subjects, such as predestination, Augustine, and Schleiermacher. This gave me the opportunity to outline the five points of Calvinism. After lunch I asked him if he would be interested in meeting weekly to study the Bible, using some studies that I had prepared. He agreed, saying that it would be a useful form of religious dialogue.

First Bible Study: January 9

On January 9, 1990, we held our first meeting for Bible study. We talked for almost three hours. After a half hour of small talk, we began our study. Going through the introduction brought many questions from Rahman. We discussed the books of the Bible and its major divisions, the names of God in Hebrew, the forms of writing used in the Bible, how we can have a personal relationship with God, and the New Testament manuscripts.

In the first study, Rahman seemed to have difficulty understanding God as a spirit, as taught in John 4:24. This led to an extensive discussion of the difference between men and animals, with men being the pinnacle of God's creation. Rahman was familiar with terms like *omniscient* and *omnipresent*, as they are described in Psalm 139. At this point, our discussion got sidetracked on the subject of God's revelation to all people. He was asking questions like "What is the Word of God?" "Don't people from other religions have the word of God in their scriptures?" "How can a God whose major characteristic is mercy and compassion condemn millions of people who have never had the Bible?" It appeared that much of Rahman's thinking had been influenced by the teaching given at the university's religion department. Its approach was universalistic and looked for a convergence of all religions. Rahman also gave indications that he believed that there was evolutionary progress in religion. It seems that he had been reading from John Hick, *God Has Many Names*, as he mentioned that book at one point in our conversation. Of course, this kind of thinking departs in some ways from orthodox Islam. We then discussed some of the differences between orthodox Christianity and cults coming out of it, like Mormonism and Jehovah's Witnesses. We concluded our conversation by looking at Philippians 2:1–11, where the Bible says that every knee shall bow and every tongue confess that Jesus Christ is Lord.

Second Bible Study: January 23, 1990

This time we had only one and a quarter hours together. Our discussion focused on five verses from Proverbs (16:4, 9; 19:21; 21:30, 31). We discussed at length the sovereignty, foreknowledge, and foreordination of God. This led into much discussion of the problem of evil, its source, God's control over it, and our responsibility in the face of it. I recounted some of the history of Israel, in which God used the Assyrians and Babylonians to punish the Israelites for their disobedience. I also gave the example of God hardening the heart of Pharaoh in order to reveal his power by the plagues brought on the Egyptians. Although God was in control, I said, Pharaoh and the Egyptians were responsible for their actions and their response to God. Our discussion ended with my sharing of Luke 13:1–5 with Rahman. This passage deals with Jesus' response to calamity and how we must repent or all likewise perish.

Third Bible Study: January 29, 1990

The week before, I noticed that Rahman seemed very interested in the details of the history of Israel. So this week I brought with me a time line of Old Testament history from the front of a Bible. So for most of our time together, we discussed the history of Israel. He found it very enlightening. Old Testament prophets and people are mentioned in the Qur'an, but not in any kind of historical context. We talked a bit about Israel taking over the land of Canaan and who the people were who lived there at the time. Rahman was very interested in what land was included in Israel. Eventually our discussion moved to the JEDP hypothesis[1] and my belief in the Mosaic authorship of the Pentateuch. (This diversion was needed because of the liberal perspective he was being taught in his university courses.) From there we discussed Noah, his three sons, and the curse on Ham. We ended by reading through passages in Genesis 16, 17, and 21 on the life of Ishmael. This discussion included mention of the relationship between Ishmael and Isaac and the covenant of God with Abraham. Unfortunately, time did not allow me to discuss this important topic in much depth. Again, in reading the history of Ishmael, Rahman was very interested in the names of places mentioned, and he was trying to figure out if they corresponded with familiar places in Islamic tradition. This week we did not get into the prepared Bible study series.

Fourth Bible Study: February 6, 1990

We began this week by discussing the *hajj* (pilgrimage) to Mecca, as I looked through a book of Rahman's photographs of it. I asked him about its significance and the significance of the black rock in the Ka'aba, which people either kiss or touch. He mentioned that he was thinking of going on the *hajj* sometime from the U.S., since it was cheaper to travel to Mecca from the U.S. than from Indonesia.[2]

After half an hour, we began our two-hour study, beginning with Isaiah 55:8–9, including Isaiah 6:3 and Habakkuk 1:13, and ending with Leviticus 11:44. The Isaiah 55 passage describes the transcendence of God. We discussed how God's thoughts and ways are not like ours. When we began studying the character of God, some new concepts were introduced to Rahman. First John 1:5 describes God as "light," which is a term commonly used by Muslims. However, we understand "light" to include purity, holiness, and truth, which Rahman apparently did not. Next, 1 Timothy 6:15b–16 was a difficult passage to explain. What is meant by God living "in unapproachable light, whom no one has seen or can see"? I described God's holiness and hatred for our sin. Rahman then asked about Moses having seen God. I replied that anthropomorphic language is used to describe what occurred on Mount Sinai, and that God did not fully reveal himself to Moses; God hid Moses with his hand and showed Moses his back. When Moses returned from Mount Sinai, his face shone so that he had to wear a veil. The really difficult part came when Rahman asked how this verse related to our understanding of Jesus. I described the two natures of Christ and how Jesus identified himself with the Father in his words, works, and ministry. At first, Rahman understood me to say that just the message of Jesus was from God. But I corrected that by saying that not only the message, but also Jesus' very presence, manifested the Father, as Jesus told Philip in John 14.

The holiness of God was discussed at some length. It was a new concept, which made Rahman ask about the source of evil. I told him that the Bible does not tell us the source of evil. We discussed the Fall and the power of Satan. Rahman came to the conclusion on his own that Christians believe there are two kingdoms, the kingdom of God and the kingdom of evil, which is very powerful. I explained the Christian's fight against the power of Satan, as described in Ephesians 6, which portrays the Christian in complete armor. He found this interesting. Also, the idea that we are to be holy, as God is holy, was new to him. I described how the Israelites were to be separate from the pagan idol worshipers in the nations around them. This again raised the question of the nations that did not have the revelation that was given to Israel. I described the commandments of God to Israel to show love and concern for the alien, and pointed out that many aliens from the surrounding nations became worshipers of the true God. This led us to discuss missions, God's concern for the lost, the mixture of colonialism and missions, and Christians' failure to carry out God's command to preach the gospel to all nations. When we returned to the point that God required us to be holy, I had an opportunity to describe his provision for our holiness through the sacrificial death of Jesus for our sins. We got back to the question of the source of evil. I described the life of Job and how it teaches us to trust the Lord fully, even though he may severely test us.

We ended our session together by looking at some Bible maps, which gave him a better understanding of Palestine in Old Testament and New Testament times. This was to follow up on our discussions from the previous week.

Fifth Bible Study: February 13, 1990

In looking at Deuteronomy 4:23–24, we discussed the meaning of covenant. This was new material for Rahman. The passage goes on to mention idols. I showed him in Exodus 20 the commandment not to make or worship any idols. Our discussion included statues in churches and the crucifix. The statement that the Lord is "a consuming fire, a jealous God" was difficult for Rahman to accept. He had trouble reconciling that with God's mercy. God's jealousy also seemed contradictory to his goodness and holiness. I explained how this is all part of God's character and consistent with his holiness. We then discussed God's punishment of, and hatred for, our sin and his provision of Jesus to take our sins as a substitutionary atonement. The idea of Jesus being our substitute did not seem reasonable to Rahman. I explained that we, being sinners, could not do anything to save ourselves. Only God could provide a way for our sin to be washed away.

The next verses, Proverbs 21:12; 17:15; 3:33; 2:7–8, made it clear that justice and righteousness are part of God's character. Therefore, his curse is on the wicked. The song of Moses in Deuteronomy 32:3–6 likewise emphasizes God's perfection, goodness, and justice. Again, the question of evil came up. What does God do to counteract the forces of evil? I said that God is doing something to address the problem of evil. He did that by the death and resurrection of Jesus. Jesus said that he came to destroy the work of the devil. That work to destroy evil is in process today and will be completed upon Christ's return. Rahman did not seem satisfied, considering that there is so much suffering and evil around us today. Even though there were some things that were difficult for Rahman to accept, we both thoroughly enjoyed our time together.

Sixth Bible Study: March 13, 1990

After not being able to meet for three weeks, due to Rahman being ill and a scheduling conflict, it was good to continue our studies. During our first hour together, we discussed a variety of things, including the resurrection of Christ. This came up because of something he had read about the religious leaders' response to Christ's resurrection. Our Bible study began with the section on God's condescension to man. Rahman asked what *condescension* meant. The passages I used here to speak of God as our Father (Deut. 32:6; James 1:17) did not seem to communicate the concept clearly enough. Rahman asked if this concept of God as Father was also found in Judaism. My reply was that, although the term *Father* is used in a couple of places in the Old Testament, the term was not familiar to the Jews, and they took offense at Jesus using it to call God "my Father." After reading the passages from 1 John on God's love for us, I tried to explain his close relationship to us. I explained that although in Islam it is said that Allah is closer than your jugular vein, in Christianity the closeness to God is of a different nature, like that of a father and a son. Rahman then thought of the type of closeness to Allah understood by the Sufis. Then I mentioned that we understand God to be not only transcendent, but also imminent. I still was not sure that Rahman understood the biblical concept of being close to God, but I mentioned that God's Holy Spirit lives within the Christian.

In looking at Isaiah 57:15, Rahman asked the meaning of "contrite" and "lowly in spirit." The latter phrase he initially understood as being a negative characteristic from his Muslim perspective. I tried to emphasize the imminence of God. Somehow this got us into discussing what had come up earlier when we discussed 1 John 4:7–8 on the love of God. Rahman asked, "How does the love of God fit in with God's justice?" I read to him Hebrews 12:4–11, which describes how a father who loves his son disciplines him. In the same way, I said, God disciplines us when we do wrong, so that we may be taught to live holy lives. Then Rahman asked, "What about those whom he is sending to hell?" My reply was, "That shows the justice of a holy God in punishing our sin. Love and justice must both be held as attributes of God. One cannot simply see his love. All of us are sinners and deserve God's punishment and wrath, but out of his great love for us he saved us by sending Jesus to be our Savior. Jesus bore the punishment for sin that we deserved, so that we could be saved." This Rahman had trouble accepting. How could Jesus be punished for our sins? My reply was, "Unless Jesus paid the penalty for our sins, no one could be saved." Then I showed him Romans 3:21–26 and 5:1–2, 6–11. Justification by faith was a totally new concept for him. He asked, "What does 'faith' mean here? Does it mean faith in Jesus dying for your sins that you can be saved?" I said, "Yes." He asked if this was just my interpretation or if this was what all Christians believed. I said that this was what orthodox Christianity teaches and all accept, with the exception of liberal Christians, such as those who taught in this university's religion department. Rahman took note of these references.

Seventh Bible Study: March 27, 1990

The day before we met, Rahman called me and asked if we could discuss the basics of what all Christians agreed on, aside from those having a liberal theological orientation. When we met, I first explained the three different forms of church government—episcopal, congregational, and presbyterian. He commented that in Islam, the word *government* always referred to the authority ruling a country.

I brought with me a copy of the Apostle's Creed and the Lord's Prayer. In looking at this, Rahman first asked what was meant by the word "Apostle's." My response was that the Apostles' Creed was not written by the apostles of Christ, but by later Christians who developed it on the basis of apostolic teaching. We discussed each phrase, which went pretty smoothly until we reached the statement that Jesus "descended into hell." This Rahman found difficult to understand and accept, and I found it difficult to explain. So we decided just to go on.[3] Next we discussed Jesus' return to judge the living and the dead. This Rahman found interesting, as he compared that teaching to the Islamic understanding of Jesus' return. He noted that Jesus' power to judge was a divine attribute.

Next we briefly went through the Lord's Prayer. When we reached the petition "give us this day our daily bread," Rahman associated this with the Lord's Supper. I explained the difference and how often we participate in the Lord's Supper. Rahman did not understand the word "debtors" in the prayer. At the end of our meeting, I showed Rahman a copy of the Westminster Confession of Faith and the Longer and Shorter Catechisms. I explained what this confession was, when and where it was written, and that other confessions were similar. Also, I pointed out to Rahman the explanation of the Lord's Prayer at the end of the Shorter Catechism. I ended up giving my copy of the Confession of Faith to him.

Eighth Bible Study: April 10, 1990

Since Rahman was observing Ramadan this month, I began by asking him what Ramadan meant for him. He saw it as a discipline and as something that helps one remember God.

Then Rahman asked me what I thought about religious dialogue. I responded, "I think it is good to understand one another, but dialogue will not bring the different religions together to form one world religion. One has to come to the dialogue with convictions about one's own faith. For me, learning about Islam from Muslim friends and classes has been a valuable experience, but it has not made me want to become a Muslim. Also, I cannot convert anyone to the Christian faith; only God can do that."

When we got back to my prepared Bible study, we went over Isaiah 57:15 again. Rahman had trouble accepting the concept of "lowly in spirit" as a positive characteristic. The question I asked after the verse, "Does this mean God can live with us?" he found to be superficial. He thought that of course God can live with us, since the Sufis claim to have the embodiment of Allah in them and the Qur'an says that Allah is closer to us than our jugular vein. I found it difficult to come back with a response that showed the distinction between Islam and Christianity at this point. I said that when we speak to God and he hears our prayers, we have a relationship with him; Rahman said they have the same thing in Islam. I found his views on this to be somewhat different than other Muslims, who emphasize more the transcendence of Allah.

As we compared the Islamic and the Christian understandings of God, Rahman did not find any significant differences. When I mentioned God's holiness, his immutability, and his righteousness, Rahman said that the Islamic view of God was similar. The next section on application brought up the distinction between God's incommunicable and communicable attributes. Rahman took notes on these two kinds of attributes. It appeared to be a new concept for him that we should model our lives on the character of God. Again I explained God's jealousy as a positive attribute in light of the fact that God demands our total allegiance.

After finishing this study, it occurred to me that looking at the character, life, and teachings of Jesus might clarify the distinctive aspects of God not found in Islam. One example of this would be that Jesus is the Good Shepherd.

Ninth Bible Study: June 26, 1990

Finally we were able to meet again, but only for one hour. Rahman wanted to meet only occasionally now because of his busy schedule and because his family would soon be arriving from Indonesia. He did not seem interested in going through the prepared Bible study I had brought. Instead, he wanted me to tell him what was distinctive about the Presbyterian church within Protestantism. I explained each of the five points of Calvinism as he took notes. He seemed very interested in this topic. I explained the Atonement and how it was God's plan to have Jesus die on the cross for our salvation. He asked if Jesus could have kept himself from dying on the cross. I replied that he could have, but he willingly obeyed his Father's will that he should suffer and die.

Then I mentioned that Jesus was going to be our judge on the last day. He asked if it was not God who would be the judge. I answered that God the Father has entrusted all judgment to his Son

Jesus. Jesus said, "All authority in heaven and on earth has been given to me" (Matt. 28:18). Rahman then replied, "Then God is like in retirement on his throne, having given everything to Jesus to do." I found it a bit difficult to know how to respond to this. I said that there is one God, but the different persons within the Godhead have different roles. Then Rahman asked, "How can God be infinite and be in Jesus? God must be finite." I replied, "No, God is infinite in his knowledge, power, presence, eternity, and love. But when Jesus came, he willingly limited himself by taking on the form of a man. So Jesus had two natures, divine and human. After his resurrection, he was glorified and exalted to where he sat at the right hand of the Father, the place of honor. Then he no longer was limited as a man."

After I explained the five points of Calvinism, Rahman asked about the historical background to this. I explained about Arminius, and Pelagius and Augustine before him. Rahman asked how Martin Luther fitted in. I said that Luther was basically Calvinistic in soteriology, though not in all of his theology. He wrote *The Bondage of the Will*, explaining how we are bound in sin and can do nothing to save ourselves apart from the grace of God. At this point I had to leave.

Our studies were not able to continue after this, because of the arrival of Rahman's family from Indonesia. His schedule became very busy, as he was preparing for his comprehensive exams. We met a few more times for lunch on campus quite a while later for informal discussions before he left for Indonesia.

For Reflection/Action

What are your thoughts about the Bible studies as described in this appendix? Would you have presented the biblical themes differently? Would you have responded to Rahman differently? If so, how?

Notes

Chapter One

1 Diana L. Eck, "Neighboring Faiths: How Will Americans Cope with Increasing Religious Diversity?" *Harvard Magazine*, September–October 1996, 44.

2 Ahmad H. Sakr, *Islam and Muslims: Myth or Reality* (Milwaukee: Al-Qur'an Foundation, 1994), 119–20.

3 W. O. Blake, *The History of Slavery and the Slave Trade, Ancient and Modern* (Columbus: H. Miller, 1860), 94–95.

4 Walter Dean Myers, *Now Is Your Time! The African-American Struggle for Freedom* (New York: HarperTrophy, 1991), 11–27.

5 Mark Horne, "A Bad Moon Rising: The Growth of Islam in the U.S.," *Tabletalk*, April 1998, 13.

6 Andrea W. Lorenz, "Canada's Pioneer Mosque," *Aramco World* 49, no. 4 (July–August 1998): 28–31.

7 Yvonne Haddad, *A Century of Islam in America: The Muslim World Today—Occasional Paper No. 4* (Washington: American Institute for Islamic Affairs, 1986), 1, 10.

8 Derk Kinnane Roelofsma, "Muslims in U.S. Defend the Faith," *Insight*, November 3, 1986, 69.

9 George W. Braswell, Jr., *Islam: Its Prophet, Peoples, Politics and Power* (Nashville: Broadman & Holman, 1996), 241–42.

10 Jeff Gammage, "Iraqi Americans Watch and Worry," *Philadelphia Inquirer*, February 22, 1998, A21–22.

11 The American Muslim Council estimates that there are between four and eight million American Muslims.

12 Carl Ellis, "Project Joseph: A Ministry Concept" (unpub. paper, n.d.), 5.

13 Alan Sipress, "Keeping Faith in Growing Numbers," *Philadelphia Inquirer*, July 25, 1993, A10.

14 Ibid.

15 Kerry Lovering, *Islam on the March*, reprinted from *Africa Now* (Sarborough, Ont.: Sudan Interior Mission, n.d.), 9.

16 Sakr, *Islam and Muslims*, 123–24.

17 George W. Braswell, Jr., *Understanding Sectarian Groups in America*, rev. ed. (Nashville: Broadman & Holman, 1994), 287.

18 William R. Macklin, "Growing Up in the Nation of Islam," *Philadelphia Inquirer*, February 4, 1997, D5.

19 C. Eric Lincoln, "The American Muslim Mission in the Context of American Social History," in *The Muslim Community in North America*, ed. Earle H. Waugh, Baha Abu-Laban, and Regula B. Qureshi (Edmonton: University of Alberta Press, 1983), 221.

20 "United States of America," in *World Christian Encyclopedia*, ed. David B. Barrett (Oxford: Oxford University Press, 1982), 712.

21 Braswell, *Understanding Sectarian Groups in America*, 291, 294.

22 Monica Yant, "Grays Ferry Gets Focus on National TV," *Philadelphia Inquirer*, April 14, 1997, A1, A8.

23 "Farrakhan: 'It's Time for Us to Show the World Our Brilliance,'" *Philadelphia Inquirer*, April 15, 1997, A12.

24 "Prison Disfellowship," *World* 13, no. 46 (November 28, 1998), 10.

25 Bawa Muhaiyaddeen, "A Contemporary Sufi Speaks on Peace of Mind," (Philadelphia: Bawa Muhaiyaddeen Fellowship, 1997), www.bmf.org/pamphlets/pomen2.htm.

26 Jay Smith, "The Attraction of Islam, and a Christian's Response," 99 *Truth Papers* (London: Hyde Park Christian Fellowship, 1992), 5.

27 Evangelical Christians are those who believe that the Bible is God's authoritative and inerrant Word, that salvation from our sins is received only through faith in Jesus Christ, and that we are commanded to share our faith in Christ with the world.

28 Ellis, "Project Joseph," 6–7.

29 Ronald C. Potter, "No Spiritual Wimps," *World* 11, no. 7 (May 11/18, 1996), 25.

30 Richard P. Bailey, "Why Americans Convert" (unpub. paper, 1998), 1.

31 Carl Ellis, "How I Witness to Muslims," *Moody Monthly* 83, no. 5 (January 1983): 52.

32 Eck, "Neighboring Faiths," 40.

33 Braswell, *Understanding Sectarian Groups in America*, 282.

34 Douglas Pasternak, "American Colleges Are 'Weapons U.' for Iraq," *U.S. News & World Report* 125, no. 9 (March 9, 1998): 32.

35 Jan Goodwin, *Price of Honor* (Boston: Little, Brown and Company, 1994), 12–13.
36 Ibid., 13.
37 "Muslims in School in the U.S.," *Reach Out to the Muslim World* 7, no. 1–2 (1994): 22.
38 Arthur Clark, "Books for a New World," *Aramco World* 49, no. 1 (January-February 1998): 34–37.
39 Lovering, "Islam on the March," 10.
40 Braswell, *Islam*, 243.
41 Eck, "Neighboring Faiths," 43.
42 Alice Dembner, "Saudi Grant to Put Harvard at Fore of Islamic Studies," *Boston Globe*, June 16, 1993.
43 Iranian Christians International, "The ICI Partner Prayer Letter," October 1993, 2.

Chapter Two

1 H. L. Ellison, "Ebionites," in *The New International Dictionary of the Christian Church*, ed. J. D. Douglas, 2d ed. (Grand Rapids: Zondervan, 1978), 326.
2 Mostafa Vaziri, *The Emergence of Islam: Prophecy, Imamate, and Messianism in Perspective* (New York: Paragon House, 1992), 7.
3 Ibid., 10–11.
4 Ibid., 15.
5 Ibid., 18–20, and Tor Andrae, *Mohammed: The Man and His Faith* (New York: Harper Torchbooks, 1960), 118.
6 Varizi, *The Emergence of Islam*, 52–53.
7 Anis A. Shorrosh, *Islam Revealed: A Christian Arab's View of Islam* (Nashville: Thomas Nelson, 1988), 52–53.
8 Richard Bell, *The Origin of Islam in Its Christian Environment* (London: Frank Cass and Co., 1926), 136, 140.
9 Kenneth Cragg, *The Call of the Minaret* (New York: Oxford University Press, 1956), 263.
10 Nestorianism was condemned as heretical at the ecumenical Council of Chalcedon in 451.
11 Harold Coward, *Pluralism: Challenge to World Religions* (Maryknoll: Orbis Books, 1985), 46.
12 Andrae, *Mohammed*, 116, 120–23, 126.
13 Ibn Ishaq, quoted by Vaziri, *The Emergence of Islam*, 48.
14 "Go forth, light-armed and heavy-armed, and strive with your wealth and your lives in the way of Allah! That is best for you if ye but knew" (Surah 9:41). "And fight them until persecution is no more, and religion is all for

Allah" (Surah 8:39). In the *Hadith,* Muhammad says: "Every prophet had some profession (for livelihood), and my profession is *Jihad;* and in fact my means of subsistence are placed under the shadow of my spear." Quoted by Muhammad Hamidullah, *The Muslim Conduct of State,* 7th ed. (Lahore, Pakistan: Sh. Muhammah Ashraf, 1977), 12.

15 Mohammed Marmaduke Pickthall, *The Meaning of the Glorious Koran* (New York: New American Library, 1953), 300.

16 There are conflicting *Hadith* which say he had nine, eleven, and fifteen wives. One year he took four wives. One source, Ahmad Ya'qubi, indicates he had twenty-one or twenty-three wives, having divorced a few and not slept with all of them.

17 Two Muslim authorities report that A'isha was six years old (at-Tabari, IV, 1291, and Ibn Athir, I, 124), and another reports that she was nine (Mostaufi, 140).

18 Vaziri, *The Emergence of Islam,* 24.

19 Ahmed ibn Hanbal, *Musnad,* I, 63, quoted by Andrae, *Mohammed,* 154.

20 Varizi, *The Emergence of Islam,* 39.

21 J. Dudley Woodberry, "Interfaith Dialogue," unpub. paper at Fuller Theological Seminary, 5.

22 Andrae, *Mohammed,* 129.

23 Jack Budd, comp., *Studies on Islam: A Simple Outline of the Islamic Faith* (Northants: Red Sea Mission Team, 1978), 16.

24 John B. Taylor, *The World of Islam* (New York: Friendship Press, 1979), 43.

25 Kenneth Scott Latourette, *A History of Christianity,* rev. ed. (New York: Harper & Row, 1975), 414.

26 Joseph Smith, "Is the Qur'an the Word of God? Debate Between: Dr. Jamal Badawi and Joseph H. Smith," with "Commentary on a Challenge to the Authenticity of the Qur'an," by Abdul-Rahman Lomax (World Wide Web: Hyde Park Christian Fellowship, 1996).

Chapter Three

1 "The Willowbank Report: The Lausanne Committee for World Evangelization," in *Perspectives on the World Christian Movement: A Reader,* ed. Ralph D. Winter and Steven C. Hawthorne (Pasadena: William Carey Library, 1981), 508–9.

2 Tor Andrae, *Mohammed: The Man and His Faith* (New York: Harper Torchbooks, 1960), 78.

3 Yvonne Yazbeck Haddad and Adair T. Lummis, *Islamic Values in the United States: A Comparative Study* (New York: Oxford University Press, 1987), 60.

4 Aaron Epstein, "Rehnquist Rejects Request to Remove Muhammad Art," *Philadelphia Inquirer,* March 13, 1997, A16.

5 Haddad and Lummis, *Islamic Values in the United States*, 157.
6 Ibid., 171.
7 Some of this material is taken from Michael Diamond and Peter Gowing, *Islam and Muslims: Some Basic Information* (Quezon City: New Day Publishers, 1981), 90–93.
8 See discussion of this topic by Muhammad Asad in "Appendix IV" of *The Message of the Qur'an* (Gibraltar: Dar al-Andalus, 1984), 996–98. See also *Sahih al-Bukhari*, I, 345; IV, 429; V, 227.
9 Most of this section is based on a lecture given by Paul Hiebert at a conference in Wheaton, Illinois, in 1991.

Part Three

1 David Brown, *A New Threshold: Guidelines for the Churches in Their Relations with Muslim Communities* (London: The British Council of Churches and the Conference of Missionary Societies in Great Britain and Ireland, 1976), 13.

Chapter Four

1 Badru D. Kateregga and David W. Shenk, *Islam and Christianity: A Muslim and a Christian in Dialogue* (Grand Rapids: Eerdmans, 1980), 101.
2 'Allamah Sayyid Muhammad Husayn Tabataba'i, *Shi'ite Islam* (Albany: State University of New York Press, 1975), 146.
3 Seyyed Hossein Nasr, *Islamic Life and Thought* (Albany: State University of New York Press, 1981), 8.
4 Al-Haji A. D. Ajijola, *Qur'an in the Classroom* (Lahore: Islamic Publications, 1977), 4–5.
5 David L. Johnson, *A Reasoned Look at Asian Religions* (Minneapolis: Bethany House, 1985), 150–51.
6 Canon Sell, *The Historical Development of the Qur'an* (reprint, Chicago: People International, n.d.), vii–viii.
7 Toby Lester, "What Is the Koran?" *Atlantic Monthly* 283, no. 1 (January 1999): 43–56.
8 Patricia Crone and Michael Cook, *Hagarism: The Making of the Islamic World* (Cambridge: Cambridge University Press, 1977), as quoted in Lester, "What Is the Koran?" 46.
9 Jay Smith, "The Bible and the Qur'an: An Historical Comparison," 99 *Truth Papers* (London: Hyde Park Christian Fellowship, n.d.), 2–8.
10 Ajijola, *Qur'an in the Classroom*, 8.
11 Ibid., 23–24.
12 Ibid., 50–51.

13 Ajijola's translation.
14 Johnson, *A Reasoned Look at Asian Religions*, 155–57.
15 See Lester, "What Is the Koran?" 43–56.
16 W. Montgomery Watt, *Bell's Introduction to the Qur'an* (Edinburgh: Edinburgh University Press, 1970), 156.
17 Richard Bell, *The Origin of Islam in Its Christian Environment* (London: Frank Cass and Co., 1926), 157.
18 Watt, *Bell's Introduction to the Qur'an*, 157.
19 Quoted in Phil Parshall, *The Cross and the Crescent* (Wheaton: Tyndale House, 1989), 42.
20 Bruce J. Nicholls, ed., *Christian Witness to Muslims* (Wheaton: Lausanne Committee for World Evangelization, 1980), 15.
21 See James Montgomery Boice, *Standing on the Rock* (Grand Rapids: Baker, 1994); John Wenham, *Christ and the Bible*, 3d ed. (Grand Rapids: Baker, 1994).
22 From a conversation with missiologist Samuel Schlorff.

Chapter Five

1 Samuel M. Zwemer, *The Moslem Doctrine of God* (Edinburgh: Oliphant, Anderson and Ferrier, 1905), 21.
2 Muhammad Taqi-ud-Din al-Hilali and Muhammad Muhsin Khan, "Glossary," in *The Noble Qur'an* (Riyadh: Maktaba Dar-us-Salam, 1994), 1002.
3 'Allamah Sayyid Muhammad Husayn Tabataba'i, *Shi'ite Islam* (Albany: State University of New York Press, 1975), 130.
4 Zwemer, *The Moslem Doctrine of God*, 30–31.
5 Isma'il R. al-Faruqi, "On the Nature of Islamic Da'wah," *International Review of Mission* 65, no. 260 (October 1976): 406.
6 Jamal Badawi and Harry Almond, *Bridgebuilding Between Christian and Muslim* (Newberg, Ore.: Barclay Press, 1982), 3–4.
7 Al-Hilali and Khan, "Glossary," 1003.
8 Harold Spencer, *Islam and the Gospel of God* (New Delhi: ISPCK, 1956), 6.
9 L. Bevan Jones, *Christianity Explained to Muslims*, rev. ed. (Calcutta: Baptist Mission Press, 1952), 64–65.
10 Lois Gardet, *Mohammedanism* (New York: Hawthorne Books, 1961), 38.
11 Badawi and Almond, *Bridgebuilding Between Christian and Muslim*, 4.
12 Letter from Bassam Madany, February 9, 1999.
13 Zwemer, *The Moslem Doctrine of God*, 82–83.
14 W. Montgomery Watt, *Bell's Introduction to the Qur'an* (Edinburgh: Edinburgh University Press, 1970), 158.
15 Gardet, *Mohammedanism*, 39.

16 Nestorius (d. 451) was a theologian of Persian origin who became the patriarch of Constantinople. He split Jesus Christ into two persons, one human and one divine. He believed that there was no more than a sympathetic and moral union between the two persons. He was anathematized as a heretic at the Council of Ephesus in 431. His followers took his views further, seeing Jesus as having a double personality: not the God-man, but the God-bearing man. Nestorian missionaries established churches in Arabia which had contacts with Muhammad.

17 Monophysitism was a movement among the Eastern churches in response the Council of Chalcedon in 451. They insisted that there is only one nature in Jesus Christ, rather than two. Chalcedon had said that Jesus Christ was truly God and truly man, one in person and substance, not divided into two persons. The Monophysites thought that to say Jesus has two natures is to deny the possibility that man could have ultimate oneness with God, the goal of salvation. But the Monophysite view resulted in reducing the humanity of Christ to insignificance. Their views developed out of Eastern monasticism, which believed that our humanity needed to be destroyed. So it was unthinkable that Christ would share our humanity.

18 Giulio Basetti-Sani, *The Koran in the Light of Christ* (Chicago: Franciscan Herald Press, 1977), 29, 31.

19 Jones, *Christianity Explained to Muslims*, 67.

20 Zwemer, *The Moslem Doctrine of God*, 84.

21 Watt, *Bell's Introduction to the Qur'an*, 155.

22 Jones, *Christianity Explained to Muslims*, 69–70.

23 Compiled from Phil Parshall, *Bridges to Islam* (Grand Rapids: Baker, 1983), 123–26; Ahmad H. Sakr, *Islam and Muslims: Myth or Reality* (Milwaukee: Al-Qur'an Foundation, 1994), 18–21; poster produced by Ta-Ha Publishers (London, n.d.); Zwemer, *The Moslem Doctrine of God*, 34–46.

24 Spencer, *Islam and the Gospel of God*, 1.

25 Ibid., 4–5.

26 Zwemer, *The Moslem Doctrine of God*, 71.

27 Ibid., 75.

28 Tabataba'i, *Shi'ite Islam*, 135.

29 Ibid., 54.

30 Spencer, *Islam and the Gospel of God*, 4–5.

31 Tor Andrae, *Mohammed: The Man and His Faith* (New York: Harper Torchbooks, 1960), 65–66.

32 Zwemer, *The Moslem Doctrine of God*, 55.

33 Andrae, *Mohammed*, 67.

34 Norman L. Geisler and Abdul Saleeb, *Answering Islam: The Crescent in the Light of the Cross* (Grand Rapids: Baker, 1993), 26.

35 Zwemer, *The Moslem Doctrine of God*, 47–49.

36 Ibid., 58–59.

37 Ibid., 49.

38 William M. Miller, *A Christian's Response to Islam* (Phillipsburg, N.J.: Presbyterian and Reformed, 1980), 72–73.

39 Quoted in *Threshold: A Journal of Sufism* (Brattleboro, Vt.: Threshold Books and the Threshold Society, 1997) 11.

Chapter Six

1 Hammudah Abdalati, *Islam in Focus* (Malaysia: Polygraphic Press, 1980), 153.

2 Lois Gardet, *Mohammedanism* (New York: Hawthorne Books, 1961), 39.

3 Ibid., 40.

4 Frithjof Schuon, *Dimensions of Islam* (London: George Allen and Unwin, 1970), 77.

5 Comment made by Harvie M. Conn.

6 Giulio Basetti-Sani, *The Koran in the Light of Christ* (Chicago: Franciscan Herald Press, 1977), 136.

7 Seyyed Hossein Nasr, *Islamic Life and Thought* (Albany: State University of New York Press, 1981), 209.

8 Samuel M. Zwemer, *The Moslem Doctrine of God* (Edinburgh: Oliphant, Anderson and Ferrier, 1905), 86.

9 W. Montgomery Watt, *Bell's Introduction to the Qur'an* (Edinburgh: Edinburgh University Press, 1970), 158.

10 Muhammad Taqi-ud-Din al-Hilali and Muhammad Muhsin Khan, "Glossary," in *The Noble Qur'an* (Riyadh: Maktaba Dar-us-Salam, 1994), 998.

11 *Christian Witness Among Muslims*, standard ed. (Achimota, Ghana: Africa Christian Press, 1971), 60–61.

12 Gardet, *Mohammedanism*, 38.

13 Basetti-Sani, *The Koran in the Light of Christ*, 136.

14 Gardet, *Mohammedanism*, 38–39, and comment from Harvie M. Conn.

15 Schuon, *Dimensions of Islam*, 81.

16 Ibid., 82–83.

17 'Allamah Sayyid Muhammad Husayn Tabataba'i, *Shi'ite Islam* (Albany: State University of New York Press, 1975), 149.

18 Nasr, *Islamic Life and Thought*, 210.

19 Schuon, *Dimensions of Islam*, 79; Nasr, *Islamic Life and Thought*, 210.

20 Of course, Jesus did not receive an eternal book from heaven, written in Arabic, as some Muslims believe.

21 John Elder, *The Biblical Approach to the Muslim* (Fort Washington, Pa.: W.E.C., 1978), 106–7.

22 Gardet, *Mohammedanism*, 40.

23 Richard Bell, *The Origin of Islam in Its Christian Environment* (London: Frank Cass and Co., 1926), 154–55.
24 Samuel M. Zwemer, *Mohammed or Christ* (New York: Fleming H. Revell, 1915), 229–30.
25 Abdalati, *Islam in Focus*, 158.
26 Zwemer, *Mohammed or Christ*, 230.
27 Nasr, *Islamic Life and Thought*, 210.
28 David Brown, *A New Threshold: Guidelines for the Churches in Their Relations with Muslim Communities* (London: The British Council of Churches and the Conference of Missionary Societies in Great Britain and Ireland, 1976), 16.
29 Watt, *Bell's Introduction to the Qur'an*, 158.
30 Abdalati, *Islam in Focus*, 160, 162.
31 L. Bevan Jones, *Christianity Explained to Muslims*, rev. ed. (Calcutta: Baptist Mission Press, 1952), 96, 97.
32 Comment from Harvie M. Conn.
33 Jones, *Christianity Explained to Muslims*, 90.
34 Ibid.
35 Zwemer, *Mohammed or Christ*, 230.
36 Al-Hilali and Khan, "Glossary," 1041.
37 Kenneth Cragg, *The Call of the Minaret* (New York: Oxford University Press, 1956), 245–46.
38 Nasr, *Islamic Life and Thought*, 211.

Chapter Seven

1 Seyyed Hossein Nasr, "Sufism and the Integration of Man," in *God and Man in Contemporary Islamic Thought*, ed. Charles Malik (Beirut: American University of Beirut, 1972), 144, 151.
2 Kenneth A. Cragg, *Sandals at the Mosque* (New York: Oxford University Press, 1959), 122–23.
3 J. N. D. Anderson, "Islam," in *The Inadequacy of Non-Christian Religion*, ed. H. A. Evan Hopkins (London: Inter-Varsity Fellowship of Evangelical Unions, 1944), 11–12.
4 Isma'il R. al-Faruqi, "On the Nature of Islamic Da'wah," *International Review of Mission* 65, no. 260 (October 1976): 404.
5 Badru D. Kateregga and David W. Shenk, *Islam and Christianity: A Muslim and a Christian in Dialogue* (Grand Rapids: Eerdmans, 1981), 101.
6 Isma'il Ragi al-Faruqi, *Christian Ethics* (Montreal: McGill University Press, 1967), 202.
7 Ibid., 201.
8 Kenneth A. Cragg, "Islamic Theology: Limits and Bridges," in *The Gospel and Islam*, ed. Don M. McCurry (Monrovia, Calif.: MARC, 1979), 202.

9 Ibid.
10 'Allamah Sayyid Muhammad Husayn Tabataba'i, *Shi'ite Islam* (Albany: State University of New York Press, 1975), 144–45.
11 Samuel M. Zwemer, *The Moslem Doctrine of God* (Edinburgh: Oliphant, Anderson and Ferrier, 1905), 53.
12 Hazrat Mirza Bashiruddin Mahmud Ahmad, "What Is Sin?" *The Muslim Sunrise* 49, no. 3 (July 1982): 13–16.
13 David L. Johnson, A *Reasoned Look at Asian Religions* (Minneapolis: Bethany House, 1985), 155.
14 Zwemer, *The Moslem Doctrine of God*, 50–51.
15 Ibid., 51.
16 Ibid., 52.
17 Ibid., 53.
18 Yusuf al-Qaradawi, *The Lawful and the Prohibited in Islam*, 2d ed. (Salimiah, Kuwait: International Islamic Federation of Student Organizations, 1989), 203.
19 From J. Lenk's unpublished report on his Bible study with two Turkish students, 1988.
20 Cragg, "Islamic Theology: Limits and Bridges," 201.

Chapter Eight

1 Isma'il R. al-Faruqi, "On the Nature of Islamic Da'wah," *International Review of Mission* 65, no. 260 (October 1976): 392.
2 Syed Muhammad al-Naquib al-Attas, "Islam: The Concept of Religion and the Foundation of Ethics and Morality," in *The Challenge of Islam*, ed. Altaf Gauhar (London: Islamic Council of Europe, 1978), 40–41.
3 Bruce J. Nicholls, "New Theological Approaches in Muslim Evangelism," in *The Gospel and Islam*, ed. Don M. McCurry (Monrovia, Calif.: MARC, 1979), 156.
4 David W. Shenk, "Conversations Along the Way," in *Muslims and Christians on the Emmaus Road*, ed. J. Dudley Woodberry (Monrovia, Calif.: MARC Publications, 1989), 12.
5 Nicholls, "New Theological Approaches in Muslim Evangelism," 156.
6 Kenneth A. Cragg, *Sandals at the Mosque* (New York: Oxford University Press, 1959), 123–24.
7 Ibid.
8 Muhamed S. El-Awa, *On the Political System of the Islamic State* (Indianapolis: American Trust Publications, 1980), 120.
9 Ibid., 76.
10 R. W. J. Austin, "The Prophet of Islam," in *The Challenge of Islam*, ed. Altaf Gauhar (London: Islamic Council of Europe, 1978), 75–76.

11 Gholam Hossein Dargahi, *The Development of Islam as the Ideology of Arab Unity,* A.D. *622–632* (Ann Arbor: University Microfilms, 1970), 211.
12 Ibid., 212–13.
13 Ibid., 218.
14 Ibid., 215–16.
15 Cragg, *Sandals at the Mosque*, 124–25.
16 Kenneth A. Cragg, "Islamic Theology: Limits and Bridges," in *The Gospel and Islam*, ed. Don M. McCurry (Monrovia, Calif.: MARC, 1979), 203.
17 Nicholls, "New Theological Approaches in Muslim Evangelism," 156.
18 Ibid., 156–57.
19 Ibid., 157.
20 Ibid., 157–58.
21 Ibid., 159.
22 Ibid.
23 Geerhardus Vos, *The Kingdom of God and the Church* (Phillipsburg, N.J.: Presbyterian and Reformed, 1972), 42, 46–47.
24 Ibid., 51.
25 Ibid., 56.
26 Ibid., 89–90.
27 Ibid., 88–89.
28 Ibid., 103.
29 *The Vision* (Chicago: Institute of Islamic Information and Education, 1998), 2.
30 Isma'il R. al-Faruqi, "Islam and Other Faiths," in *The Challenge of Islam*, ed. Altaf Gauhar (London: Islamic Council of Europe, 1978), 100.
31 El-Awa, *On the Political System of the Islamic State*, 77.
32 Nicholls, "New Theological Approaches in Muslim Evangelism," 159.
33 Ibid., 161.

Conclusion to Part Three

1 Badru D. Kateregga and David W. Shenk, *Islam and Christianity: A Muslim and a Christian in Dialogue* (Grand Rapids: Eerdmans, 1981), 170.
2 Isma'il Ragi al-Faruqi, *Christian Ethics* (Montreal: McGill University Press, 1967), 225.
3 Kateregga and Shenk, *Islam and Christianity*, 169–70.

Chapter Nine

1 D. Macleod, "Sovereignty of God," in *New Dictionary of Theology*, ed. Sinclair B. Ferguson, David F. Wright, and J. I. Packer (Downers Grove, Ill.: InterVarsity Press, 1988), 654–56.

2 Meditate on the following passages on the sovereignty of God: Ps. 33:11; Prov. 16:33; Matt. 17:22; John 19:11; Acts 2:23; 4:28; Eph. 1:11; Heb. 6:17.

3 Harvie M. Conn, *Evangelism: Doing Justice and Preaching Grace* (Grand Rapids: Zondervan, 1982), 82.

4 Ibid., 74.

5 Ibid., 85.

6 Ibid., 86.

7 John Piper, *Let the Nations Be Glad! The Supremacy of God in Missions* (Grand Rapids: Baker, 1993), 11.

8 Richard P. Bailey, "The Muslims Are Here," *Action* 49 (1990): 4–7.

9 Anthony Hoekema, *The Bible and the Future* (Grand Rapids: Eerdmans, 1979), 109.

Chapter Ten

1 Phil Parshall, "Other Options for Muslim Evangelism," *Evangelical Missions Quarterly* 34, no. 1 (January 1998): 38–42.

2 See Stan Guthrie, "Carnegie or Rushdie?" *World Pulse* 26, no. 17 (September 13, 1991): 2–3.

3 For an apologetic for using this method of reaching Muslims, see Jay Smith, "Courage in Our Convictions," *Evangelical Missions Quarterly* 34, no. 1 (January 1998): 28–35. For a response from two other perspectives, see "Two Other Views," by an anonymous writer and Phil Parshall, in the same issue, pp. 36–42.

4 J. Dudley Woodberry, "Interfaith Dialogue" (unpub. paper, n.d.), 1.

5 Ibid., 4.

6 John Cammarata, "Intercultural Evangelism" (unpub. paper, 1997), 3–4.

7 Letter from Rick Hicks to Operation Mobilization supporters, November 19, 1996.

8 We recommend material on this subject from Dr. John DeVries, president of Mission 21 India. He has produced a six-part video and devotional prayer guide to help teach the principles of prayer evangelism. Order from Mission 21 HOPE, P.O. Box 141312, Grand Rapids, MI 49514–1312; tel. (616) 453–8855.

9 Andreas D'Souza and Diane D'Souza, "Reconciliation: A New Paradigm For Missions," *Word & World: Theology for Christian Ministry* 16, no. 2 (Spring 1996): 210.

Chapter Eleven

1 These guidelines are particularly applicable to friendships with Muslim international students. Usually they are in North America for a few years and

then return to their home country. But the principles have broader application to others as well.

2 Charles H. Kraft, *Communication Theory for Christian Witness* (Nashville: Abingdon, 1983), 162.

3 Jim Reapsome, "Final Analysis," *World Pulse* 29, no. 24 (December 16, 1994): 8.

4 Some ideas here come from Carl Ellis, "How I Witness to Muslims," *Moody Monthly* 83, no. 5 (January 1983): 52–53.

5 David L. Ripley, "Suggestions for Ministry to Muslims," in *Going Among the Nations Without a Passport*, comp. David Housholder (Marietta, Ga.: ETHNOServe, 1997), pt. 4, p. 2.

6 For the *Jesus* video in numerous languages, see "Further Ministry Resources" at the back of this book. The *International Opinion Game* was formerly available from International Students, Inc., P.O. Box C, Colorado Springs, CO 80901.

7 Roger Steer, *George Muller: Delighted in God!* rev. ed. (Wheaton: Harold Shaw, 1981), 247.

Chapter Twelve

1 I. Coulter, "Ministry Report for Church Without Walls," July 1997.

2 Jamal Badawi and Harry Almond, *Bridgebuilding Between Christian and Muslim* (Newberg, Ore.: Barclay Press, 1982), 1–2.

3 Muhammad A. Nubee, Introduction to *Christian-Muslim Dialogue*, by H. M. Baagil (Aldahieh, Kuwait: Revival of Islamic Heritage Society, 1984), iii.

4 Samuel M. Zwemer, *The Moslem Christ* (Edinburgh: Oliphant, Anderson and Ferrier, 1912), 183–84.

5 Abdullah Yusuf 'Ali, *The Meaning of the Holy Qur'an*, new ed. (Brentwood, Md.: Amana Corporation, 1992), 998–99.

6 Muhammad Asad, *The Message of the Qur'an* (Gibraltar: Dar al-Andalus, 1984), 416.

7 Ibid., 735.

8 Wahiduddin Khan is president of the New Delhi–based Islamic Center and editor in chief of *Alrisala* magazine.

9 Irfan A. Omar's interview of Wahiduddin Khan in "Islam: An Ideological Movement for a Peaceful Co-Existence," *The Minaret* 18, no. 12 (December 1996): 36–37.

Chapter Thirteen

1 Thomas A. Thomas, *A Reason for the Hope* (Rochester, N.Y.: Backus Book Publishers, 1988), 10–11.

2 This is an insight gained from a Turkish believer in the U.S.

3 Bruce J. Nicholls, "Contextualization," in *New Dictionary of Theology*, ed. Sinclair B. Ferguson, David F. Wright, and J. I. Packer (Downers Grove, Ill.: InterVarsity Press, 1988), 164–66.

Chapter Fourteen

1 Carl Ellis, "Project Joseph: A Ministry Concept" (unpub. paper, n.d.), 5.

2 Archie Hensley, "Ministering in the Shadow of Mecca: Reach Out to Muslims in North America!" *Mission Frontiers* 13, no. 4–5 (April/May 1991), 43. Reprint from AIM International Magazine.

Appendix One

1 Mrs. Adam is involved in ministering to Muslims in North America, formerly with Arab World Ministries.

Appendix Two

1 This theory of the origin of the Pentateuch was expounded by Julius Wellhausen (1844–1918) and others in the late nineteenth century. The view holds that the Pentateuch is a composite document, whose sources were written hundreds of years after Moses and woven together as if written by him. These sections supposedly represent the Yahwist (Jehovistic), Elohist, Deuteronomist, and Priestly traditions (hence, JEDP). This hypothesis is used to explain an evolutionary development of monotheistic religion apart from the inspiration of Scripture. It is still held by liberal scholars, but has been ably refuted by evangelical scholars. See Raymond B. Dillard and Tremper Longman III, *An Introduction to the Old Testament* (Grand Rapids: Zondervan, 1994), 40–48.

2 The next year he did go on the *hajj*, and we discussed his experience over lunch. As part of the ritual, he had an animal sacrificed in his hometown in Indonesia on his behalf, rather than in Mecca, where there was too much meat to be used. At his home, the meat was distributed to needy families and friends.

3 J. I. Packer provides a good explanation of this term in his book *Growing in Christ*. He explains how the term *hell* changed in meaning during the seventeenth century from the place of the dead (Hades) to the place of eternal punishment (Gehenna). In the creed, "hell" has the older English meaning, indicating that Jesus really died physically.

Glossary of Islamic Terms

Note that in transliteration from Arabic to English, there are variations in spellings. For example, many words may end in either *a* or *ah*, such as *Shari'a* or *Shari'ah*.

'abd—"servant" or "slave."

abu—"father of."

adhan—the call to prayer made five times a day.

Ahl al-Kitab—"people of the book," a term designating Jews and Christians in the Qur'an.

Al-Fatihah—"the opening"; the name of the first surah of the Qur'an, which is repeated several times during each of the five times of prayer each day. It contains in condensed form all the fundamental principles of the Qur'an.

alhaji—a Muslim who has made the pilgrimage (*hajj*) to Mecca.

Al-Hamdu-lil-lah—"Praise to God." Often said as an expression of thanks.

Allah—"God."

Allahu-Akbar—"Allah is the Most Great." Repeated as part of a Muslim's prayers.

amir—"prince"; leader.

ansar—"helpers," "supporters"; companions of Muhammad in Medina who helped and supported him and his followers.

ayah (pl., *ayat*)—verse of the Qur'an.

baraka—"blessing."
bent (or *bint*)—"daughter of."
bin (also *ibn*)—"son of."
bismillah—the phrase: In the name of God, the Merciful, the Compassionate. This general invocation of Allah prefaces each Surah of the Qur'an except Surah 9, and is often used in speech and at the beginning of written documents.
caliph—Islamic ruler who was a close associate of Muhammad or the descendant of one; head of the Muslim community; imam.
caliphate—the Muslim state headed by a caliph; the last one ended in 1923 with the collapse of the Ottoman empire.
dar-al-islam—"house of peace."
da'wah—calling all people to the path of Allah, to follow divine guidance; missionary work.
dervish—Sufi mystic who often engages in whirling dance, trances, and singing or chanting of the names and attributes of Allah.
dhikr (or *zhikr*)—"recitation"; Sufi spiritual exercises, in which one is remembering or being mindful of God to perceive the oneness of all being, by concentrating on one of the names of God.
dhimmi—people of the covenant (Jews and Christians); non-Muslims living under an Islamic government's protection.
din—religion in general and religious duties in particular, including the five pillars of Islam; divine judgment.
Eid al-Adha—four-day feast in memory of the last day of Muhammad's pilgrimage to Mecca. Rams are sacrificed in memory of Ibrahim (Abraham) offering his son (Ishmael) as a sacrifice to Allah and Allah providing a ram instead. The meat is shared with the poor. The sacrifice is made as part of the *hajj* rituals, as well as in every Muslim community.
Eid al-Fitr—feast at the breaking of the fast; three-day festival to mark the end of the fast of Ramadan.
fard—"obligatory."
fatwa—legal ruling made by an expert scholar.
fiqh—Islamic jurisprudence.

fitrah—innate pure nature possessed by all people at birth; the pattern according to which God has created all things.

Hadith—the sayings, actions, and approvals of the prophet Muhammad as recorded in tradition, having been passed on by his companions and later Muslim authorities.

hadrat (or *hazrat*)—title of honor and respect.

hafiz—title of respect given to those who have memorized the entire Qur'an.

hanif—pre-Islamic monotheist.

hajj—pilgrimage to Mecca required of all Muslims once in their lifetime, if they can afford it.

halal—"permitted"; what is lawful; meat that is properly butchered in the name of Allah (Surah 22:34): with the animal's throat slit, allowing the blood to drain out, and its head facing Mecca.

haram—"unlawful"; doing that which is forbidden; sacred.

hegira—Muslim lunar new year.

henna—a dye often used by Muslim women on their hair and hands, particularly on special occasions.

hidayah—Allah's divine guidance.

hijab—scarf worn by Muslim women over their head.

hijra—Muhammad's flight from Mecca to Medina in 622; the beginning date of the Muslim lunar calendar.

Hira—a mountain near Mecca where Muhammad first received his revelation of the Qur'an.

ibadah—"worship."

ibn (also *bin*)—"son of."

iftar—meal eaten right after sunset during the month of Ramadan, often shared in the community.

i'jaz—the doctrine that the Qur'an cannot be imitated, and therefore cannot be translated.

ijmaa'—general consensus; the third source of Islamic law.

iktisab—power to appropriate all the good and evil deeds that Allah has created for man.

ilm—"knowledge."

imam—the religious leader of a Muslim community or mosque; someone who leads in prayers.

iman—"faith" (conviction); "belief."

In-shallah—"If God wills." Often said in hopes that something will happen or as plans are made.

'Isa—Jesus in the Qur'an.

islam—submitting to the will of Allah; "peace."

ismah—"inerrancy," a quality of a prophet of God in the transmission of God's revelation.

isnad—chain of authorities transmitting the traditions of the prophet Muhammad.

jahiliyyah—"ignorance."

jihad—striving in the way of Allah. The greater *jihad* is an inner struggle for remembrance of Allah; the lesser *jihad* is fighting for the cause of Allah against his enemies.

jinn—spiritual beings created by Allah from fire, which do evil, like demons, but can also aid in this earthly life. They have subtle bodies that can enter people and things.

jizya—"tax"; a tax imposed on non-Muslims living in an Islamic state.

Jumah—Friday congregational prayer at about noon.

juzw—one of the divisions of the Qur'an into thirty equal parts for memorization purposes.

Ka'aba—cubical place of worship in Mecca, with the black meteorite in the corner, to which Muslims make the *hajj*; believed to have been rebuilt by Abraham; the center of the universe.

kafir—"unbeliever" or infidel; one who rejects the message of Islam.

kalam—"speech"; academic theology.

kebira—great sins.

khalifah—the vicegerent of Allah, his administrative deputy; his representative on earth to reflect the divine names and qualities and to fulfill the divine will; the role of every Muslim.

kitab—"book"; holy Scripture.

kufi—"skullcap."

kufr—the ultimate evil of disbelief in God and his signs; rejection of revelation; thanklessness.

maulid—"birthday"; celebration of Muhammad's birthday.

manzil—one of seven portions into which the Qur'an has been divided to be recited in seven days.

Mecca—holy city in Saudi Arabia, where Muhammad began his preaching and to which Muslims make a pilgrimage.

Medina—city to which Muhammad fled upon leaving Mecca, where he established the Islamic state.

messehy—"Christian."

mihrab—the niche in the wall of a mosque indicating the direction of the Ka'aba in Mecca, toward which one should bow in prayer.

mu'azzin—the person who calls people to prayer.

munkir—someone who rejects or conceals the truth.

mushrikun—those who worship others besides Allah.

Mustafa—"the Elect"; one of the names by which the prophet Muhammad is commonly known.

Muslim—one who submits to the will of Allah; a follower of Islam.

nabi—"prophet"; informer.

nosrani (pl., *nasara*)—"Christian" (root word from *Nazarene*, having connotations of being a second-class citizen); European; conqueror (North Africa).

pir—Sufi spiritual guide (especially on Indian subcontinent); "elder."

purdah—"curtain" or "veil." Refers to the seclusion of women from the time of puberty, so they will not mix with anyone but close relatives and women friends.

qadi—"judge" in both Islamic and civil court.

qiyas—"analogical reasoning"; the fourth source for the *Shari'a*.

qibla—the direction of prayer—toward the Ka'aba in Mecca.

Qur'an (or Koran)—the holy book revealed by the angel Gabriel to Muhammad.

Rabb—"Lord." The most commonly used title for God, often in "Lord of the Worlds."

rak'at—(sing., *rak'a*) the prayers of a Muslim, consisting of one standing, one bowing, and two prostrations.

rasul—"apostle"; "messenger."

ruh—"spirit."

ruku'—a section of a *surah* of the Qur'an (divided by subject matter).

sahur—meal eaten before dawn during the month of Ramadan.

salat—ritual prostration in prayer five times each day; the second of the five pillars of Islam.

saum—"fasting."

Sayyid or *Seyyed*—"master." Used as a title name for descendants of Muhammad.

shahada—confession of faith: "There is no god but Allah, and Muhammad is the Apostle of Allah." Making this confession before two witnesses makes one a Muslim. First of the five pillars of Islam and repeated in prayer.

shaheed—"martyr."

Shari'a—the constitution of the Islamic community, the divine will applied to every situation in life. It is derived from the Qur'an, the *Hadith*, and the *Sunnah* of the prophet Muhammad, general consensus, and *qiyas* (analogy).

sheikh—"old man"; title of respect.

Shi'ite (or *Shi'a*)—the branch of Islam that follows the leadership of 'Ali, the son-in-law of Muhammad, and of the twelve Imams descended from him. Most people in Iran and many people in Iraq and Lebanon are Shi'ite.

shirk—associating partners to Allah, polytheism; the unforgivable sin.

Sirat—the conduct of Muhammad in his wars; a part of the *Hadith*.

Sufi—a Muslim who has a mystical approach to Islam in which he seeks unity with Allah and claims direct experiences of him. Sufis have special rites and ecstatic dances.

Sunnah—the practice or actions of the prophet Muhammad as recorded in tradition, which are a model to be followed. This includes every detail of Muhammad's life, from the direction in which he slept to how he brushed his teeth. So *Sunnah* is the way of faith and conduct as followed by the Islamic community.

Sunni—the major orthodox branch of Islam, which follows the leadership of the caliphs after Muhammad's death.

surah—a chapter of the Qur'an; there are 114 of them.

tahrif—the doctrine that Jews and Christians have corrupted the Scriptures.

tarawih—special prayers in the evening, in sequences of twenty, said during the month of Ramadan, usually corporately.

tarika (or *tariqah*)—Sufi order or path.

Taurat—"the Torah" (Pentateuch) revealed to Moses (Musa).

tawhid—the oneness of God; man's integration by means of the realization of the One. "Salvation" for the Muslim is the purity or totality of this belief. It is to be expressed in all aspects of life. It includes the three aspects of belief in the oneness of lordship, worship, and the names and qualities of Allah.

'ulama (sing., *'alim*)—Islamic scholars of theology or law, the custodians of Islamic teachings.

um—"mother of."

ummah—the worldwide Muslim community or the community of Islamic scholars.

wahy—"revelation."

wajib—omission of duties that are obligatory.

wali (pl., *awliya'*)—"saint"; friend of God.

wudu—"ablution" (ceremonial cleansing) performed before prayers, in which hands up to the elbows, feet, and head are cleaned with water.

Yathrib—the name of the city of Medina before the arrival of Muhammad.

Yesua—Arabic name for Jesus from the Hebrew root. 'Isa is the qur'anic name for Jesus.

Zabur—"the Psalms" revealed to the prophet David (Dawud).

zakat—alms tax of 2.5 percent of one's income, given for the cause of Islam and to the poor; the third of the five pillars of Islam.

Zamzam—well on the grounds of the Grand Mosque in Mecca, from which pilgrims on the *hajj* draw water; the spring of water that saved the life of Hagar and Ishmael.

Bibliography

Works by Muslim Authors on Islam

Abdalati, Hummudah. *Islam in Focus*. Malaysia: International Islamic Federation of Student Organizations, 1980.

Ahmad, Hazrat Mirza Bashiruddin Mahmud. "What Is Sin?" *The Muslim Sunrise* 49, no. 3 (July 1982): 13–16.

al-Attas, Syed Muhammad al-Naquib. "Islam: The Concept of Religion and the Foundation of Ethics and Morality." In *The Challenge of Islam*, edited by Altaf Gauhar. London: Islamic Council of Europe, 1978.

Badawi, Jamal, and Harry Almond. *Bridgebuilding Between Christian and Muslim*. Newberg, Ore.: Barclay Press, 1982.

Dargahi, Gholam Hossein. *The Development of Islam as the Ideology of Arab Unity*, A.D. *622–632*. Ann Arbor: University Microfilms, 1970.

El-Awa, Muhamed S. *The Muslim Conduct of State*. 7th rev. ed. Lahore: Sh. Muhammad Ashraf, 1977.

———. *On the Political System of the Islamic State*. Indianapolis: American Trust Publications, 1980.

al-Faruqi, Isma'il Ragi A. *Christian Ethics*. Montreal: McGill University Press, 1967.

———. "Islam and Other Faiths." In *The Challenge of Islam*, edited by Altaf Gauhar. London: Islamic Council of Europe, 1978.

———. "On the Nature of Islamic Da'wah." *International Review of Mission* 65, no. 260 (October 1976): 391–409.

Kateregga, Badru D., and David W. Shenk. *Islam and Christianity: A Muslim and a Christian in Dialogue*. Grand Rapids: Eerdmans, 1981.

Moktefi, Mokhtar, and Veronique Ageorges. *The Arabs in the Golden Age*. Brookfield, Conn.: Millbrook Press, 1992.

Mufassir, Sulaiman Shahid. *Jesus, a Prophet of Islam*. Indianapolis: American Trust Publications, 1980.

Nadwi, Ali Syed Abul Hasan. *Muslims in the West: The Message and Mission*. Leicester: Islamic Foundation, 1983.

Nubee, Muhammad A. Introduction to *Christian-Muslim Dialogue*, by H. M. Baagil. Aldahieh, Kuwait: Revival of Islamic Heritage Society, 1984.

Omar, Irfan A. "Islam: An Ideological Movement for a Peaceful Co-Existence." *The Minaret* 18, no. 12 (December 1996): 36–37.

al-Qaradawi, Yusuf. *The Lawful and the Prohibited in Islam*. 2d ed. Salimiah, Kuwait: International Islamic Federation of Student Organizations, 1989.

Sakr, Ahmad H. *Islam and Muslims: Myth or Reality*. Milwaukee: Al-Qur'an Foundation, 1994.

Tabataba'i, 'Allamah Sayyid Muhammad Husayn. *Shi'ite Islam*. Albany: State University of New York Press, 1981.

The Vision. Chicago: Institute of Islamic Information and Education, 1998.

Waugh, Earle H., Baha Abu-Laban, and Regula B. Qureshi, eds. *The Muslim Community in North America*. Edmonton: University of Alberta Press, 1983.

Works by Non-Muslim Authors on Islam

Anderson, J. N. D. "Islam." In *The Inadequacy of Non-Christian Religion*, edited by H. A. Evan Hopkins. London: Inter-Varsity Fellowship of Evangelical Unions, 1944.

Basetti-Sani, Giulio O. F. M. *The Koran in the Light of Christ.* Chicago: Franciscan Herald Press, 1977.

Behind the Veil: Unmasking Islam. N.p., n.d.

Bell, Richard. *The Origin of Islam in its Christian Environment.* London: Frank Cass and Co., 1926.

Braswell, George W., Jr. *Islam: Its Prophet, Peoples, Politics, Power.* Nashville: Broadman & Holman, 1996.

———. *Understanding Sectarian Groups in America.* Rev. ed. Nashville: Broadman & Holman, 1994.

Brown, David. A *New Threshold: Guidelines for the Churches in Their Relations with Muslim Communities.* London: The British Council of Churches and the Conference of Missionary Societies in Great Britain and Ireland, 1976.

Budd, Jack, comp. *Studies on Islam: A Simple Outline of the Islamic Faith.* Northants, England: Red Sea Mission Team, 1978.

Coward, Harold. *Pluralism: Challenge to World Religions.* Maryknoll: Orbis Books, 1985.

Cragg, Kenneth A. *The Call of the Minaret.* New York: Oxford University Press, 1956.

———. "Islamic Theology: Limits and Bridges." In *The Gospel and Islam,* edited by Don M. McCurry. Monrovia, Calif.: MARC, 1979.

———. *Sandals at the Mosque.* New York: Oxford University Press, 1959.

Diamond, Michael J., and Peter G. Gowing. *Islam and Muslims: Some Basic Information.* Quezon City: New Day Publishers, 1981.

Epstein, Aaron. "Rehnquist Rejects Request to Remove Muhammad Art." *Philadelphia Inquirer,* March 13, 1997, A16.

Gardet, Lois. *Mohammedanism.* New York: Hawthorn Books, 1961.

Geisler, Norman L., and Abdul Saleeb. *Answering Islam: The Crescent in the Light of the Cross.* Grand Rapids: Baker, 1993.

Goodwin, Jan. *Price of Honor: Muslim Women Lift the Veil of Silence on the Islamic World.* Boston: Little, Brown, 1994.

Haddad, Yvonne Yazbeck. *A Century of Islam in America: The Muslim World Today—Occasional Paper No. 4*. Washington: American Institute for Islamic Affairs, 1986.

Haddad, Yvonne Yazbeck, and Adair T. Lummis. *Islamic Values in the United States: A Comparative Study*. New York: Oxford University Press, 1987.

Horne, Mark. "A Bad Moon Rising: The Growth of Islam in the U.S." *Tabletalk*, April 1998, 13.

Johnson, David L. *A Reasoned Look at Asian Religions*. Minneapolis: Bethany House, 1985.

Miller, William M. *A Christian's Response to Islam*. Phillipsburg, N.J.: Presbyterian and Reformed, 1976.

Morey, Robert A. *The Moon-god Allah: In the Archeology of the Middle East*. Newport, Pa.: Research and Education Foundation, 1994.

Parshall, Phil. *The Cross and the Crescent: Reflections on Christian-Muslim Spirituality*. Wheaton: Tyndale House, 1989.

Roelofsma, Derk Kinnane. "Muslims in U.S. Defend the Faith." *Insight*, November 3, 1986, 69.

Schuon, Frithjof. *Dimensions of Islam*. London: George Allen and Unwin, 1970.

Shorrosh, Anis A. *Islam Revealed: A Christian Arab's View of Islam*. Nashville: Thomas Nelson, 1988.

Smith, Jay. "The Attraction of Islam, and a Christian's Response." In *99 Truth Papers*. London: Hyde Park Christian Fellowship, 1992.

Smith, Joseph. "Is the Qur'an the Word of God? Debate Between: Dr. Jamal Badawi and Joseph H. Smith." With "Commentary on a Challenge to the Authenticity of the Qur'an," by Abdul-Rahman Lomax. World Wide Web: Hyde Park Christian Fellowship, 1996.

Spencer, Harold. *Islam and the Gospel of God*. New Delhi: I.S.P.C.K., 1956.

Taylor, John B. *The World of Islam*. New York: Friendship Press, 1979.

Vaziri, Mostafa. *The Emergence of Islam: Prophecy, Imamate, and Messianism in Perspective*. New York: Paragon House, 1992.

Watt, W. Montgomery. *Bell's Introduction to the Qur'an*. Edinburgh: Edinburgh University Press, 1970.

Zwemer, Samuel M. *Mohammed or Christ*. New York: Revell, 1915.

———. *The Moslem Christ*. Edinburgh: Oliphant, Anderson and Ferrier, 1912.

———. *The Moslem Doctrine of God*. Edinburgh: Oliphant, Anderson and Ferrier, 1905.

Works on Muhammad

Andrae, Tor. *Mohammed: The Man and His Faith*. Translated by Theophil Menzel. New York: Harper Torchbooks, 1960.

Austin, R. W. J. "The Prophet of Islam." In *The Challenge of Islam*, edited by Altaf Gauhar. London: Islamic Council of Europe, 1978.

Ustun, Yakup. *Mohammed the Prophet*. Translated by Metin Beynam. Ankara: Turkish Religious Foundation, 1994.

Works on the Qur'an

Ajijola, al-Haji Adeleke Dirisu. *Qur'an in the Classroom*. Lahore: Islamic Publications, 1977.

Lester, Toby. "What Is the Koran?" *Atlantic Monthly* 283, no. 1 (January 1999): 43–56.

Sell, Canon. *The Historical Development of the Qur'an*. Reprint. Chicago: People International, n.d.

Smith, Jay. "The Bible and the Qur'an: An Historical Comparison." In *99 Truth Papers*. London: Hyde Park Christian Fellowship, n.d.

Interpretations of the Qur'an in English

'Ali, Abdullah Yusuf. *The Meaning of the Holy Qur'an*. New ed. Brentwood, Md.: Amana Corporation, 1992.

Asad, Muhammad. *The Message of the Qur'an*. Gibraltar: Dar al-Andalus, 1984.

al-Hilali, Muhammad Taqui-ud-Din, and Muhammad Muhsin Khan. *Interpretation of the Meanings of the Noble Qur'an in the English Language. A Summarized Version of At-Tabari, Al-Qurtubi and Ibn Kathir with comments from Sahih Al-Bukhari*. 4th ed. Riyadh: Maktaba Dar-us-Salam, 1994.

Pickthall, Mohammed Marmaduke. *The Meaning of the Glorious Koran*. New York: New American Library, n.d.

Folk Islam

Musk, Bill A. *The Unseen Face of Islam: Sharing the Gospel with Ordinary Muslims*. East Sussex: MARC Evangelical Missionary Alliance, 1989.

Parshall, Phil. *Bridges to Islam: A Christian Perspective on Folk Islam*. Grand Rapids: Baker, 1983.

Sufism

Muhaiyaddeen, Bawa. "A Contemporary Sufi Speaks on Peace of Mind." Philadelphia: Bawa Muhaiyaddeen Fellowship, 1997. www.bmf.org/pamphlets/pomens2.htm.

Nasr, Seyyed Hossein. *Islamic Life and Thought*. Albany: State University of New York Press, 1981.

———. "Sufism and the Integration of Man." In *God and Man in Contemporary Islamic Thought*, edited by Charles Malik. Beirut: American University of Beirut, 1972.

Schimmel, Annemarie. *Mystical Dimensions of Islam*. Chapel Hill: University of North Carolina Press, 1975.

Threshold: A Journal of Sufism. Brattleboro, Vt.: Threshold Books & the Threshold Society, 1997.

Islam Among African-Americans

Bailey, Richard P. "Why Americans Convert." Unpublished paper, 1998.

"Farrakhan: 'It's Time for Us to Show the World Our Brilliance.'" *Philadelphia Inquirer,* April 15, 1997, A12.

Macklin, William R. "Growing Up in the Nation of Islam." *Philadelphia Inquirer,* February 4, 1997, D1, D5.

Myers, Walter Dean. *Now Is Your Time! The African-American Struggle for Freedom.* New York: HarperTrophy, 1991.

Potter, Ronald C. "No Spiritual Wimps." *World* 11, no. 7 (May 11/18, 1996): 24–25.

Reach Out to the Muslim World 7, nos. 3–4 (1994).

Sipress, Alan. "Keeping Faith in Growing Numbers." *Philadelphia Inquirer,* July 25, 1993, A10.

Yant, Monica. "Grays Ferry Gets Focus on National TV." *Philadelphia Inquirer,* April 14, 1997, A1, A8.

Works on Muslim Evangelism and Ministry

Bailey, Richard P. "The Muslims Are Here." *Action* 49 (1990): 4–7.

Cammarata, John. "Intercultural Evangelism." Unpublished paper, 1997.

Christian Witness Among Muslims. Standard edition. Achimota, Ghana: Africa Christian Press, 1971.

Dennett, Bill. *Sharing the Good News with Muslims: Simple Guidelines for Christians.* Homebush West, N.S.W., Australia: ANZEA Publishers, 1992.

D'Souza, Andreas, and Diane D'Souza. "Reconciliation: A New Paradigm for Missions." *Word and World: Theology for Christian Ministry* 16, no. 2 (Spring 1996): 203–12.

Elder, John. *Biblical Approach to the Muslim.* Fort Washington, Pa.: Worldwide Evangelization Crusade, 1978.

Ellis, Carl F., Jr. "How I Witness to Muslims." *Moody Monthly* 83, no. 5 (January 1983): 52–56.

———. "Project Joseph: A Ministry Concept." Unpublished paper, n.d.

Guthrie, Stan. "Carnegie or Rushdie?" *World Pulse* 26, no. 17 (September 13, 1991): 2–3.

Hensley, Archie. "Ministering in the Shadow of Mecca: Reach Out to Muslims in North America!" *Mission Frontiers* 13, nos. 4–5 (April–May 1991), 42–43.

Housholder, David, comp. *Going Among the Nations Without a Passport*. Marietta, Ga.: ETHNOServe, 1997.

"Islam." *Word and World: Theology for Christian Ministry* 16, no. 2 (Spring 1996).

"Islam in America." *Reach Out to the Muslim World* 7, nos. 1–2 (1994).

Jones, L. Bevan. *Christianity Explained to Muslims*. Rev. ed. Calcutta: Baptist Mission Press, 1952.

Lovering, Kerry. *Islam on the March*. Reprinted from *Africa Now*. Sarborough, Ont.: Sudan Interior Mission, n.d.

McCurry, Don M., ed. *The Gospel and Islam: A 1978 Compendium*. Monrovia, Calif.: Missions Advanced Research and Communications Center, 1979.

———, ed. *Sharing the Gospel with Iranians: A Handbook*. Altadena, Calif.: Samuel Zwemer Institute, 1982.

Nicholls, Bruce J., ed. *Christian Witness to Muslims*. Wheaton: Lausanne Committee for World Evangelization, 1980.

———. "New Theological Approaches in Muslim Evangelism." In *The Gospel and Islam*, edited by Don M. McCurry. Monrovia, Calif.: MARC, 1979.

———. "Other Options for Muslim Evangelism." *Evangelical Missions Quarterly* 34, no. 1 (January 1998): 38–42.

Reapsome, Jim. "Final Analysis." *World Pulse* 29, no. 24 (December 16, 1994): 8.

Saal, William. *Reaching Muslims for Christ*. Chicago: Moody Press, 1993.

Shenk, David W. "Conversations Along the Way." In *Muslims and Christians on the Emmaus Road,* edited by J. Dudley Woodberry. Monrovia, Calif.: MARC Publications, 1989.

Smith, Jay. "Courage in Our Convictions." *Evangelical Missions Quarterly* 34, no. 1 (January 1998): 28–35.

30 Days Muslim Prayer Focus: February 11–March 12, 1994. Colorado Springs: 30 Days Muslim Prayer Focus, 1993.

30 Days Muslim Prayer Focus: December 20, 1998 to January 18, 1999. Colorado Springs: World Christian News, 1999.

Woodberry, J. Dudley. "Interfaith Dialogue." Unpublished paper from Fuller Theological Seminary.

———, ed. *Muslims and Christians on the Emmaus Road.* Monrovia, Calif.: MARC Publications, 1989.

Resources for Friendship Evangelism

An *American Friend Handbook.* Colorado Springs: International Students, 1984.

Bailey, Fred, comp. *Inter-Varsity Christian Fellowship International Student Ministries Guide.* Madison: Inter-Varsity Missions, 1984.

Kraft, Charles H. *Communication Theory for Christian Witness.* Nashville: Abingdon, 1983.

Resources to Be Prepared Theologically for Muslim Evangelism

The Confession of Faith; the Larger and Shorter Catechisms, with the Scripture Proofs at Large. Inverness: Free Presbyterian Publications, 1981.

Piper, John. *Let the Nations Be Glad: The Supremacy of God in Missions.* Grand Rapids: Baker, 1993.

Thomas, Thomas A. A *Reason for the Hope*. Rochester, N.Y.: Backus Book Publishers, 1988.

Discipleship Resources for Converts from Islam

Goble, Phil, and Salim Munayer. *New Creation Book for Muslims*. Pasadena: Mandate Press, 1989.

Packer, J. I. *Growing in Christ*. Wheaton: Tyndale House, 1977.

Miscellaneous

Alden, Robert L. "Malachi." In *The Expositor's Bible Commentary*, edited by Frank E. Gaebelein, vol. 7. Grand Rapids: Zondervan, 1985.

Barrett, David B., ed. *World Christian Encyclopedia*. Oxford: Oxford University Press, 1982.

Blake, W. O. *The History of Slavery and the Slave Trade, Ancient and Modern*. Columbus: H. Miller, 1860.

Chadwick, Henry. *The Early Church*. Middlesex: Penguin Books, 1967.

Clark, Arthur. "Books for a New World." *Aramco World* 49, no. 1 (January–February 1998): 32–37.

Conn, Harvie M. *Evangelism: Doing Justice and Preaching Grace*. Grand Rapids: Zondervan, 1982.

Dembner, Alice. "Saudi Grant to Put Harvard at Fore of Islamic Studies." *Boston Globe*, June 16, 1993.

Diamant, Jeff. "When Workplace and Faith Collide." *Philadelphia Inquirer*, March 22, 1998, H7.

Dixon, Thomas. "The Apology That Took a Thousand Years." *Charisma and Christian Life*, December 1997, 72–76.

Douglas, J. D., ed. *The New International Dictionary of the Christian Church*. Rev. ed. Grand Rapids: Zondervan, 1978.

Eck, Diana L. "Neighboring Faiths." *Harvard Magazine*, September–October 1996, 38–44.

Ferguson, Sinclair B., David F. Wright, and J. I. Packer, eds. *New Dictionary of Theology*. Downers Grove, Ill.: InterVarsity Press, 1988.

Gammage, Jeff. "Iraqi Americans Watch and Worry." *Philadelphia Inquirer*, February 22, 1998, A21–22.

Here's a Thought! Oak Park, Ill.: Win USA, 1997.

Hicks, Rick. Letter to Operation Mobilization supporters, November 19, 1996.

Hoekema, Anthony. *The Bible and the Future*. Grand Rapids: Eerdmans, 1979.

Iranian Christians International, "The ICI Partner Prayer Letter," October 1993.

Latourette, Kenneth Scott. *A History of Christianity*. Rev. ed. New York: Harper & Row, 1975.

Lorenz, Andrea W. "Canada's Pioneer Mosque." *Aramco World* 49, no. 4 (July–August 1998): 28–31.

Marter, Marilynn. "The Feast After the Fast." *Philadelphia Inquirer*, January 21, 1998, F1, F7.

"News in Brief." *Philadelphia Inquirer*, January 12, 1997, A2.

Pasternak, Douglas. "American Colleges Are 'Weapons U.' for Iraq." *U.S. News & World Report* 125, no. 9 (March 9, 1998): 32.

"Prison Disfellowship." *World* 13, no. 46 (November 28, 1998): 10.

Rhor, Monica. "Preaching What They Practice." *Philadelphia Inquirer*, January 20, 1998, C1, C3.

Trail, Jo Ann S. "Focus on Islamic Art and Culture at the University of Idaho." COMSEC *Newsletter*, Spring 1996, 7–8.

Vos, Geerhardus. *The Kingdom of God and the Church*. Phillipsburg, N.J.: Presbyterian and Reformed, 1972.

"The Willowbank Report: The Lausanne Committee for World Evangelization." In *Perspectives on the World Christian Movement: A Reader*, edited by Ralph D. Winter and Steven C. Hawthorne. Pasadena: William Carey Library, 1981, 507–38.

Further Ministry Resources

To receive Christian literature on Islam and materials in English and other Muslim languages, refer to the following places:

The Anis Shorrosh Evangelistic Association
P.O. Box 577
Spanish Fort, AL 36527–0577
Phone: (800) 255–3360 or (205) 621–0507

Ask for price list of books, tapes, and other resources on Muslim ministry and other topics.

Arabic Communication Center
P.O. Box 1124
Temple City, CA 91780
Phone: (818) 291–2866

Produces thirty-minute evangelistic videos in Arabic, which have been broadcast on television.

The Back to God Hour
Arabic Broadcast Department
6555 West College Drive
Palos Heights, IL 60463
Phone: (312) 371–8700

(In Canada: P.O. Box 5070, Burlington, Ontario L7R 3Y8; phone: (416) 637–3434)

This ministry has books, tracts, and tapes available in Arabic.

Biblical Institute for Islamic Studies (BIIS)
P.O. Box 27276
Philadelphia, PA 19118
Phone: (215) 784-9194

Offers training classes for outreach to Muslims. Courses also offered by correspondence.

Church Without Walls
P.O. Box 27276
Philadelphia, PA 19118
Phone: (215) 784-9194

A ministry of outreach and equipping using the model of Meetings for Better Understanding.

Fellowship of Faith for Muslims
P.O. Box 221, Station J
Toronto, Ontario M4J 4Y1
Canada

This ministry promotes prayer for Muslims and has an extensive catalog of resources for Muslim ministry.

Fellowship of Isa
P.O. Box 1206
Minneapolis, MN 55440

They publish booklets that present the Christian faith to Muslims.

Fellowship Tract League
P.O. Box 164
Lebanon, OH 45036
Fax: (513) 494–2626

Gospel leaflets are available in Kazakh, Tajik, and Uzbek.

Good Shepherd Ministries
P.O. Box 40248
Pasadena, CA 91104

They will send you a free catalog of Christian literature in Turkish.

Gospel Recordings Int'l.
122 Glendale Blvd.
Los Angeles, CA 90026

This organization has recordings of gospel messages on tape in almost any language you would want. This is especially useful for those who are illiterate.

Iranian Christians International, Inc.
P.O. Box 25607
Colorado Springs, CO 80936
Phone: (719) 596–0010; fax: (719) 574–1141

This ministry organizes regional conferences for Iranians, publishes a bilingual journal called Mojdeh, and sells Christian literature on Muslim ministry and Christian titles in Farsi. They also assist Iranian refugees in resettlement.

The JESUS Film Project
P.O. Box 7690
Laguna Niguel, CA 92607
Phone: (800) 432–1997
Website: http://www.JESUSFILM.org

They offer the two hour film *Jesus*, based on the gospel of Luke, in over 400 languages.

Middle East Media
P.O. Box 2033
Westfield, NJ 07091–2033
Phone: (908) 301–9730

They produce an Arabic/English Christian magazine called *Ultimate Questions*, a preevangelistic magazine in Arabic called *Magalati*, and videos for a Muslim audience.

Middle East Resources
P. O. Box 96
Upper Darby, PA 19082
Phone: (610) 352–2003

They provide literature for Muslim ministry, such as William Campbell's book *The Qur'an and the Bible* and John Haines's book *Good News for Muslims*.

Multi-Language Media
Box 301
Ephrata, PA 17522
Phone: (717) 738–0582
E-mail: mlminfo@multilanguage.com
Website: http://www.multilanguage.com

Order Christian books, tapes, and videos in many languages.

Muslim Ministries/WEC
Box 1707
Fort Washington, PA 19034–8707

Order literature for ministry among Muslims.

Shoenhof's Foreign Books
76-A Matt. Auburn Street
Cambridge, MA 02138
Phone: (617) 547–8855

Order Turkic- and Kurdish-language materials.

Tenth International Fellowship
1701 Delancey Place
Philadelphia, PA 19103
Phone: (215) 735-7688

A ministry to international students and scholars, including Muslims.

Voice of Preaching the Gospel
P.O. Box 15013
Colorado Springs, CO 80935

Order books, Bible correspondence courses, and cassettes for Muslim ministry.

World Christian News
P.O. Box 26479
Colorado Springs, CO 80936
Phone: (719) 380–0505; fax: (719) 380–0936

They offer resources for reading and studying about Islam and Christian witness to Muslims. They publish *World Christian News*, a digest of news and trends for mission-minded Christians, and publish *30 Days Muslim Prayer Focus* for use during Ramadan. This prayer guide is now available in many languages and via e-mail.

Bibles and Scripture Portions

To order Bibles and Scripture portions in the languages of Muslims, write to the agencies listed below and ask for their catalogue. Many of the suppliers in the previous section also have Bibles in Islamic languages.

American Bible Society
1865 Broadway
New York, NY 10023
Phone orders: (800) 322–4253; fax (212) 408–8765
Website: www.americanbible.org

For a complete listing of Scriptures in other languages, request the catalogue entitled "Scriptures in Many Languages" (AJK106069).

The Bible League
16801 Van Dam Road
South Holland, IL 60473
Phone: (708) 331–2094

Scripture Gift Mission International
P.O. Box 495908
Garland, TX 75049
Phone: (972) 226–6550; fax: (972) 226–6755
e-mail: usa@sgm.org or sgmus@juno.com

They have Scripture booklets in at least twenty-seven languages spoken primarily by Muslims.

Scripture Gift Mission (Canada) Inc.
#32, 300 Steelcase Road West
Markham, Ontario L3R 2W2
Canada

International Bible Society
P.O. Box 62970
Colorado Springs, CO 80962–2970
Phone for credit card orders: (800) 524–1588 or (719) 488–9200; fax: (719) 488–0870
Website: www.gospelcom.net/ibs
E-mail: ibs@gospelcom.net

They carry modern translations and the *Living Bible* in numerous languages. They also have available the *Jesus* movie on video in 192 languages.

Index of Bible References

Genesis
1:26–27—136
1:28—251
6:4—94
15:6—133
16—273
17—273
21—273
21:19—254

Exodus
20—276

Leviticus
11:44—274
19:34—196

Deuteronomy
4:23–24—276
18:15—43
18:18—43
18:22—43
32:3–6—276
32:6—277

1 Samuel
15:1–29—131

Job
31:32—204

Psalms
33:11—153, 294n.2
51:10—253
67:3–4—160
86:9—136
119:1—252
119:165—252
122:1—249
139—272

Proverbs
2:7–8—276
3:33—276
12:26—212
16:4—273
16:9—273
16:33—294n.2
17:15—276
19:21—273
21:12—276
21:30—273
21:31—273
25:11—86

Isaiah
1:11–20—131
2:2–3—166
6:3—274
12:3—254
19:23–25—167
43:7—136
53—179
55—274
55:8–9—274
55:11—216, 226
57:15—277, 279
60:7—166
61:1–2—223
66:1–2—249

Jonah
2:9—240

Micah
6:6–8—131

Habakkuk
1:13—274

Malachi
1:11—165

Matthew
5:16—165
5:44—162
6:5–6—248
6:10—142
6:16–18—249
6:33—144
9:35—142
9:37–38—159
11:2–6—142
11:19—197
11:27—109
16:16–17—110
16:16–18—143
16:18—253
16:27—169
17:22—294n.2
18:19–20—199
18:21–35—241
21:21–22—159
21:28–32—131, 241
23:13–33—177
24:14—146, 163, 170
24:42—169
24:44—169
28:18—281
28:19—116, 163
28:19–20—250
28:20—116

Mark
1:11—110
1:15—141
2:17—163
3:28–30—253
7:14–15—253
7:18–20—250
11:15–18—177
12:1–9—109
12:13–17—143
12:29—92
14:62—169
16:15—163

Luke
1:34–35—94
4:16–19—223
4:17–19—142
5:17–26—224
5:18—206
5:20—206
5:24—206
8:13—184
10:1—187
10:6—192
10:38–42—159
11:20—142
12:37—169
12:40—169
12:43—169
12:48—251
13:1–5—273
13:10–13—223
13:23–24—156
14:7–14—241
14:12–14—179
15—241
16:19–31—241
18:1—248
18:9–14—241
19:10—162
19:13—252
24:13–35—201
24:27—240
24:30—240
24:30–32—240
24:47—163

John
1:1—109
1:1–2—110
1:14—92, 110
1:18—92, 110
1:21—43
1:25—43
1:45—43
3:16—92
3:16–18—155
4:10—206
4:13—206
4:13–14—254
4:14—206
4:21—249
4:23—249
4:24—272
4:39—201
5:19—171
5:22–23—120
6:14—43
6:44—167
7:40—43
8:28–29—109
10:1–21—241
10:9—155
10:11—167
10:16—162, 167
12:31—142
13:34—252
13:34–35—203
14—275
14:5–6—155
14:5–11—113
14:9—109
14:16—43, 115
14:16–17—115
14:26—43, 115, 127
15:26—115
16:7—115
16:13—127
17:3—248
17:15—163
17:18—163
17:20–21—163

17:20–23—205
18:36—143
19:11—294n.2
20:21—165
20:30–31—116

Acts
1:6–8—146
1:8—116, 154, 163, 250
2:23—294n.2
2:37–40—208
3:6—206
3:22–26—43
4:12—155
4:28—294n.2
6–7—177
6:9–10—177
7:37—43
8:26–39—210
8:30–31—200
13:1—210
13:2–3—165
13:16–41—247
17:17—200
17:18—177
17:22–23—195
17:22–31—247
18:7—180
18:27–28—177
19:8–10—177
26:28–29—209
28:23—142, 177

Romans
3:10—132
3:21–22—132
3:21–26—278
3:22—156
3:29–30—156
4:3—133
4:23–25—133
5:1–2—278
5:6–11—278
5:8—105, 162
5:10—162
6:9—120
6:14—252
7:19—141
8:3–4—252
8:35–39—105
9:14–18—153
10:1–4—133
10:12–15—164
12:13—204
12:13b—179
15:20–21—164
16:5—180

1 Corinthians
1:18—158
1:21–24—158
2:2–5—158
2:12—240
2:14—86, 157, 240
8:4–6—92
9:22—200
13:3—252
13:8—211
15:14—132
15:17—132
16:2—248
16:19—180

2 Corinthians
5:11—154
5:14—154
5:18–20—154
5:20—154, 252
9:7—248

Galatians
3—158
3:28—253
4:30—166

Ephesians
1:4–5—95
1:11—153, 294n.2
2:11–13—157
2:12—260
2:19–22—251
2:20—116
3:6—253
3:14–15—253
3:17–19—105
4:4–6—253
4:24—125
5:1–2—106
5:25–27—253
6—275
6:10–12—251
6:12—199

Philippians
2:1–11—272
2:9–11—121

Colossians
1:13—142
2:16–17—250
4:2—248
4:2–4—199
4:15—180

1 Thessalonians
5:17—159, 198, 248

2 Thessalonians
1:6–10—155
3:1–3—160

1 Timothy
2:5—15
2:5–6—155
4:3–5—250
4:13—183
6:15b–16—274

2 Timothy
1:15—212
2:20–21—254
2:22—251
3:15–16—239
3:16—127
4:2—183
4:14–15—212

Titus
3:5–6—254
3:9—212

Philemon
2—180

Hebrews
1:1–3—112
1:1–12—44
1:3—109
3:3—116
4:12—86, 226, 240
6:17—294n.2
11—250
11:8–10—249
12:1—250
12:2—252
12:4–11—277
13:2—204
13:15–16—165

James
1:17—277
2:19—92

1 Peter
2:4–5—166
2:5–6—251
2:9–10—166
2:11—250
4:13–14—146
4:19—146

2 Peter
1:4—90
1:20–21—127
3:13—144

1 John
1:5—274
1:7—132
2:5–6—106
4:7–8—277
4:7–21—104

Revelation
5:8—165
5:9–10—168
6:9—252
7:9–10—161
15:4—136
21:24—166
21:26—166
22:18–19—116